MW01077288

Chris Marker |

Contemporary Film Directors

Edited by James Naremore

The Contemporary Film Directors series provides concise, well-written introductions to directors from around the world and from every level of the film industry. Its chief aims are to broaden our awareness of important artists, to give serious critical attention to their work, and to illustrate the variety and vitality of contemporary cinema. Contributors to the series include an array of internationally respected critics and academics. Each volume contains an incisive critical commentary, an informative interview with the director, and a detailed filmography.

A list of books in the series appears at the end of this book.

Chris Marker |

Nora M. Alter

**UNIVERSITY
OF
ILLINOIS
PRESS**
URBANA
AND
CHICAGO

Library of Congress Cataloging-in-Publication Data
Alter, Nora M.– Chris Marker / Nora M. Alter.
p.   cm. — (Contemporary film directors)
Includes bibliographical references and index.
ISBN-13: 978-0-252-03073-4 (cloth : alk. paper)
ISBN-10: 0-252-03073-7 (cloth : alk. paper)
ISBN-13: 978-0-252-07316-8 (pbk. : alk. paper)
ISBN-10: 0-252-07316-9 (pbk. : alk. paper)
1. Marker, Chris, 1921—Criticism and interpretation.
I. Title. II. Series.
PN1998.3.M366A48   2006
791.4302'33092—dc22   2005028936

For Arielle and Zoë

Contents |

Preface and Acknowledgments |

The idea to write a monograph on the work of Chris Marker had its origins about a decade ago when he extended his hospitality and invited me to meet with him for a conversation. When I visited Marker in his residence located, incidentally, in a poor neighborhood still reverberating with echoes of the Commune's last stand in May 1871, I was struck by the self-sufficiency of the space. The studio/workplace was filled floor to ceiling with written matter, audiovisual materials, a vast array of technological devices, and computers. As Marker explained, he could produce an entire film without ever leaving his home. Even more impressive than the workplace was the man himself, and our conversation (which I would never have presumed to record) left me with the feeling that I had met a rare and remarkable individual. It was upon leaving that I decided that I would at some point engage with a full-time study of his work.

To write about such a multifaceted filmmaker, who has consistently tried to elude all categorization, is an endeavor fraught with peril. Indeed, the existent literature on Chris Marker (Christian-François Bouche-Villeneuve) is surprisingly scant. Marker's humble self-effacement of his importance as a cultural worker and intellectual and his reclusive nature, combined with a reluctance to grant interviews or make public appearances or engage in written statements, make writing on his work a challenge. It is out of respect for the filmmaker's desire not to be interviewed that the interviews and writings included in this volume are, for the most part, from his earlier period. Thus, when approaching a Marker film, it is really the work that must speak for itself. It follows naturally that Marker has consistently refused to be fixed in any one role; his identity has never been static but labile and changing, and, although this book is part of the Contemporary Film Directors series, it is less about a person than about a body of texts.

Marker's impact has been considerable in three areas of filmmaking: His explorations in nonfiction filmmaking have pushed this genre forward in significant ways; his politically engaged films have provided a model for other committed filmmakers all over the world to follow; and his experimentation in new media and technology has developed a distinct style of art film that has impacted visual artists. Indeed, it is in this last area that his production has increased, not only in numbers but also in interest over the years, and has in the past decade resulted in several museum exhibitions. The following book is organized according to these three facets of Marker's work; however, my groupings are not definitive, and there are significant overlappings in the categories that merely underscore the intricacies of their interrelationship. Although I try to touch upon most of his audiovisual productions, due to spatial constraints I have omitted some. In addition, though in his mid-eighties, Marker has not slowed down but continues to be active. Even during the writing of this book, Marker has started or completed two new important projects: the first is an ongoing news and information blog, *Un Regard Moderne* (2004–present); the second, an installation, *Owls at Noon Prelude: The Hollow Men* at New York's Museum of Modern Art (May–June 2005).

Unless otherwise noted, all translations from foreign sources are my own. The titles of Marker's works are given in the original French on initial citations, and subsequent references are made to English translations. Exceptions are those films that were released in English with their French titles and are commonly referred to as such, for example, *Le joli mai* and *La jetée*.

| | |

To a certain extent, this book is collaborative, and there are many individuals who shared in its production. First, I would like to thank Rebecca Crist, Carol Burwash, and other members of the staff at the University of Illinois Press. In particular, I would like to express my gratitude to the series editor, James Naremore, for his belief in the project and his willingness to accept creative solutions when difficulties arose. In addition, special thanks go to Joan Catapano, editor in chief, both for her support of this book as well as more generally for her commitment over the years to publish excellent texts in film and media studies. Thanks go to Adam Nikolaidis for his expertise in image reproduction as well as to Will Lehman for his research assistance and final manuscript preparation and to Margit Grieb for preparing the index. I also would like to thank Peter Latta of the photo archives of the Filmmuseum Berlin—Deutsche Kinemathek for his permission to reprint four of the images in this book and Marie-Odile Masson at *Le Monde* for granting me reproduction rights for two interviews. The writing of this book was aided by a research fellowship from the Alexander von Humboldt Stiftung. In addition, I am grateful to the department of Germanic and Slavic Studies and to the dean's office of the College of Liberal Arts and Sciences at the University of Florida for granting me the necessary leave time to complete this project. I would also like to thank my immediate colleagues for their support and enthusiasm: Keith Bullivant, William Calin, Susan Hegeman, Eric Kligerman, Carol Murphy, Robert Ray, Maureen Turim, Gregory Ulmer, and Philip Wegner. Thanks, too, go to colleagues elsewhere who, when I had my doubts, gave me their encouragement to pursue this book: Timothy Corrigan, Thomas Elsaesser, Anton Kaes, Gertrud Koch, Lutz Koepnick, Molly Nesbit, Gerald Prince, Eric Rentschler, Kristin Ross, Alan Sekula, and Frank Trommler.

As I conducted research for this project, I was struck by the network of shared information and materials that exist on Marker. Those interested in his work have the same intellectual generosity and willingness to help that characterize Marker himself. Without this spirit of sharing of resources and collaboration this book could never have been written. I am, therefore, grateful to individuals such as Adrian Miles, who began and maintained a very comprehensive Web site, and to Thomas Tode, whose German edition *Chris Marker: Film Essayist* provides a comprehensive resource: both of these sources were invaluable in helping me to compile the bibliography and filmography. Further, Tode was very generous in providing me with copies of rare Marker films. Nuria Enquita, contemporary curator of the Fondacio Antoni Tapies in Barcelona, shared her material from a 1998 show and allowed me to excerpt part of Marker's statement from that exhibition. Kerry Oliver-Smith, contemporary curator at the Samuel P. Harn Museum of Art, has been a wonderful collaborator and has always indulged my screening requests for the most recent Marker releases. In particular, special thanks go to Sam DiIorio, who shared with me his own excellent work on Chris Marker as well as helped me locate videos, essays, and other sources. Finally, I am indebted to Caroline Constant for her careful consideration and reading of my manuscript and her genuine enthusiasm, which came at just the right time.

In many ways, this was also an extended family project: Michelle Caroly was extremely helpful in sending me materials from France as well as in assisting me to negotiate various bureaucracies during my archival research and, most importantly, for providing me with initial contact information for Marker; Ana Lizon patiently entertained my questions about liberation movements and politics in Latin America; Jean-Marie Frodon generously "donated" his interview with Marker; Ginette and Pierre Billard both kept me abreast of "Marker news" over the years and more recently read through the completed manuscript with their immeasurable "insider's knowledge" of the cultural scene in France that allowed for invaluable insights, feedback, and corrections; the translations of the interviews could not have been completed without the assistance of my parents, Maria P. Alter and Jean V. Alter, the latter who supported my intellectual pursuit of Marker from the beginning.

This book is dedicated to my immediate family: Alex Alberro, my intellectual interlocutor, collaborator, and partner, who shared in my enthusiasm, interest, and respect for Marker. Without his participation at every stage in its development, this book would never have been realized. And to our daughters Arielle, who, despite the periodic surfacings of "Guillaume-en-Egypte," had to endure many hours watching often black-and-white, mostly unsubtitled, and almost always nonfictional films, and Zoë, whose presence during the final writing stages was already evident. It is my hope that some of the spirit behind Chris Marker's production may have entered into them.

And finally thanks go to Chris Marker, not only for his remarkable cultural and intellectual contribution over the past half a century but also for his openness and willingness to engage in dialogue with me during the past decade. I would like to acknowledge his cautionary words from an earlier communication with me: "I am the cat who walks by himself, and if there is something I'm not looking for it's recognition, be it great or small. My works have their way to go around and meet their audience, sometimes I'm amazed at the response, and to achieve that I don't need to be locked between two covers." In the pages that follow, I hope I have respected the essence of Marker's message and that my essayistic text provides not closure but rather an opening and starting point for readers in order that they may pursue their own investigations.

Chris Marker |

"The Cat Who Walks by Himself"

Introduction: The Solitary Cat

But the wildest of all the wild animals was the Cat. He walked by himself, and all places were alike to him.

—Rudyard Kipling, "The Cat Who Walks by Himself"

"All right," said the Cat; and this time it vanished quite slowly, beginning with the end of the tail, and ending with the grin, which remained some time after the rest of it had gone. "Well! I've often seen a cat without a grin," thought Alice; "but a grin without a cat! It's the most curious thing I ever saw in my life."

—Lewis Carroll, *Alice's Adventures in Wonderland*

We do not have cats, cats have us. Cats are our Gods, the most expansive and approachable of Gods, that goes without saying.

—Chris Marker

The first of these epigraphs, repeated at rhythmic intervals throughout
Rudyard Kipling's story, "The Cat Who Walks by Himself," refers to the
elusive, mysterious, independent, and only half-domesticated nature of
the common breed of cats. The tale evokes a prehistoric era when all
creatures were wild, and "the wildest of all the wild animals was the Cat."
Through a slow but steady series of compromises, animals such as the
dog and the horse trade their independence for a guarantee of safety
and food. The only animal clever enough to strike a pact with humans
in order to preserve its wildness, solitariness, and independence is the
cat. In turn, the cat prompts the envy and dislike of both the dog, who
will forever be destined to chase it, and the man, who will periodically
kick it but rarely outwit it. The second epigraph, taken from a passage
in *Alice's Adventures in Wonderland,* comes at the conclusion of Alice's
perplexing encounter with the Cheshire Cat. During the course of their
conversation, the Cat declares that everyone is mad, including Alice, and
supports his claim with the logic that, if she were not mad, she "wouldn't
have come here." The rest of the exchange is punctuated by the Cat's
appearances and disappearances until, as in the preceding quote, all
that remains is his evasive grin. In both stories cats are emblematic of
mysterious, elusive, transitory, and stubbornly independent figures. They
navigate through the world of humans largely on their own terms.

    "The Cat Who Walks by Himself" is an autobiographical description the French independent filmmaker Chris Marker uses as an e-mail subject header, and *A Grin without a Cat* is the title with which he released *Le fond de l'air est rouge* (1977), now reedited and updated, in 1993.[1] Figures of animals, including owls, wolves, horses, elephants, and mammoths, are not uncommon within Marker's oeuvre, but the cat's status is special. Hence, it seems appropriate to employ what is perhaps Marker's first citation of the figure of the cat in his texts (specifically, from a review of a 1952 cat show in Paris) as the third epigraph.[2] True, Marker uses the occasion to discuss the status not only of cats but of a whole spectrum of domestic and wild animals put on display and thereby transformed into "statues." He ends with the hope that in the future animals will be cared for the way that medicine and music are presently treated. Marker keeps returning to cats. Felines, whether live, imaged, or in the form of sculptures, appear in almost all of his films. Marker's CD-ROM self-portrait, *Immemory* (1997), figures the filmmaker's alter ego in the form of a red cartoon cat named Guillaume. Even his greeting cards feature Guillaume, who is also often summoned in salutational closings. Thus it comes as no surprise to hear that when asked for a photograph of himself, Marker sends one of a cat instead.

That Marker would choose the cat as his personal mascot is not surprising given his own cultivation of a reclusive, elusive, and mysterious identity. Marker does not allow himself to be photographed and rarely grants interviews. Deprived of direct information, authors of reviews, essays, and Web sites naturally resort to apocryphal anecdotes about Marker's life. They range from various myths about his origins—birth in Mongolia, aristocratic ancestry, son of a very wealthy colonialist in South America—to speculations about his "professional past": a paratrooper, a member of the French Resistance, an interpreter for the U.S. army. So much for stories. A search for facts yields somewhat more reliable, albeit still ambiguous, information: Marker was given the name Christian François Bouche-Villeneuve at his birth in late July 1921, probably in Neuilly-sur-Seine, a suburb of Paris.[3] He seems to have adopted his nom de plume in the late 1940s, with credits to a "C. M." first appearing in print in the early 1950s. Whether his pseudonym is meant to connote the act of inscription, or that of leaving a trace—a mark—remains unclear.[4] In addition, the alias does not immediately indicate a specific ethnicity or class, as did Marker's birth name. Then there is the matter of the peculiar punctuation of the name: until the early 1990s, film credits almost always recorded it as *Chris. Marker;* more recently the period after *Chris* has been dropped, and *Chris Marker* has become standard. Marker is not entirely innocent in the proliferation of these myths. He has contributed to this phenomenon, even if only indirectly, by doing little to dispel the cult of personality that has developed around him, never addressing (let alone correcting) the rumors and claims about his past. One of these was made by his friend Alain Resnais, who recalls that Marker favored a 1951 English translation of his prizewinning (Prix Orion, 1950) novel *Le Coeur net* (The Forthright Spirit, 1949), precisely because it had so little resemblance to the original (Resnais, "Rendez-vous," 207). Resnais' recollection is significant because it reveals that Marker has maintained a vehemently antiproprietary stance regarding his intellectual output from the very beginning of his career—a disposition that was no doubt due to his commitment to avant-garde cultural production. Marker's standpoint belies his lifelong involvement in leftist movements and his many collective endeavors. Part of this intellectual history can be traced to the existentialism of Jean Paul Sartre (with whom, some say, Marker studied), who proposed that man is ultimately responsible not only for himself but for all other men. This positioning should not be confused with an antiauteurism, however, for, during the 1950s in France, when Marker was establishing his career as a filmmaker, auteur theory was one the dominant modes of understanding filmic production. Auteur theory included not only the notion that each director had a recognizable style but also implied a sincere belief in film as an art form that was fundamentally related intellectually to the other arts, especially literature.[5] Thus, Marker's auteurism derives more from his literariness or, as we shall see, essayistic tendencies than from any cultivation on his part of a director-as-genius myth. In that spirit, the author/artist should be decentered when contemplating the films that bear Marker's name, and the interpretative and analytical stress should be placed on the deep sociopolitical structures that determine textual production. The more irrelevant the author to the process of understanding, the better the reader or viewer will be able to produce interpretations that derive from the very texts or films in question.

Marker has consistently refused to be fixed in any one role. Rather than static, his identity has been labile, changing, and dynamic. This mobility may explain why he has granted relatively few interviews and has avoided making theoretical statements regarding his work. Marker has been a writer (screenwriter, novelist, storyteller, critic, and poet), a photographer (producing books of photos *Coréennes* [Korean Women], *Le dépays* [The Un-country]), as well as a filmmaker (directing many shorts, fictional and nonfictional features, television programs), a visual artist exhibiting in museums, an editor, a publisher, an organizer, a producer, and an assistant to numerous cultural projects throughout the world in the past half-century. Little binds all of this work together. Only a certain heterodoxy of thought; an aleatory approach characterized by chance, playfulness, wit, and humor; and a commitment to rescuing from the "dustbin" of history various figures and events, thread through the entire oeuvre. No wonder, then, that Marker's pronounced influence on a number of interrelated fields—film, art, letters, and politics—is due not to particular writings or films but to a *practice* that is multiple and slides as easily from medium to medium as it does from text to context. The diversity of his reception is indicative of this multiplicity. For instance, it would be difficult to agree on what else figures such as filmmaker Terry Gilliam (who based his feature film *12 Monkeys* on *La jetée*), author Henri Michaux (who provocatively proclaimed that the "Sorbonne should be razed and Chris Marker put in its place!"), and artist Jonas Mekas (who averred that "Chris Marker is pure spirit!") would share in common. Marker's influence and assistance on films and other projects over the years have been large, though a prevailing sense of humbleness has led him to downplay his role. That humbleness, as I am calling it here, has also led to an underestimation of the artist's significance—a misjudgment that the present book aims to redress.

The diverse nature of Marker's work parallels his peripatetic journeying around the globe. From Peking to Paris, Tokyo, Siberia, Santiago, Jerusalem, Bissau, Berlin, Havana, Hanoi, Helsinki—all of these locations appear in his oeuvre. Indeed, his film *Si j'avais quatre dromadaires* (*If I Had Four Camels*, 1966), made entirely of stills, claims to include photographs taken in twenty-six countries during the years 1955 through 1965. Marker traveled to all of the continents (with the exception of Antarctica) and several islands in between, such as Iceland, Bijagos, Cape Verde, and Hokkaido. As this very cursory list already reveals, locating Marker in fixed geographical terms and categorically assigning to him a national profile is a difficult, if not impossible, task. His work is marked precisely by a transnationalism that eschews facile classifications. Although the literary and philosophical allusions and references in his films are primarily to French intellectuals (such as Michaux, Giraudoux, and Sartre), it would be too reductive to define Marker and his work as typically French. Indeed, Marker publicly refuses to dispel rumors that he was born in Ulaanbaatar, or on the Ile-aux-Moines, or that his mother was Russian. As his oeuvre reveals, his operative principle is to ignore ultimately constraining and divisive national and cultural identities and boundaries. He prefers to seek commonalities through unusual and unpredictable geographical and historical juxtapositions, however exotic they may be. His aversion to any conformity and to any mode of patriotism may be related to a social philosophy that aligns with those who are oppressed and abused by authoritarian regimes, regardless of nationality. As the commentary in *A Grin without a Cat* categorically asserts, "the cat is never on the side of power."

Beginnings

> Chris Marker is the prototype of the 19th Century man. He managed to achieve a synthesis of all appetites and obligations without ever sacrificing any of them to the others. In fact a theory is making the rounds, and not without some grounds, that Marker could be an extra-terrestrial. He looks like a human, but perhaps he comes from the future or from another planet. . . . There are some very bizarre clues. He is never sick or ill, he is not sensitive to cold, and he doesn't seem to need any sleep.
>
> —Resnais, "Chris Marker," 52–53

Lore has it that Marker was a student of Sartre's in the 1930s when the former studied at the Lycée Pasteur, located in the upper-middle-class Neuilly-sur-Seine suburb of Paris. His role as editor of *Le Trait d'union,* a student newspaper, provides an early indication of his cultural ambitions.[6] Nothing substantial is known of Marker's activities during World War II. Immediately after the war, however, he became very active on the cultural scene in Paris. Actor Gérard Lorin remembers that, after the liberation, Marker was part of a forward-looking avant-garde group that included filmmaker Resnais, theorist Alexandre Astruc, critic André

Bazin, and actor Roger Blin. The group would meet regularly at 5 rue des Beaux-Arts in the fifth arrondissement to discuss cultural initiatives.[7] They formed the basis of Travail et Culture (Work and Culture), a left-wing cultural organization composed of writers, filmmakers, theater directors, playwrights, and other cultural activists. The puppeteer Remo Forlani recalls that members of the group would frequent the Café Flore, then a popular meeting spot for intellectuals such as Sartre and Simone de Beauvoir.[8] In the evening, Marker, Resnais, filmmakers Roger Vadim, François Truffaut, and others would go to the Filmclub organized by Bazin and initially held at the Maison de la Chimie in the rue Saint-Dominique. Travail et Culture had divisions of theater, music, literature, and film. It subsidized and provided logistical support for projects by artists, writers, and filmmakers on the left; it also distributed discount tickets for a variety of performances. Marker, rumored to be quite wealthy, had an office at Travail et Culture. Resnais remembers seeking him out there and soliciting him to finance the production of his films.[9] A slightly different version of events has it that Marker was at the time a young actor in the theater division of Travail et Culture and first met Resnais during debate centered on whether the latter's film *Van Gogh* was viable in 16 mm or had to be reshot in 35 mm. According to this account, Marker also became acquainted with Bazin during these discussions and was so taken by the latter's views that he decided to quit theater and assist Bazin in the film division instead (Andrew 90). The leading role that Bazin played on the cinephilac group cannot be underestimated. It should be noted, however, that Bazin was neither a Communist nor a Marxist but rather a Socialist-Christian.

In 1946, another cultural group, Peuple et Culture (People and Culture), which had been founded in Grenoble in 1944, moved to Paris and immediately began to draw on the membership of Travail et Culture. The latter was under the sway of the Parti Communiste Français (PCF), whereas Peuple et Culture was more Socialist in its leanings. Both groups worked closely together, however, and sought to rethink and radically democratize the traditional role of culture, especially in its relationship to the working class. Joseph Rovan, founder of Peuple et Culture, recalls that "in the documentation center, we worked on 'reading cards' which were written by a 'team of unemployed intellectuals' and we hired, among others, Chris Marker as a typist" (Rovan 209).

Peuple et Culture produced Marker's first feature-length film, *Olympia 52* (1952). Despite various internal differences and conflicts between the two groups, one cannot underestimate the vibrant and diversified intellectual community they offered to Marker at the war's end. Many of the individuals belonging to the two groups had played a part in the Resistance during the occupation, others had just returned from concentration camps, and all positioned themselves politically somewhere on the left.

Marker worked as an animator following his move from theater to film at Travail et Culture. By the late 1940s, however, he had already become involved in writing, filming, and organizing activities. Little is known about his early film work. Resnais recalled that Marker made several 8 mm productions in the 1940s, including one, *La fin du monde vu par l'Ange Gabriel* (The End of the World as Seen by the Angel Gabriel), that consisted of mostly blurry and sometimes unidentifiable images shot in a devastated Berlin at the end of the war. Although Resnais found the film visually unremarkable, he was impressed by both the verbal commentary and the interplay with the musical score—two features that stand out in Marker's subsequent audiovisual productions (Resnais, "Rendez-vous," 207).

At the same time, from the mid-1940s to the mid-1950s, Marker was very active on the literary scene, writing poetry, novels, short stories, essays, reviews, translations, and creating cartoons.[10] He also edited the first four volumes of the cultural review *DOC*, published jointly by Peuple et Culture and Travail et Culture.[11] The journal translated and published texts by intellectuals such as Bertolt Brecht and John Dos Passos as well as writings by Bazin, Marker, and other members of the group. In addition to his work for *DOC,* Marker was a regular contributor to *Esprit,* a leftist Catholic review edited by Emmanuel Mounier, and to *Cahiers du Cinéma* and other French film journals. In that decade alone, he published close to one hundred pieces on topics ranging from music (*Du jazz considéré comme une prophétie;* Jazz as Prophecy), literature (C. S. Lewis: *Le grand divorce;* The Big Divorce), film (*Blood of a Poet*), and theater (Le théâtre du peuple en Angleterre; Theater of the People in England) to politics (*L'affaire Tito vue de Yougoslavie;* The Tito Affair) and anthropology (*L'art noir;* Black Art). He also published a number of texts that focused on techniques such as animation (*L'esthétique du dessin animé;* The Aesthetics of Animation), trick films (*Der Trickfilm*), and cinerama (*And Now This Is Cinerama*) as well as meditations on animals such as *Le chat aussi est une personne* (The Cat Is Also a Person). Marker wrote several book-length studies at this time, including *Veillée de l'homme et de sa liberté* (Vigil of a Man and His Liberty, 1949) and an academic study of the French writer Giraudoux: *Giraudoux par lui-même* (Giraudoux by Himself, 1952). In 1952, he coedited, with Cacérès Benigno, *Regards sur le mouvement ouvrier* (Reflections on the Worker's Movement), a collection of texts from Peuple et Culture published by Editions du Seuil. From 1954 to 1958, Marker edited a special series for Seuil, *Petite Planète,* which specialized in texts with illustrations, graphics, and photographs. The highly pictorial nature of the books in this series reflected Marker's own interests and inclinations and led directly to his later "photo essays." Although Marker continued to be active in the publishing world, his critical journalistic essays became more infrequent as his preoccupation with film increased. Furthermore, his writing became more self-reflexively concerned with elements of film. Indeed, his collection of film commentaries, *Commentaires* (1961) and *Commentaires II* (1967), features a vast number of film stills and other illustrations alongside his written narrative. In some instances, the texts address films that remained in the project stage. For example, the descriptions of his two "imaginary films," *L'Amérique rêve* (America Dreams, 1959) and *Soy Mexico* (I Am Mexico, 1965), are accompanied by illustrations, cartoons, and photographs. In *Soy Mexico,* however, Marker problematizes the role of the text, explaining that "it is more of a commentary than a description, with the voice of the person reciting the text taking over that of the narrator without there being any indication in the typeface" (Marker, *Commentaires II* 40). This reflection on the function of a text or commentary as transmitted by voice-over or read by a narrator in a film would have a significant impact on much of his later work.

Marker's next two books, *Coréennes* (1959) and *Le dépays* (1982), are highly idiosyncratic photo essays. The subtitle of *Coréennes* is "Court-Métrage" (short film), indicating the author's attempt to blur distinctions between the media of film and print. In the case of *Le dépays,* Marker questions the traditional limits of photojournalism and the photo essay, in which there is a correspondence between the text and the image.

More specifically, Marker seeks to rupture the constraining bond between text and image, rejecting the idea that the latter illustrates the former as thoroughly as the idea that the former comments on the latter. As he states in his advice to the reader at the beginning of *Le dépays:* "The text is no more a commentary for the image than images are illustrations of the text. They are two different series of sequences that inevitably cross each other and interact now and then. But it would be pointless and tiring to have one confront the other." Marker thus clearly separates text and image and theorizes a structural rather than a supplemental relationship between them. Neither system of signification is granted precedence over the other, a point of view that propels the medium in a new direction.

Marker also explores the nature of film as a moving image. These investigations culminate in two productions, *La jetée* and *If I Had Four Camels,* made almost entirely with still photographs. His curiosity regarding, and preoccupation with, the relationship of photographic images to text, context, and historical narrative resurfaces in 2001 with *Le Souvenir d'un avenir* (Remembrance of Things to Come)—an homage to photographer Denise Bellon. Marker has explained his turn to cinema in the 1950s by saying that he realized he would never amount to much as a photographer—that he would "never be, say, Robert Frank."[12] Yet Marker's interest in the moving image can also be located in another strand in his intellectual formation: the encounter with surrealism. André Breton's dictum that "images come spontaneously" could just as easily be Marker's. Indeed, Breton's peculiar blend of text and image in works such as *Nadja* bears a remarkable similarity to Marker's own practice and to the central importance the latter places on circumventing any form of rational logic or expectations in images. In every one of Marker's films there is an element of chance and surprise. Like Bazin and others in his circle, Marker was interested in fusing existentialism and surrealism.[13] Yet what distinguishes him is his steadfast refusal to diminish the importance of Marxism in this mix.

The Cinematic Landscape

> Love the radio more than literature, cinema more than radio, and music more than anything else.
> —Chris Marker, *Le Coeur net*

"Guillaume-en-Egypte" in *Cat Listening to Music*

In 1949 and 1950, Marker made several radio broadcasts. One of these, "Jusqu'à la fin des temps" (Until the End of Time, 1949), was transmitted through the program "Club d'essai" (Essay Club). The text of this radio broadcast, published two years earlier in the journal *Esprit*, in many ways anticipates *La jetée*. From 1950 onward Marker devoted an increasing amount of time to filmmaking. According to Resnais, when he first met Marker the latter was already in possession of a 16 mm camera (an innovation at the time) and wanted to make films. Resnais and Marker collaborated on the thirty-minute short *Les statues meurent aussi* (1953), which was censored for more than a decade by the Centre National de la Cinématographie because of its condemnation of French colonialism. Marker was mainly responsible for the commentary on this project and Resnais for the cinematography.

Marker's first feature-length film was *Olympia 52*, an eighty-two-minute documentary filmed in 16 mm (later enlarged to 35 mm) during that year's Olympic Games in Helsinki. Also in the mid-1950s, he experimented with the new medium of television. One of these investigations, titled *La clé des songes* (The Key of Dreams), after the eponymous canvas of 1930 by the surrealist painter René Magritte, was organized around the idea that people would send their dreams to the producers to be filmed and broadcast. In one of the last episodes of *La clé des songes*, Marker's commentary blatantly states that neither psychoanalysis nor

French television actually exists. The program seems to have had quite an impact; it was immediately cancelled by the studio and a control commission was put into place to ensure that nothing like it would ever be broadcast again. Marker did not return to the medium of television until the 1970s. Since *Olympia 52*, Marker has produced more than fifty audiovisual works as well as many collaborative and collective projects. As a rule, his films range from a couple of minutes to four hours in length; they never fit the standard of ninety minutes.

The decade during which Marker emerged as a filmmaker was extremely important for French culture generally and cinema in particular. During the years of the Fourth Republic in the 1950s, it was generally believed that French postwar cinema was in a state of crisis and stagnation. Disparaging terms such as *papa's cinema* were used to refer to the productions of classic directors, and there was a concerted effort to revitalize the film industry by introducing and supporting younger filmmakers. Thus, an editorial by Pierre Billard in 1958 entitled "Forty under Forty," placed hopes for a renewal in forty first-time directors, including Louis Malle, François Truffaut, and Claude Chabrol. Many of these directors had started their cinematic careers as writers or critics in serious film journals that proliferated the cultural scene, such as *Cahiers du Cinéma, Cinéma, Positif,* and *Jeune Cinéma.* At this time, the figure of the public intellectual and cultural critic emerged, and the highly innovative productivity of Bazin, Resnais, Jean-Luc Godard, Truffaut, and others in the 1950s elevated the status of filmmaking in France to a serious art form.[14] In addition, economic plans in the form of taxes and restrictions helped provide financial resources and support to bolster the languishing film industry. In order to provide a counter to the deleterious effects of the Blum-Byrnes Agreement of 1946 that opened French markets to U.S. products, including film, a tax was added to the entrance fee of all cinema tickets. Any funds generated by this tax had to be invested directly into French film production.[15] The mechanism necessary to develop a vibrant film culture was already plainly evident in the beginning of the decade. The same period also saw a dramatic increase of ciné clubs and cinémathèques. For film buffs, to view two to three new films a day was not unusual. As Jean-Michel Frodon chronicles in his study of postwar French cinema, a steady growth in cinematic production in France took place between 1950 and 1958, culminating in the well-known explosion of new films in 1958. If there is a term that best describes the conditions of the French film industry of the 1950s when Marker began to make his forays into cinema, then, despite the seemingly contradictory tag of stagnation, it surely would be *thriving*.

The birth of the Nouvelle Vague or French New Wave is conventionally dated 1959, the same year, incidentally, as the instauration of Charles de Gaulle's Fifth Republic. Truffaut observed in a 1961 *France-Observateur* interview with Louis Marcorelles that fifty new names emerged from the explosion of new cinema in the late 1950s. He used this circumstance to explain why he thought that the press found it necessary to define this striking period of vitality and rich production with a new term: Nouvelle Vague. Among the many filmmakers whose work came to be known at this time were Marker, Chabrol, Jacques Demy, Georges Franju, Malle, Resnais, Jacques Rivette, Eric Rohmer, Jacques Tati, Truffaut, Roger Vadim, Agnès Varda, and others. Many of these directors were writers for film journals, and their knowledge of film theory and criticism helped them produce viable alternatives to traditional cinema. Yet the films made by these directors defied easy categorization because they incorporated a wide range of cinematic styles, narrative structures, and editing techniques. Despite the convenient tag Nouvelle Vague, which has now come to encompass a considerably broad swath of work, the cohesiveness of the filmmaking community was not as smooth as presented by the press. Truffaut was arguing already by 1961 that Nouvelle Vague was a deceptive label that did not adequately capture the great diversity of films then being produced. He distinguished between two different types of cinema: the *branche Lumière* and the *branche Delluc*. In effect, this distinction continued the conventional division between the Lumières and the Méliès legacies of film, which also broke down into fiction and nonfiction. But Truffaut's aim in summoning Delluc was more complex. Delluc, who was also a novelist and a critic, thought that the camera could be used to film ideas and actions that had a significance beyond that which was evident and that cinema could become a new and independent art. According to Truffaut, the Delluc branch was represented by Jean Epstein, Marcel L'Herbier, Jacques Feyder, Jean Grémillon, Alexandre Astruc, and others for whom cinema was a language unto itself. In turn, Truffaut called for a Cinéma des Editions de Minuit, reminiscent of the literary series that published Nouvelle Vague authors such as Alain Robbe-Grillet, which would include the films of, among others, Resnais, Varda, and Marker. Many of these young directors were making works with a strong sociopolitical dimension, which is not entirely surprising because they were all in one way or another affiliated with Travail et Culture and Peuple et Culture.

Several years earlier, in 1953, Resnais, Marker, Varda, and Astruc were among the newly formed Groupe des Trente (Group of Thirty), which promoted the development of the short film. (The group's name referred to the maximum length of what they determined to be a short film.) Their initial manifesto/proclamation read: "Next to the novel and other extensive works, there is the poem, the short story, or the essay, which often plays the role of a hothouse; it has the function of revitalizing a field with the contribution of fresh blood. The short film has the same role. Its death will also be the death of film, since an art that ceases to change is a dead art." These filmmakers sought to use the form of the short film to experiment with the medium and impel it in new directions. But this did not prevent many of the practitioners of the short film, including Marker, from going on to make lengthier production, as all eventually did.

A year after Truffaut proposed the Branche Delluc, U.S. critic Richard Roud came up with the designation Left Bank (Rive Gauche) to refer to the work of Marker, Resnais, and Varda. Roud described the films of these directors primarily as documentary productions marked by political and social problems. In his view, the generation these directors represented "have inherited the legacy of the Thirties," and especially that decade's "passionate concern about political and social problems and a conviction that these problems have their place in the realm of art" (Roud, "The Left Bank," 25–26). The Left Bank, Roud continues, has come to represent avant-garde aesthetic practice in France. The filmmakers connected to this movement have developed an "interest in problems of form" that is more thorough than their Right Bank (Rive Droite) counterparts, which includes directors such as Godard, Rohmer, and Truffaut. (Revisiting the topic a few years later, Roud observes that Godard eventually switched sides to join the Left Bank group.) Whatever the designation of his films, whether they be based on biography, geography, or medium specificity, Marker's attempt from the beginning of his career was to expand the possibilities of cinema.

Filmed Intelligence

"Cinema and not film"
—*The Last Bolshevik*

In his October 30, 1958, review of *Letter from Siberia,* only days prior to his death in November of that year, Bazin observes that Marker's film is unlike any other documentary.[16] The closest *Letter from Siberia* comes to another film, he argues, is Jean Vigo's *A propos de Nice* of 1930. Bazin praises Marker's film for its formal innovations, in particular its introduction of a new mode of editing and the establishment of a "horizontal montage" that moves sideways from *l'oreille à l'oeil* (ear to eye). He also applauds Marker's insertion of playful sequences into the flow of the film, such as animated images of wooly mammoths. But it was the guiding "intelligence" driving the film that Bazin found most remarkable. As he puts it: "The primary material is intelligence, and language is its direct expression. The image only intervenes in the third position, in reference to this verbal intelligence" (180). Thus, for Bazin, Marker's development of a truly innovative form of filmed intelligence made his work outstanding.

Bazin also praised the narrative sequence in *Letter from Siberia* that features a triad of different commentaries superimposed over the same visual track. The commentaries project "three intellectual beams" onto that single track, and receive "their reverberation" *(envoyer trois faisceaux intellectuels et recevoir l'écho)* in return. Bazin's metaphor of beams evokes the dynamic and vibrating rays of light projected by cinema. Yet, with the suggestion that the intellectual beams are simultaneously cast from three directions and create a medley of equally dynamic and vibrant images upon a screen, Bazin crystallizes the filmic practice of Marker: a practice that is at once sensitive to the intellectual nature of texts and to the traces of their audiovisual echoes. Marker's attention is drawn to at least three overlapping, intertwined, and interdependent planes. None can be addressed adequately without reference to the other two. I will use the three to structure my analysis of Marker's work.

The first area plane encompasses the audiovisual essay. It focuses in particular on Marker as a film essayist who steadfastly explores the parameters of nonfiction cinema and pushes that genre in new ways, such as into the three-dimensional form of installations. The second plane concerns pedagogy. It explores Marker's contribution to the development of contemporary cinema through an examination of the varying degrees of assistance he has provided to other filmmakers, his support for counter media, and his attempt to put into practice a public sphere that would provide an alternative to the dominance of mass media. Importantly, these strategies are remarkably similar to those of Brecht, who was persistent in his attempt to teach individuals how to resist ideology, and how to read authentic images. That Marker's productions have in the past fifty years had a unique influence on many politically committed filmmakers throughout the world attests to the success of this facet of his practice. The third plane of my analysis will explore Marker's development of innovative formal techniques. Indeed, Marker was one of the first directors to use 16 mm film, portable synch cameras, television, Super 8, the Portapak, computer graphics, and most recently CD-ROM. He has been consistent in his attempt to remain abreast of new technologies. In each instant, the intellectual beams are directed toward illuminating and spotlighting previously underexposed areas of film production. Whether it be generic, thematic, or technological, preestablished conventions and traditions are disrupted and at times dismantled by Marker's cinematic practice. If one examines these three intellectual beams in tandem, then the remarkable diversity of his production and the breadth of its influence can be better understood. The following study of Marker's work will elucidate these three planes in their vibrant complexity and address the intricacies of their interrelationship.

The Elephant's Memory: The Filmed Essay

"Did you know," said Elena Andréivna leaning over the samovar, "they have a flute in South America which can be heard only by its player?"
—Pouchkine, as cited by Marker

I am an essayist. . . . Film is a system that allows Godard to be a novelist, Gatti to make theater, and me to make essays.
—Marker

Statue of Elephant from alley leading to Ming tomb in *Sunday in Peking*

In his review of Marker's *Letter from Siberia,* Bazin expands on his praise of the "intelligent" film by describing it as "an essay in the form of a filmic reportage on the past and present reality of Siberia. . . . An essay documented by film." The term *essay,* he continues, should be "understood in the same way it is in literature: an essay is both historical and political, while being written by a poet" (180). Bazin's mobilization of this term in the context of cinematographic practice was not entirely new. As early as 1940, Hans Richter, the German avant-garde director, had written a short text entitled "The Film Essay: A New Form of Documentary Film." There, Richter describes the emergence of a new genre of film that enables the director to make "problems, thoughts, even ideas" perceptible and to "render visible what is not visible." He dubbed this genre the *essay film,* noting that it "deals with difficult themes in generally comprehensible form." Indeed, unlike the documentary film that presents facts and information, the essay film, according to Richter, produces complex thoughts that are not necessarily grounded in *reality.* These thoughts are occasionally contradictory and not always rational. The filmmaker is thus no longer bound to the rules and parameters of traditional documentary practice and is given free rein to use his or her imagination with all of its artistic potentiality (198). Richter justifies his use of the term *essay* for this new type of filmmaking by noting that like the latter the written essay is a subgenre between major genres—the philosophical treatise and the literary excurses—and as such is inherently transgressive, digressive, playful, contradictory, and at times even political. In short, Richter posited the essay film as a subgenre situated between documentary and experimental or artistic filmmaking. That it also combines these genres testifies to the inherent creativity of this new filmic form.

Richter's concept of the essay film was further developed by French filmmaker and theorist Astruc, a close associate of Marker, who was also involved in Peuple et Culture and in the Groupe des Trente. Astruc stressed the new genre's literary and philosophical antecedents. Already in 1948, he speculated in "Naissance d'une avant-garde: la caméra stylo" (Birth of an Avant-garde: The Camera-Pen) that if Descartes were to write his *Discours* today, it would be "written" in the form of a 16 mm essay film. Astruc described the new subgenre as "filmed philosophy" and advanced the notion of a *camera-stylo* (camera-pen) that within the context of cinema would "become a means of writing, just as flexible and subtle as written language, . . . [rendering] more or less literal 'inscriptions' on images as 'essays.'" *To essay*, within the French tradition at the time, meant "to assay," "to weigh," as well as "to attempt," suggesting an open-ended, evaluative, and speculative search. This supposedly objective prospect is haunted and constrained by the presence of the individual subjectivity of the "essayist." The current French use of the word *essay* as a distinct genre can be traced to the sixteenth-century social critic and philosopher Michel de Montaigne, whose *Essais* (1580) exerted a deep influence not only on Enlightenment philosophers but also on a number of social critics. By *essay* Montaigne meant the testing of ideas, himself (slyly qualified as "the most frivolous of topics"), and society. His essayistic approach can be summed up by the phrase "que-sais-je" (What do I know?), which reveals that any investigation of society is concomitantly an investigation of one's own relationship to that society.[17] The Montaignian essay was a wide-ranging form of cognitive perambulation and meditation that reflected upon fundamental questions of life and human frailty, tensions, and overlaps between "fact" and "fiction" and their consequences for social order and disorder. Since Montaigne, the essay has retained some of its distinguishing features. Its weapons are humor, irony, satire, and paradox; its atmosphere is contradiction and the collision of opposites.

The definition of the written essay has always encompassed the essay film's philosophical and literary dimensions. The subgenre is even more of a hybrid within the realm of film. For one thing, it weaves in and out of the two established dominant modes of film categorization: fiction and documentary. For another, it neither follows a clear narrative trajectory nor shuns storytelling. Furthermore, the essay film often self-reflexively offers its own film criticism, supplying a theoretical flavor to its narratives. Like its ancestor, the written essay, it poaches across disciplinary borders or transgresses conceptual and formal norms. That Marker would choose to work in this genre when making films is not surprising given his mastery of the literary essay. One of the tenets of the Groupe des Trente was that the short film should function in a manner similar to the written essay and that it would advance and expand the filmic genres of the feature and the documentary in significant ways. By the mid-1950s then, essayistic tendencies can be found not only in the work of Marker but also in that of Resnais and others, and the term *essai cinémathographique* (cinematographic essay) was in frequent use. Indeed some of the cinémathèques exhibiting primarily documentaries and avant-garde films were referred to as art and "essai" theaters. Yet it was Marker's filmic work that most pointedly represented this new genre, and the director came to be described by film critics as the "1 to 1:33 Montaigne" (Roud, "The Left Bank," 27).

Marker's filmic essays are heavily multilayered: an image track, which often contains writing on the screen, and a sound track usually accompanied by a dominating voice-over commentary. Graphic marks are sometimes literally inscribed onto the celluloid, but most often intertitles are used. The sound track or layer is occasionally in direct contradiction with the image track, creating within the total filmic text a jarring collision of signs and various levels of meaning that the audience must coproduce. More generally, both the literary and the audiovisual essays are positioned against relatively more stable genres of feature and documentary and thus directly problematize these binary systems of representation. Thus, Bazin's description of Marker's work not only as a form of intelligence but also as a constant formulation of questions is absolutely appropriate and is further supported by Marker's identification with the "insatiable curiosity" of the Elephant Child (Marker interview 2003).

But there are other reasons for the multifaceted diversity of Marker's essay films. Just as the literary and philosophical essays often combine autobiography, biography, history, social commentary, and forms of critical exegesis, essay films, too, adopt various formal schemes. Hence, it is not uncommon to encounter internal tensions within an essay film because by its very nature such a film is pulled in different directions by its constitutive elements. For the purposes of clarity, however, Marker's filmic essays will be here grouped into categories and discussed as travel essays that often adopt epistolary forms, humorous essays with anecdotal digressions that playfully deal with the banality of everyday life, self-reflexive essays that refract and critique the image, and portrait essays that occasionally include elements of autobiography.

Sunday in Peking

> I write to you from a faraway place.
>
> —*Letter from Siberia*

> With his four dromedaries, Don Pedro d'Alfaroubeira traveled around the world and admired it. He did what I would like to do.
>
> —*If I Had Four Camels*

Many of Marker's films are set in faraway places. He does not always foreground the journey to these locations. Yet the images recorded once Marker reaches his destination make it possible to connect these films both to the genre of the written travel essay and to popular film travelogues. Travel in general, despite or because of its very transitory condition, has long provided Marker with a rich supply of resources. Often, it has led him to innovative and fragmentary modes of presentation, such as letters describing the experience of the traveler, notebooks filled with fleeting observations, or diaries and journals that record the geographical and psychological dimensions of the journeys. The encounter with foreign, often exotic, cultures at once provides new knowledge about specific conditions and greater insight into the structures of human behavior.

Marker's fascination with alien customs and the details of everyday life inevitably trigger comparisons with writers such as Montaigne

"An image from childhood" in *Sunday in Peking*

and others who have published their travel journals. The magic-lantern shows of the nineteenth century established a full-fledged subgenre that came to be known as the travel lecture. These shows thrilled audiences with photographic images of distant lands. Early cinema developed this subgenre to the extent that in 1903 approximately half of internationally produced films concerned travel. Filmic travelogues continued to expand throughout the twentieth century, with offshoots in ethnography and anthropology. Even fictional narratives were set in exotic locations. Film became a form of travel, transporting audiences to remote lands. At the same time, travel became increasingly cinematic; voyagers came to structure their experiences in a filmic manner. Marker alludes to this symbiotic relationship in *Sunday in Peking* (1955) in which the commentary notes that "it really is China, like in the movies. One expects that Humphrey Bogart wearing a white suit will emerge from an opium den." This highly mediated filmic or photographic way of seeing the world became second nature for an increasing number of U.S. viewers who, according to Marker in *America Dreams*, travel around the globe armed with a Kodak and accumulate images to consume back home in the secure comfort of an armchair. The simulation of images overtakes the narrator of *Sunless*, Sandor Krasna, almost a quarter of a century later: "I remember that month of January in Tokyo, or rather I remember the images I filmed in that month of January in Tokyo. They have replaced my memory. They *are* my memory."

The sites to which Marker travels in his first decade of filmmaking are highly significant. China, the Soviet Union, the United States, Israel, and Cuba are all marked by novelty in one way or another. Three of these countries experienced Socialist revolutions in the twentieth century, and one achieved statehood as a direct result of the Holocaust. Marker also makes films that allude to travel even though they were mostly shot in Paris. For instance, *Les statues meurent aussi* (Statues Also Die, 1953), a collaboration with Resnais, also constitutes a travelogue of sorts. The two directors explore the fate of a number of African cultural objects that were displaced from their native environment and recontextualized in Europe. The insinuation is that travel and exploration are often accompanied by plunder and colonialization. With his short *Sunday in Peking*, however, Marker explicitly strives to film China—a place historically viewed as "exotic"—from a perspective that is marked neither by Orientalism nor by a colonizing gaze but instead by intelligence.

Sunday in Peking was shot during the fifteen days that Marker spent in China on a trip organized by the association Amitiés Franco-Chinoises (French-Chinese Friends). The twenty-two-minute, 16 mm film was made as part of the Groupe des Trente films. In his preliminary notes to the published written commentary, the filmmaker stresses that "this film is not, can not, does not want to be an essay on China, that would be an enterprise which would take far more time, much more effort and infinitely more humility" (Marker, *Commentaires*, 29). Indeed, the sense of humility is key to understanding both Marker and his work. Neither the director nor the films presume to have all the answers, neither present ideas as definitive expressions of thought, and both view thinking as a process. Marker's insistence that *Sunday in Peking* is not, can not be, and certainly does not claim to be an essay is clearly overstated, especially given that the film's essayistic traits are so prominent and foundational.

One of the essayistic characteristics of *Sunday in Peking* is located in the nature of the commentary. With its personal and conversational style, much of the commentary stands in sharp contrast to the "objective" voice-over that was the norm in contemporary documentaries. From the onset of the film, the spectator is immediately drawn into its intimacy with the words "Nothing is more beautiful than Paris, unless it is the memory of Paris. And nothing is more beautiful than Peking, unless it is the memory of Peking. And me in Paris, I remember Peking, and I count my treasures." The commentary is highly subjective, beginning with the aesthetic judgments that Paris, Peking, and the memories the two cities invoke are beautiful. Unlike documentaries that present viewers with the visual and verbal information needed for them to draw their own conclusions, what is presented in this instance is stated as fact—not only the beauty of the two cities but even more remarkably the director's personal and intangible *memory* of the cities. Even the opening shot is deliberately confusing. A close-up of an object whose details suggest something vaguely "exotic" or "oriental" transforms into a symbol of modernity as the camera pulls back and the Eiffel Tower suddenly emerges at an odd angle in the frame. This device of a disorienting opening shot recurs in films by Marker, as for example in *Le joli mai,* which opens with a shot of a building being scaled by elusive Fantômas. Marker was surely aware that directly challenging and disorienting the visual experience of the viewer, transforming the screen image into a strange vision, harkens back to the visual experiments of the Russian Constructivists and in particular to the literary theories of Russian and Czech Formalists, such as Victor Schlovsky, who argued that the task of literature was to "make strange" *(ostranienie)* and hence interesting the most ordinary events. This strategy of making the banalities of life look as if they were seen for the first time, stripping away the varnish of habit and ideology, is a defining characteristic of Marker's work. More than merely details, however, this trait can be applied to entire films such as *Sunday in Peking.* Bazin noticed this when he remarked that *Sunday in Peking* clearly aimed to be "an original work, belonging at the same time to literature, cinema, and photography. . . . Neither a poem, nor a reportage, nor a film, but a dazzling synthesis of all of the above" (Bazin, "Sur les routes").

Marker's commentary in *Sunday in Peking* is remarkable: "I had been dreaming about Peking for thirty years, without knowing it. In my mind's eye, I see an engraving from a children's book, without having known from where exactly it came . . . and it was exactly from the gates of Peking: the alley which takes you to the Ming tomb. It was a beautiful day, and I was there." The viewer thus immediately enters into a world in which the present is shrouded in dreams and memories from the past. Next comes a phrase that recalls a passage from *La jetée:* "It is rather rare to be able to walk in an image from childhood." The oneiric opening of the film sets the tone for a meditation that will be characterized by a blurring of past, present, and future, making these time frames as hazy as the mist through which Marker's camera shoots its images and foreshadowing the opening of *Le joli mai.* The short then recaptures a day in Peking and ends with an ambiguous final commentary that at one and the same time brings images together spatially and separates them temporally. Time and space are contrasted to each other in a film that purposefully confuses reality with dreams and memories: "All of that is far away like China, but at the same time as familiar as the Bois de Boulogne or the river banks of the Loing. . . . In this decor filled with a bygone grandeur, in these avenues of this Mongolian Versailles, one can easily ask questions about the past and the future."

The presentation of historical "fact" in *Sunday in Peking* is just as confusing. The film betrays an open lack of concern for historical veracity; the aforementioned statue-lined alley does not lead to where the Mings are buried. As the narrator slyly remarks, "Where they are [buried] that's their business." The alley is thus a misleading or false path without a teleological direction, similar to what in German is called a *holzweg,* a wood path leading nowhere that rhetorically refers to the way that essayistic thoughts often digress without a clear end in sight. Recall that the structure of the essay emphasizes process over conclusions. For the film narrator, it does not make a difference whether the Mings are actually buried at the end of the alley; what is important is the beauty of the path, the figures of animals erected to guide the travelers, the experience of the journey down the alley, and the memories that journey evokes. Such disregard for factual truth persists in the commentator's efforts to convey a different sort of truth, one that seeks to impart the complexity of a revolution "that has been waged against capitalists, yes, but also against dust, against microbes, against flies. The result is that one can still find capitalists in China, but there aren't any more flies." The tone is at once gently mocking and ironic. When the film was released, the tone connoted an admiration that was interpreted as being Communist propaganda by West German censors who would not allow it to be screened in Berlin.[18]

As the narrator of *Sunday in Peking* enters the old city, the camera lingers on picturesque scenes that evoke a bygone era before modernity and revolution (or revolution and then modernity) swept through China. The nostalgic reverie is suddenly interrupted as the camera fixes on an elderly woman who is barely able to walk because of her mutilated feet. The voice-over continues, "But the price of modernism would have perhaps appeared to us too heavy, had not the price of the picturesque suddenly been inscribed before our eyes: a woman with mutilated feet, a survivor from the time of the emperor." With that image, the ever-lurking dangers of a reactionary nostalgia surface, and the viewer is reminded of Brecht's famous dictum "Let us not praise the good old days, but welcome the bad new ones."

Yet no trip or film would be complete for Marker without the appearance of friends, both human and animal. Representations of animals abound in this film, from stone statues of camels and elephants that line the Avenue of the Mings to elaborate images of horses adorning battle scenes; from costumed monsters, dragons, and tigers that appear in the theater to poetic turns of phrase such as "et les yeux des lionnes qui dévisagent le soleil" (and the eyes of lionesses that stare at the sun). Late in the afternoon of that Sunday in Peking, the film takes us to the zoo where resides a bear named Joris Ivens, a gift from the filmmaker Ménegoz. Whether or not this animal's name is really Joris Ivens remains in question. But by hailing it as such in the film, Marker acknowledges his respect for his colleague, just as he does with Agnès Varda, whom the credits identify as his "sinologist." Such gestures of recognition toward friends and comrades permeate Marker's oeuvre. In *Le joli mai* the camera lingers on a wall with the graffitied name Gatti; in *Description of a Struggle* a Varda hairdressing salon appears on the screen; and a shot of people exiting from a movie theater featuring *Hiroshima, mon amour* is highlighted in *Cuba Si!* Paradoxically, Marker's solitariness is coupled with his loyalty and commitment to a close-knit community of friends with whom he will collaborate throughout his career.

Letter from Siberia

In August 1957, four years after the death of Stalin, Marker traveled to Siberia with his friends Pierrard, Armand Gatti, and Sacha Vierny to make his next film, *Letter from Siberia*. The film, Marker insists, rejects

Mammoths in *Letter from Siberia*

the documentary style of Soviet social realism in which "the rule was that all images, like the wife of Stalin, had to be above suspicion. Positive - Positive - Positive until infinity—something which is very strange coming from the country of the dialectic" (Marker, *Commentaires,* 43). To distance himself from the documentary style sanctioned by the Soviet state, Marker presents the film in the form of a personal letter, which begins with the famous line, "Je vous écris d'un pays lointain" (I write to you from a faraway country). The epistolary form Marker employs also signals the essayistic nature of the film. Essay travelogues have traditionally been cast as meditative letters.[19] That genealogy harkens back to the public documents of classical antiquity. Isocrates tested his Athenian oratory style in a series of epistles, and Epicurus put much of his philosophical writing in letter form. Roman writers such as Seneca, Horace, and Ovid developed the essayistic epistolary genre further. Late Renaissance and early modern essayists also used public letters to convey their ideas. Montaigne, for instance, turned to the epistolary essay after the death of his interlocutor, Etienne de la Boetie, in order to maintain the spirit of the dialogue.

Marker has employed the letter form in some of his most significant films: *Letter from Siberia, Sunless,* and *The Last Bolshevik.* As with Montaigne's turn to the epistolary essay, Marker's *The Last Bolshevik* was inspired by the death of a good friend, Alexander Medvedkine, in 1989. The film outlines the cultural history of the Soviet Union through the lens of a portrait of this important Russian filmmaker. But Marker may not even have been aware of the existence of Medvedkine when making *Letter from Siberia*. Rather, the latter focuses more on the possibilities of essayistic filmmaking and experimentation than on the Soviet Union. In fact, it has been observed that in his coverage of things Siberian, Marker neglected to mention what Western audiences most commonly think of when Siberia is summoned: the Gulags and the masses of political prisoners who were sent by Stalin to their deaths there.[20] Instead, Marker's "letter" focuses on other, less grim, and perhaps more surprising and visually striking aspects of life in this remote region of Eurasia.

The film opens with a long tracking shot that depicts a rich and colorfully textured landscape: nothing grey, bleak, or frozen here. A Russian song bursts from the sound track and threatens to overwhelm the image as the countryside passes by as viewed from the window of a moving train. Throughout the film the camera tracks slowly from right to left and then back again, traversing space like a dancer. Then comes the voice-over—"I write to you from a faraway country"—followed by images of trees in a forest. Minutes later, a slight variation of the opening sentence is spoken over more shots of trees. This time it says "Je vous écris du bout du monde," evoking a phrase from the surrealist *Plume précédeé de Lointain intérieur* (1938) by Henri Michaux: "I am writing to you from the end of the world. You should know it. The trees are often shivering. Leaves are gathered. They have a crazy number of veins. Friends, what is the use? There is no longer anything between them and the tree." The shots of woods take on a different meaning, as if they were there to visually represent and continue the lines of the poem that the commentator has started to read aloud. Finally, after a few minutes, the first cut to shots of men working on telephone poles and electricity line appears. They put into place the technology that abolishes distance and brings the region into the twentieth century. This is followed by a series of sharp cuts, most of which are announced by the ring of a bell. Whether or not the image track is cut to the audial or the audial to the images remains unclear. Yet Bazin's review of the film favored the former: "The primordial element is the sonorous beauty and it is from there that the mind must leap to the image. The editing is done from ear to eye" (Bazin, "Chris Marker," 180). From ear to eye, from audial to visual, this is a process that reverses the standard editing practice. In fact, the relationship between the sound track and the image track is continuously questioned throughout *Letter from Siberia*.

The sound track is entirely nondiegetic and is composed of music, dramatic noises, and the guiding voice of the narrator. Each of these registers has a special relationship with the images and is edited accordingly. Furthermore, many of the transitions are effected through sound bridges. Interestingly, Marker even uses sound bridges between different films, as for instance when he adapts Eisler's haunting musical score from *Night and Fog* to a sequence of *Far from Vietnam* and thereby painfully highlights the atrocious nature of the war being waged in Southeast Asia. Elsewhere he couples shots of nature with an overpowering musical composition. For instance, a passage that focuses on the river Léna commences with a song in praise of the tributary and ends with a series of highly dramatic chords as the current pounds and churns, representing a powerful force of unchanneled energy. In another sequence, a Siberian song about the profound effect that Yves Montand's voice has on the singer summons Paris in Siberia. Songs, like images, transport the audience to faraway places. In a sense, images also have to be heard, as the narrator explains at the end of *Sunday in Peking:* "I who am recording these images, and breathing them, and listening to them." Indeed, the commentator's role in Marker's films is both to breathe life into the pictures and to listen to their sounds. In one of the most celebrated passages of *Letter from Siberia,* three different commentaries (three intellectual beams) accompany the same image, producing very different effects. The sequence concerns an image of Yakutsk:

1. Yakutsk, capital of the Socialist republic of Yakutia, is a modern city where comfortable buses used by the common people are constantly coming across powerful Zim, the crown of Soviet cars. Thanks to the joyful competition offered by Socialist labor, the happy Soviet workers, among whom we recognize picturesque inhabitants of the boreal regions, are intent to make out of Yakutia a blessed country for its residents.

2. Yakutsk has a terrible reputation. It is a dark city where the common people squeeze uncomfortably in blood-red buses, while the powerful authorities insolently parade the luxury of their Zims, actually quite expensive and uncomfortable. Bent over like slaves, the miserable Soviet workers, among whom we notice the presence of alarming Asiatic types,

are applying themselves to a symbolic labor: bringing down equality to the lowest possible level.

3. In Yakutsk, where modern housing replaces, little by little, the dark old districts, a bus that is less crowded than in Paris at rush hour is coming across a Zim, an excellent car produced in small quantities and reserved for public services. With courage and determination, under very hard conditions, Soviet workers, among whom we notice the presence of a squinting Yakut, are working hard to beautify their city, which needs it a lot.

Each of the previous commentaries is accompanied by appropriate, albeit clichéd, "mood" music. Marker thus illustrates the manipulative and deceptive effects of sound tracks and their powerful ability to alter the meaning of an image. By the same token, he calls into question the possibility of a true or pure image with a stable meaning in cinema, because the medium does not exist without a sound track. As will be shown later, the semiological nature of the image will continue to preoccupy Marker throughout his career. But to return to the sequence at hand, critics who have discussed it have consistently failed to note that it actually appears not three but four times in the film. Furthermore, the sound track used in the first instance of the sequence's appearance has never been addressed. Importantly, although the sound track seems to be spontaneous, it points directly to the essayistic nature of the film:

> A labor, an energy, and an unquestionable enthusiasm—a very heavy past and a striking faith in the future—enormous gaps and a firm will to fill them up—while recording as objectively as possible these images of the Yakut capital, I confess I wondered whom they would please since it is well known that the only way to talk about the USSR is in terms of hell or paradise. (Marker, *Commentaires*, 61)

Hell or paradise are binaries of course, as diametrically opposed to each other as truth and nontruth. Yet essays—including the essay film—by their very nature seek to disrupt all rigid (and absolute) forms of categorization. They favor instead an in-between area, one that reserves a place for contradictions and presents them in a productive and thoughtful manner. No orthodoxies, no clear definitions, appear in the ideal essay. Almost forty years after *Letter from Siberia*, a "level 1" personality in the film *Level Five* is defined (and dismissed) as someone who accepts classifications that render things black and white.

Binaries will not suffice for Marker. Phenomena such as history (especially history!) are much more complicated. As the narrator stresses at the end of the sequence discussed previously: "But objectivity is not right either. It does not deform Siberian reality but it stops it for a moment—the time needed for judgment—and thereby it deforms it all the same. What counts are its impetus and diversity. A walk through Yakutsk's streets will not make you understand Siberia; you would need an imaginary newsreel recorded everywhere in the country." And that is precisely what Marker sets out to do. The rest of the film is presented as a series of "actualities" or snapshots of life in Siberia: the gold rush, a mythical bear, space exploration. The true image of reality flashes before the viewer between the world of fiction and imagination and just as rapidly disappears. Marker further develops this idea in his next text, the imaginary film *America Dreams,* in which he deconstructs U.S. society based on a vision of reality derived from photographic images. "For many Americans," he states, "reality is nothing more than the antechamber of photography" (Marker, *Commentaires,* 95).

Marker thus advocates stripping away all disguises, postures, and masks. Paradoxically, he sees Mardi Gras celebrations as an anticipation of that process. These medieval celebrations "have lost none of their original violence: the costumes are a confession, the masks a confidence. It is the one day of the year where one does not disguise oneself" (Marker, *Commentaires,* 114). In other words, the mask in this case does not disguise anything at all. An exemplary reality paradoxically emerges from a performance that is at once improvised and staged. Similarly, Marker presents the reality of social inequality and violence in modern-day Mexico in the figure of a young boy who risks his life by diving off a cliff in Acapulco to the roaring applause of tourists in another imaginary film, *Soy Mexico.* Such scenes go a long way toward clarifying Marker's fascination with live performances by the Peking Opera and provide a clue as to why some of the last sequences in *Letter from Siberia* record the remarkable theater performances of the Yakoute Opera. For Marker, it seems, it is often in the imaginary that reality reveals itself.

Although the sound track of *Letter from Siberia* calls into question the veracity of the visual track, it still retains a documentary quality. By this I mean that the images that unfold before the viewer were filmed on location, unstaged, and in no way manipulated technologically. Some of these (moving) images are striking and their content obscure. This is the case, for example, when the camera rectangle frames the meeting of a modern forty-ton truck and a donkey-drawn cart or when a Soviet airplane lands in an ice field and is greeted by riders on reindeer and dogsleds. For the first of these two scenes, the narrator self-reflexively observes, "These are just the images that I have been waiting for, that the whole world has been waiting for, without which there could not be a serious film about a country undergoing a transformation: the opposition between the past and the future." He continues, "Look at them closely, I am not going to show you again." This explanation is somewhat spurious because tenuous juxtapositions occur throughout the film. Yet the commentary reflects full awareness of the conventions of this type of film and of the stock scenes required to lend it a reassuring predictability. A more conventional documentary about the region of Siberia would be produced if these rules were followed. Instead, Marker's *Letter* is full of startling and delightful surprises, their reading suspended in the image and its description.

The camera tracks all of the detectable manifestations of daily life in the dense forests of the remote taiga, pausing to record scenes of sheep and cattle being herded and fields populated by ducks. Marker's commentary playfully directs the meaning of these scenes. The ducks, for instance, are presented as "naturally collective animals [who,] despite the frigid morning temperatures, agree, out of sympathy for the cinematographers and out of friendship between the two peoples, to go swimming in the glacial waters at the risk of being frozen—a misfortune that occurred in this vicinity to a much larger animal, more celebrated and moreover more rare, the mammoth." Anthropomorphic images of animals are one of Marker's signature traits. Indeed, animals are consistently privileged in his films, often used as markers or as placeholders that grant the viewer a moment to pause, breathe, and catch his or her breath before moving on to the next section. Marker treats animals as special friends, and several species make regular appearances in his films.

But then, as if the denotative elements of the footage had not been sufficiently mediated by the subjective and playful commentary on the sound track, a visual element appears that ruptures the remaining vestiges of objectivity. More specifically, an animated cartoon sequence of mammoths marching across the terrain suddenly interrupts the passages of landscapes and domesticated animals. The narrator chants a poem over this scene:

> Mammoths, mammoths of Siberia
> Only dreamed of spending winter in Paris
> Fleeing ukases and knout
> Many got lost on the way
> They would be found thirty centuries later
> But in a slightly knockout shape.

What follows is a charming cartoon sequence about mammoths: their possible affinity with moles, the initial discovery of their frozen bodies, and problems in removing, transporting, and reconstituting them. The insertion of this highly amusing digression is consistent with the tacit parameters of the essay, in which the element of play constitutes a crucial rhetorical strategy, at once complex and disarming. That Marker employs the figure of the mammoth in particular is also not without significance. Although extinct for thousands of years, remains of this wooly creature have been preserved in the tundras of Siberia. Unlike dinosaur fossils, which must be reconfigured and leave many details about the animal to the imagination, frozen mammoths are sometimes discovered in their full materiality. The effect is uncanny. Whether it confirms Bazin's theory of the *mummy complex*, which maintains that aesthetic preservation is the driving force behind all representation, is a moot point. Yet the fact remains that the recording of life by photographic or filmic means serves to freeze it in a way that parallels the preservation of the wooly mammoth. Marker also employs imaginary drawings of prehistoric cavemen in this film, and three decades later in *The Last Bolshevik* he draws an analogy between dinosaurs and Communists, suggesting that the utopianism of the latter is kept alive by children who cherish the former.

In another scene from *Letter from Siberia,* Marker visits a subterranean science station where experiments on the effects of freezing are performed. Amid the battery of studies calculating a variety of pressures, melting points, and transformations, Marker finds astonishing specimens of frozen flowers. The flowers represent what the narrator refers to as "a pretty parentheses in the work of the technicians of Iakoutsk" who have invented "the refrigeration of nostalgia." Nostalgia is thus linked to frozen time, without any problematic connotations. Marker uses these sequences to comment on his own filmmaking practice, which will forever freeze in time late summer 1957 in Siberia. Significantly, the theme of preservation will reappear in many of his later projects. These will reflect on the role of museums, technology, and memory and on the difficulties of making audiovisual portraits of friends, whether living (Christo, Roberto Matta), dying (Tarkovsky), or dead (Medvedkine). Films are thus posited as death masks, as memento mori of even that which is not yet dead.

Once back above ground, the camera visits the counterpart of the underground scientific activity: empty spaces designated as culture parks. This in turn leads to the skeptical (and somewhat morbid) reflection that "culture is what remains when everyone has left." One may find in this sentiment an echo, or a continuation, of the opening words of Marker's commentary in the earlier *Statues Also Die:* "When people die they enter into history; when statues die, they enter into art. This botany of death is what we call culture." But what about mammoths, and by extension other animals and wildlife? Do their remains become history or culture? Or do they occupy a space in between?

The cultural destiny of the mammoth is the museum of natural history, one of the oddest of institutions. The function of these museums is in some ways similar to that of zoos, though they preserve dead animals rather than exhibit live ones. Indeed, in some instances, as in the Jardin des Plantes in Paris, the two institutions are located side by side, an irony that does not go unnoticed by Marker, who uses this (double) site as the setting for one of the scenes in *La jetée.* But the museum of natural history has another, more personal, appeal for Marker; it is a hybrid, a location where what was once animate is now preserved and displayed. With its prehistoric remains and dioramas, the natural history museum operates like a film set; both reconstitute an imaginary world. Special pains are taken by the curators of the natural history museum, as by a filmmaker, to research the object of study meticulously and to re-create its context as precisely as possible. By contrast, museums that exhibit artifacts of civilization are filled with items wrested from their original environment. Thus, for instance, African statues and objets d'art in Western museums are largely disconnected from their origins. They are presented as dead objects alienated from the milieu that brought them into being and gave them purposeful meaning, as stated in *Statues Also Die:* "An object is dead when the living gaze that was once cast upon it has disappeared. And when we disappear, our objects will go where we send those of the Africans: to the museum." Hence, it is the "living gaze" that grants an object life, and that gaze is not to be found in a museum.

In contrast, Marker's camera comprehensively records a series of live ritualistic and theatrical performances in Siberia. One features an annual reindeer race, another the festival of spring, and another a play about a young Mongolian warrior whose fiancée has been stolen by demons. The society in which these performances take place is in the midst of a dramatic transformation, rapidly becoming modernized. The rituals captured on film by Marker retain a certain "authenticity," which is in sharp contrast to the African objects, theatrical performances, and dances featured in *Statues Also Die* that have been reified for Western markets. Marker seems aware, however, of the anthropologist's paradox that the very process of documenting these rituals in *Letter from Siberia,* openly turning a camera upon them, produces a significantly different type of performance and undermines the authenticity of the footage. In other words, to nominate an object or act as art necessarily deculturates it. Yet this is a double-edged sword, because recording "primitive" rituals before they are lost or transformed for tourist consumption preserves them in a manner that recalls the mammoth encased in ice.

The second animated sequence in the film, a mock publicity spot for a very contemporary reindeer, is as innovative as the first. Animation was fairly common in postwar France, but this cinematic technique was not considered to be capable of treating serious issues—a prejudice not shared by audiences in Canada, Britain, and several Eastern European countries. The creative dimension of animation was then intricately linked with its craft aspects. Prior to the advent of digital editing, each frame had to be painstakingly drawn by hand and the sequence gradually transformed to give the illusion of life. As a hybrid medium bringing together drawing and movement, animation is entirely imaginary. Animation is the antithesis of film, in which trace elements always link back

Horn Flakes in *Letter from Siberia*

to the analogical surface. Hand-drawn, animated images rely entirely on connotation; they may have as much or as little resemblance to objective reality as the animator desires. Related to this, the experimental aspects of animation allow the characters and themes treated to elude easy classification.[21] Given the highly creative dimension of the medium, as well as its usual restriction to shorts, it is not surprising that Marker would feel an affinity toward animation. Indeed, he had started his filmic career as an animator for Travail et Culture. The animated sequences pushed the other footage of *Letter from Siberia* beyond the documentary and more fully into the domain of the essay. Within the realm of actuality, the cartoon spots create spaces where the imagination is given full reign. Marker's attraction to this aspect of animation returns in his CD-ROM, *Immemory,* in which the cartoon character, the feline Guillaume, serves as the guide.

Like the brief interlude with the mammoth, the digressive animation sequence with the reindeer functions as a palimpsest with multiple meanings. The sequence is framed by the commentary that announces with some irony: "And if I had the means, I would make a short publicity in its praise. At the intermission, or better yet between two reels of film [the actual sequence appears twenty minutes into *Letter from Siberia*], the image would be interrupted and suddenly one would see something like . . . United Productions of Siberia Presents." During the commentary, animated reindeer appear in a variety of delightful guises, including as a mode of transportation, as decorative wall pieces, and even as a variety of packaged cereal (Horn Flakes). The latter is presented by a small stuffed owl that reappears on the "Chris" bookshelf in *Level Five*. The highly amusing nature of the sequence draws attention away from the complexity of technical expertise (through pixilation and montage) needed to set the owl in motion. A voice, imitating the intonation of a commercial announcer, introduces the reindeer sequence:

> If I interrupt this projection for a small instant, it is not in order to boast of a new product, but it is in order to remind you of the existence of an older product, a unique product, an absolute product that will replace all the other products, and it is—the reindeer. Not only will the reindeer satisfy as a domestic animal, less burdensome than a dog, less intimidating than a cat, less insidious than a flea, but—for those of you who complain about your car, the reindeer will transport you,—for those of you who complain about your tailor, the reindeer will clothe you,—for those of you who complain about your doctor, the reindeer will cure you,—for those of you who complain about your interiors, the reindeer will decorate for you,—for those of you who complain about your destiny, the reindeer will protect you—and don't forget, for the small and large, the reindeer is a complete meal that even contains chlorophyll! Managers of the entire world listen to me, in Moscow, in Rome, in New York, in Peking, or Paris . . . beware of copies: neither the stag nor the elk, always insist on: the reindeer!

The idea of a U.S. style commercial produced in the Soviet Union, where such advertising was nonexistent, is highly ironic. The interlude obliquely points to the not-so-funny, rapidly growing consumerism in which everything, including nature, is reified. Yet Siberia was not Marker's real target. Consumer culture, proliferating in the United States, was already by the 1950s making deep inroads in France.[22] Marker prophetically warns at the end of *America Dreams*, which might as well have been named America Nightmares, "it is too easy to isolate America in its foreignness. This type of life which is the most 'decried' throughout the world, is the most imitated, and it is perhaps that which will be in Europe in twenty years. And if America dreams, and if this dream will be ours tomorrow, perhaps it would well be worth the trouble to carefully consider it, before we go to sleep" (Marker, *Commentaires*, 121).

As foreseen by Marker, consumerism swept over France in the 1960s and '70s, dramatically transforming French society. Thus, *Letter from Siberia* is as much about this remote region of Eurasia as it is about this new moment in the United States and France. Analogies and visual quotations reinforce this invasion by U.S. consumer culture: allusions abound to the gold rush and to the West, with its music, frontier towns, trading posts, and even cowboys and Indians.

Letter from Siberia is also a film about filmmaking. Just as the essay was for Montaigne primarily a form about writing, the essay film always has a self-reflexive aspect. For instance, *Letter from Siberia* tries to implement a new form of montage, "from ear to eye." It also mixes various styles, forms, and conventions and rethinks the use of commentary and the role of fiction and imagination. This is further underscored in Marker's *Commentaires,* the printed version of the film, in which the narrator reveals his desire to travel to the moon, to Mars, and straight on through to the constellations of the large bear, the small fox, the North Star, the eagle, the reindeer, Orion, Antares, Hydra, the small horse, and the little dog. The real constellations are intermixed with imaginary ones, identified with the animals that Marker encountered in Siberia, as well as with the inventions of Méliès, the father of science fiction films.

The Koumiko Mystery

> A Horse is a friend to whom you can talk.
> —*The Last Bolshevik*

Marker's early films rarely focus on specific individuals. Rather, they mostly deal with anonymous people. Exceptions include the footage of Fidel Castro and Che Guevara featured in *Cuba Si!* Generally, however, the genre of landscape prevails in these films and that of portraiture plays a minor role. Yet in the 1960s Marker began to make filmic portraits. The first of these is *The Koumiko Mystery* (1965). The film focuses on a young Japanese secretary in her twenties. Marker introduces her as someone whom he met by chance during the 1964 Olympic Games in Tokyo. She likes Giraudoux (recall that one of Marker's early written works was a critical monograph on the French writer), detests lies, was

Horse statuette in *The Last Bolshevik*

student at the Franco-Japanese school, adores Truffaut, and abhors electric typewriters and Frenchmen that are too gallant! The rest of the film follows her through the streets of Tokyo, with Marker gently asking her questions that range from the banal, "You have a serious face?" to more politically probing queries, "Don't you read the news? Haven't you heard about Krushchev? The Chinese bomb? The British elections? The satellite?" Her responses, in a Japanese-accented French, are often vague and inconclusive. The camera presents a number of intimate close-ups of the young woman's face—a stylistic effect that will be repeated in *Level Five* and *Silent Movie*—and the dialogue between Koumiko and her invisible but audible interlocutor, played by Marker, takes place on an informal level.

The Koumiko Mystery is exceptional in that it is one of the few films in which Marker reads his own lines. The casual tone of the banter is misleading, however. Although the film is ostensibly about Koumiko, who is really not that much of a mystery, it doubles as a personal essay about the filmmaker's quest to discover Japan. Similar to Roland Barthes' *Empire of Signs*, which enabled the author to explore an entirely different symbolic system from that of the West, *The Koumiko Mystery* presents Marker with a segue into the culture of Japan, a country to which he will return periodically over the next thirty years.

The Koumiko Mystery fuses the forms of literary biography and artistic portraiture within the medium of film. Marker observes that

Koumiko "is very surprised to find herself in the center of a film which bears her name. History is a tiger that devours itself, but she is the tiger. She has not read Borges, but she knows of him. She knows that she hasn't made history, but she *is* history, like you, like me, like Mao Tse-tung, the Pope, and the opossum." Marker presents her as a microcosm of a much larger social historical phenomenon. Koumiko is chosen because "around her, is Japan." The film thus at once focuses on the figure of Koumiko and on the culture of modern Japan, a Japan that hosts the Olympic Games and presents itself as a vital democracy that has left behind its Fascist, imperial past. As a news broadcaster announces: "The Japanese have not participated in the Olympic Games since 1940—but then it was not the same Japan. In 1940, the Japanese did not make transistors, the emperors did not show reverence." Marker's wandering camera captures everyday life in Tokyo. The narrator relates statistics in a manner that recalls *Le joli mai.* Interspersed throughout the film are news broadcasts reporting an array of sports events and the arrest of nine students demonstrating against the presence of nuclear-equipped U.S. submarines in Japanese waters. The rapidly encroaching process of Westernization is illustrated by a proliferation of blonde mannequins in department stores, posters advertising Hollywood films, and Koumiko's fascination with "European blue eyes." Tokyo is full of signs, many in-scribed in Western letters. The signs often belong to advanced forms of advertising, including a large animated owl that blinks at passersby on the streets below.

The Japanese are shown by Marker to lose themselves amid the signs of modernity, thereby obliterating memories of the not-so-distant past and distracting the population from events taking place outside of the islands. Koumiko, despite her knowledge of a foreign language ("the French of Robbe-Grillet"), makes abundantly clear that she is not interested in world events. In one remarkable sequence, Marker films her with a companion on a riverboat tour in a Disney-like adventure park where a mechanized mammoth crosses their path. Prehistory is treated as mass entertainment, offering cheap thrills and scary rides. By contrast, contemporary history is completely disregarded. The only mention of it comes toward the end of the film when Marker directly asks Koumiko if she thinks that world events have an effect on her existence. She hesitatingly answers, "yes, perhaps," and recalls that not a long time ago "people went to war, they were prisoners, they resisted, they cried out, and their flesh was destroyed." During this exchange, the film cuts to shots of the ultramodern monorail, the transportation of the future that effectively blocks out the past. Koumiko's naiveté is shocking. Yet Marker's response is even more problematic, as the film ends with an odd excuse for her ignorance: "There are 50 million women in Japan. And on the earth, a billion and a half." As if ignorance were a matter of gender.

Marker recorded half of the film's sound track in Tokyo. The other half is based on a cassette tape that Koumiko sent to Marker in Paris in answer to his questions. Once again, then, a traditional form (i.e., the epistolary model) is transformed by technology. Not without irony, Marker describes Koumiko's letters as being "between 6.35 mm in width and 180 meters in length" (Marker, *Commentaires* II, 26). What is important is that both sources—recording and letters—become grist for Marker's own personal essay, which reveals as much about himself as about the medium in which he has chosen to work. As Nietzsche once noted, any biography is at one and the same time also an autobiography. It is not by chance that Koumiko is a fan of Giraudoux, a cat lover, and speaks the language of Robbe-Grillet (a contrived French). "She is not a case, not a cause, not a class, not a race," but indefinable—like Marker himself. Many of the latter's portraits feature elements of self-portraiture and pay homage to those whose influence has been significant. In *The Koumiko Mystery*, the camera lingers on film posters. The name Kurosawa stands out as well as an extended sequence of Japanese umbrellas filmed from a bird's-eye perspective against a sound track borrowed from Jacques Demy's *Les parapluies de Cherbourg* (The Umbrellas of Cherbourg). Whether a mere allusion or an explicit sign of respect for a fellow film-maker, Marker was surely aware that he was evoking "the umbrellas of Tokyo." Yet this was but a fleeting intertextual moment; a few more years pass before Marker makes films that focus on the work of other filmmakers.

The Koumiko Mystery, essentially the portrait of an unknown figure, also serves as a preliminary sketch for the quasi-political portraits that Marker makes in the early 1970s. These begin with his contribution to a series entitled *On vous parle de . . .* (Report on . . .), produced by the collective SLON, of which Marker was a member. The films ranged between fifteen and thirty minutes in length and treated an array of topics from around the world. The subtitle of the series, "Magazine de Contre-Information" (Magazine of Counterinformation), indicates how important it was for the collective to present news from a perspective other than that of the dominant mass media and culture industry. Not surprisingly, the films were never shown commercially. Rather, they were screened by leftist groups and organizations eager to develop a countercinematic practice. Marker made five films for this series. These include *On vous parle de Prague: Le Deuxième Procès d'Artur London* (Report on Prague: The Second Trial of Artur London, 1969), about one of the few survivors of the Prague purges of the 1950s; *On vous parle de Brésil: Tortures* (Report on Brazil: Tortures, 1969), that focuses on torture and human rights abuses; *On vous parle de Brésil: Carlos Marighela* (Report on Brasil: Carlos Marighela, 1970), featuring the Brazilian guerilla combatant; *On vous parle de Paris: Les mots ont un sens* (Report on Paris: Words Have a Meaning, 1970), concerning the left-wing book dealer and publisher François Maspéro; and *On vous parle de Chili: Ce que disait Allende* (Report on Chile: What Allende Said, 1973), about Chilean President Salvador Allende. In each case, the subtopic or theme addresses the increasingly difficult conditions faced by left-wing intellectuals and the importance of maintaining political honesty and integrity. In 1974, Marker made *La solitude du chanteur du fond* (The Loneliness of the Long-Distance Singer), which follows Yves Montand as he prepares a benefit concert for Chilean refugees.[23] That Montand had not performed live in many years made his participation in this concert all the more significant. The portrait of Montand is intercut with footage from films in which he starred, including Costa-Gavras's *Z* (1969) and *L'aveu* (1970), both filmed in Chile with the support of Allende. Montand reflects on the role of politics in culture and on the nature of political films, topics of considerable interest to Marker. In addition, the latter film included footage smuggled out of Chile that tracks the final days of the democratically elected government of Allende before the coup of September 11, 1973.

Ten years later, Marker resumed his essay portrait series. The first of these films, *A. K.* (1985), focused on Akira Kurosawa during the shooting of *Ran. A. K.* details Kurosawa's meticulous directorial role. The film is filmed exclusively in the foothills of Mount Fuji, the setting for *Ran.* Marker's film opens with Kurosawa's proclamation: "I always say to my crew, to create is to remember. Memory is the basis of everything." Marker evokes the fist of this phrase almost a decade later when in an epigraph to *The Last Bolshevik* he quotes George Steiner: "It is not the literal past that rules us. It is images of the past." *A. K.* details the production of visual spectacle based on memory, exploring how images of history are artfully created and crafted. For instance, the film reveals that Kurosawa always set up three cameras to record three different angles that could later be edited together. Marker's documentary footage establishes one more perspective. Furthermore, his images, shot in 35 mm, rival those of Kurosawa's. But, whereas *Ran* plunges us into a medieval world of shoguns, samurai, and beautiful horses, *A. K.* portrays the workers of the film industry and depicts a very contemporary scenery of cars, trailers, and scaffolding. It also captures the lengthy preparations, the boredom of waiting for optimal weather conditions, and the tedious process of waiting for the actors and the crew to get into position. In short, Marker's film focuses specifically on the extensive labor that goes into making the magic of a film. As such, *A. K.* stands in sharp contrast to *The Koumiko Mystery,* completely disregarding Tokyo and modern Japan for the imaginary filmic world of Kurosawa. Only the icon of Mount Fuji indicates the location of the film. *A. K.* is essentially an essayistic homage to a style of filmmaking that is radically different from Marker's own and yet one that he evidently respects and admires.

While working on *A. K.* in the mid-1980s, Marker made several videotape portraits. These culminated in his installation project *Zapping Zone: Proposals for an Imaginary Television* (1990). Although in *A. K.* he described video technology as "small but imperfect," now he was working with it quite extensively. What interested him in particular was that this technology made for a very different type of portrait than did 35 mm film, giving the impression of informality, spontaneous creation, and humility. *Matta* (1985), the first in the series, is filmed entirely within the space of museum. Marker follows Matta through one of the latter's retrospective exhibitions, as the artist discusses his paintings hanging on the walls. By contrast, in *Christo* (1985), another product of this series, the video camera remains in the streets as Marker records the responses of passersby to the artist's wrapping (and later unwrapping) of the Pont Neuf in Paris.

One Day in the Life of Andrei Arsenevich

The next portrait in this series, *Tarkovsky* (1986), was made at the time of the Russian director's death in Paris. The film was subsequently expanded and rereleased in 1999 with the title *One Day in the Life of Andrei Arsenevich* (an allusion to Alexander Solzhenitsyn's *One Day in the Life of Ivan Denisovich*). The narrator in *One Day in the Life of Andrei Arsenevich* intones: "It rains a lot in Tarkovsky's films, like in Kurosawa's," thus establishing an interfilmic relationship. As Wim Wenders did with *Nick's Film: Lightning over Water* (1980), which focuses on the terminally ill Nicholas Ray, Marker chronicles Tarkovsky's last days, intercutting scenes of the latter's films with conversations with the dying director. *One Day in the Life of Andrei Arsenevich* opens with a shot from *Nostalghia* (1983) showing a woman with her back to the camera, her hair in a bun, sitting on a fence. The voice-over announces: "Larissa searched the sky for the plane from Moscow." The commentary then continues to discuss the image on the screen, concluding that in Tarkovsky's productions a shot of a woman's hair bun from the back consistently signifies waiting. This scene is followed by a rapid cut to a full-screen video image of a different woman with a bun, also photographed from behind. The footage is from Orly airport in Paris, and the woman is Larissa, Tarkovsky's wife. She awaits the arrival from Moscow of her son, whom she has not seen in five years. It is now 1986, and the boy has finally been allowed to join his father at his deathbed. Marker's video camera captures all the intimacy and spontaneous affection prompted by their reunion.

Close to the beginning of *One Day in the Life of Andrei Arsenevich*, Tarkovsky hails Marker with the words "Chris, you have it all?" He thus signals to the audience that he has authorized Marker to record his final days. The audiovisual essay that follows presents sequences from Tarkovsky's own films interwoven delicately with videotape images shot by Marker. The celluloid world and the "real" world become intermixed. Tarkovsky's son recounts that when officials came to notify him that he would finally be allowed to visit his father, his immediate reaction was one of fear; he was afraid that they were coming to arrest him. The commentary explains, "an image that said a lot about other times, one that came straight from the past." Then the film cuts to a scene from one of Tarkovsky's earliest productions, a gangster film made when he was still a student, which features the director playing the role of one of the shady characters. The Russian officials are thus doubled with fictional characters from Tarkovsky's oeuvre. Marker uses this tactic throughout to create a tapestry of Tarkovsky's life and works, reading the director's biography through his films and vice versa. Indeed, the blending of fact and fiction, life and art, recalls Tarkovsky's own working method, which mixed documentary with fictional footage, professional with nonprofessional actors, and invoked an inconsistent array of time periods.[24]

The montage of sequences from Tarkovsky's films featured in *One Day in the Life of Andrei Arsenevich* does more than merely comment on the Russian director's life. It also illustrates Marker's reading of Tarkovsky's work, his interpretation of the director's films, and the commonalities and unexpected linkages that he finds between them. Tarkovsky's seven films are shown to relate to one another, as Marker fluidly moves back and forth between them in a manner that parallels Andrei's movement through his "imaginary house, a unique house where all the rooms open on to one another and lead to the corridor." Opening a door by chance, Marker continues, "the actors of *The Mirror* could cross paths with those from *Nostalghia*." *One Day in the Life of Andrei Arsenevich* is the cinematic equivalent of just such a house. Thus, it functions as an expository essay on Tarkovsky's oeuvre.

Marker suggests in *One Day in the Life of Andrei Arsenevich* that each of the director's films "knits a plot between the four elements." One of the most powerful moments in Marker's films is of footage of Tarkovsky at work on site in Sweden in 1985, directing a scene of what will be his last film, *Sacrifice* (1986). The segment consists of a seven-minute single take. Marker shows that Tarkovsky's shooting method, though very different from Kurosawa's, is no less rigorous. He reveals the extent to which the scene had to be meticulously orchestrated. But he also tries to explain why a single take was imperative for Tarkovsky, who is said to have used tracking shots first to raise moral issues and subsequently to connote metaphysical concepts and ideas. Marker then compares two shots, one that focuses on a painting of a tree, in order to demonstrate the remarkable degree of concentration and attention to detail that Tarkovsky devoted even to parts of a film that are normally carried out by assistants.

The most remarkable aspect of *One Day in the Life of Andrei Arsenevich* is the way it functions as a vehicle for film criticism and analysis. For instance, Marker makes a case for the important role that paintings played in Tarkovsky's films, buttressing the latter's self-proclaimed goal "to place cinema on a par with the other arts." Furthermore, Marker points to the fact that Tarkovsky's first film opened with a shot of a child and a sapling, and his last film ended with a scene of a child resting prostrate under a dead tree. This leads Marker to conclude that "Some [filmmakers] deliver sermons, the greats leave us with our freedom. . . . [Tarkovsky is] the only filmmaker whose work lies between two children and two trees." The mode of criticism practiced by Marker's *One Day in the Life of Andrei Arsenevich* is thus reminiscent of his early film reviews for *Esprit* and *Cahiers du cinéma.* But now criticism of film is mediated through the film itself—a practice facilitated by recent developments in editing technology that have made it easier to mobilize filmic examples and illustrations. Such a reading, however, like any true essay, does not attempt to draw conclusions or "deliver sermons" but limits itself to providing openings and pathways for discussion.

One Day in the Life of Andrei Arsenevich also reveals aspects of Tarkovsky's work that have had a profound impact on Marker's own filmmaking practice. A case in point is Tarkovsky's conceptualization of a space he calls the "Zone" in *Stalker* (1979). Marker summons the Zone as a trope in *Sans soleil,* and it will go on to become the main ordering principle in his *Zapping Zone.* *Stalker's* protagonist describes the Zone in *One Day in the Life of Andrei Arsenevich:* "The Zone is a complicated system of traps, mortal traps when it is empty. I don't know, but as soon as humans are there everything starts moving, traps disappear, others appear, the right trails are blocked, the route is clear, and then indecipherable again. That's the Zone. It may seem capricious, but at each moment it is what our conscience makes it." What is striking about this passage is the extent to which the structure of the Zone resembles that of the essay. No wonder, then, that it becomes such an important trope for Marker.

Marker also hints at the limitations of the filmic medium and in particular at its inherent artificiality. He remarks in a personal aside over images from Tarkovsky's *Boris Godunov:* "*Boris Godunov* is not a film. It was a play staged in London, and for the author of this portrait [i.e., *One Day in the Life of Andrei Arsenevich*] the occasion for a very Russian confession, which is that he stole the fancy opera glasses they rent out at Covent Garden, and for a reason even more unmentionable than the crime—in the hope that one day by magic they would give back the images they had seen." This nostalgia for the live performance is echoed later in the film in an anecdote about Stalin being so moved by a concert of Mozart's music that he demanded a record of the performance, only to be disappointed by the latter's artificiality. Even absolute power, Marker suggests, cannot re-create life. Nor can cinema, which freezes and mummifies what it records.

Marker began to make *One Day in the Life of Andrei Arsenevich* in 1985 as an homage to the director. A section of early footage in which Tarkovsky rubs the back of his head subsequently becomes prescient. As Marker observes: "Among the more funny gestures, there was one that should have worried us. But we didn't know—yet." Only later did it become known (even to Tarkovsky) that he had cancer. As Marker states several times in *A Grin without a Cat,* always with a note of astonishment: "You never know what you are filming."

The Last Bolshevik

> It is not the literal past that rules us, but images of the past.
> —George Steiner, as cited in *The Last Bolshevik*

Among those shown mourning Tarkovsky's death in *One Day in the Life of Andrei Arsenevich* is a fellow Russian filmmaker from a different generation, Alexander Ivanovich Medvedkine.[25] The latter is the central subject of Marker's *The Last Bolshevik* (1993).[26] In this latter film, too, a sense of mourning prevails. Yet in this instance the lament is not for a lost filmmaker but for the end of the utopianism that brought the Soviet Union into existence and maintained it at least through its early years.

The Last Bolshevik, like *The Koumiko Mystery,* focuses on an individual figure to make sense of history. The film is composed of six letters addressed to the recently deceased Medvedkine. It opens with a 1984 interview with the filmmaker in which he admonishes Marker: "You lazy bastard, why don't you write—just a few lines, like this?" as he holds up his hand showing the space between the thumb and forefinger. Marker's commentary nearly ten years later is spoken over a freeze-frame of Medvedkine's thumb and forefinger: "Dear Alexandre Ivanovitch: Now I can write. Before, too many things had to be kept quiet, and today too many things need to be said. I will try to tell you about them, even if you are no longer here to listen. But I warn you: what I have to say is more than can be enclosed between those two fingers." The still of Medvedkine's hand gesture is followed by an engraving of a hand writing, clearly evoking the epistolary form. The allusion is to Montaigne's mode of dialogue about philosophical and social concerns with a deceased friend. But for Marker, much more than his friend Medvedkine died in 1989.

Marker employs Medvedkine's biography as a vehicle with which to reflect on the former Soviet Union. The Russian director was born in 1900, participated actively in the Russian Revolution, made all of his films during the existence of the Soviet Union, and died in 1989 as the Eastern bloc fell apart. Confluences of dates appeal to Marker. He juxtaposes a photograph of Prince Youssoupov, also born in 1900, with one of Medvedkine: "This offers a good beginning to a history where miracles are but a little more striking than forms of daily life" (Marker, "Le tombeau d'Alexandre," 1993, 19). The narrator observes that Medvedkine was five years old when Lenin wrote *What Is to Be Done?* seventeen in 1917 when "you knew," twenty during the Russian Civil War, in his thirties during the Moscow trials, fifty-three when Stalin died, and his own life ended on the eve of perestroika. Medvedkine's personal history is thus interwoven with the history of Soviet Communism in the twentieth century.

Marker became friends with Medvedkine in the early 1970s when he focused on one of the Russian director's early projects, the ciné-train, for the subject of the short film *Le train en marche* (The Train Rolls On, 1971). But this does not fully explain Marker's convergence of man and history, for he could have tracked the rise and fall of the Soviet Union through a politico-historical documentary. Rather, Marker's attraction to the personal letter seems to have been related to this genre's ability to raise pointed questions. Most pertinent was a reassessment of Medvedkine's filmic practice. This relates directly to Marker's citation of Steiner's claim that it is "not literal history that rules us, but images of the past," a pronouncement that is rephrased later in the film when the director observes: "Images of heroes don't come from life but straight out of the movies." Like all filmmakers, Medvedkine was a maker of such images. Yet as Marker reminds the imaginary recipient of the letters at the end of Part One, "my work is to question images." And question he does, opening up the closed book of history that, like a matrioshka doll, reveals stories upon stories hidden within.

The Last Bolshevik is a dialectical film. Marker offers neither an apology nor a condemnation of the Soviet Union but seeks instead to show the beauty and frailty of utopian dreams and the catastrophic consequences of their abuse. Analyzing a documentary clip of the Romanov's celebration of their tricentennial in 1913, Marker focuses on a "fat official" who condescendingly gestures to the crowd to remove their hats and show their respect to the czar. The official's humiliating command leads Marker to observe that at the end of the century when "the fashionable sport is to rewind time" and look for past crimes, people should remember that there was "before Stalin, before Lenin, this fat man who ordered the poor to bow to the rich." In other words, Marker encourages his audience in the late twentieth century to bear in mind what the Russian Revolution sought to change, for it will also help to understand Medvedkine, who was born into the peasantry and became a "pure Communist" in a world of "would-be Communists." Without the revolution, Marker notes, there would have been no filmmaker named Medvedkine. Yet this is only half of the equation, for Marker also shows that without a number of uncomfortable compromises with reality, Medvedkine would not have lived to be eighty-nine.

Much of Medvedkine's later life was spent in obscurity, but he did survive. A former film student in the USSR recalls that when he first saw Medvedkine's Happiness (1934), with its erotic images of nuns with transparent habits, he assumed that the director did not live through the Stalin purges. At one moment in The Last Bolshevik, Marker, while interviewing people who knew Medvedkine, turns his attention to life in the newly reconstituted Russia in spring 1992. Two important news items are recounted. The first occurs in Moscow and concerns revelations about the extent to which Bishop Pitirim collaborated with the KGB. What Marker finds incredible is that the media discussion centers not on whether the church collaborated but on the question of how *much* it did. This then leads him to ask, "Did you all take a short walk with evil?" (Marker, "Le tombeau d'Alexandre," 1993, 21). In other words, did everyone have to collaborate to get by? A sequence follows in which Medvedkine is contrasted to Isaac Babel, the former as "an enthusiast" and the latter as "an inquirer." Babel, a Jew, is set up as a foil to Medvedkine and to the Catholic Church. The passage closes with more contemporary shots of the church and another news item. This time the story centers on the Ukraine, but the issue remains the same: How far did Philarète, bishop of Kiev, collaborate with the KGB? Marker announces: the "decades of Lenin may have passed, but the Church is always there" (23). Indeed, it was not just the Russian Orthodox Church that survived, but others survived as well. Many Jews like Babel, who posed questions, were not so fortunate, however. Marker goes on to suggest that Medvedkine's "enthusiasm" for communism might have been a substitute for a form of religious belief. The first letter ends with the camera lingering on an old man, the same age as Medvedkine, listening to music at a church in Moscow. Marker finds a clip of this man, years earlier, playing the role of a simpleton in *Boris Godunov* while singing, "Misfortune, misfortune of Russia, weep, weep, Russian people, people who are hungry."

Although he raises these political questions, Marker also shows another side of Medvedkine—the talented artist whose horse theater astonished the cavalry division of the Red Army during the Russian Civil War. The second letter begins with the news that the exceptional success of the theater led to Medvedkine's promotion to the rank of general. This leads Marker to ask what "a cat, a very young army general, and the statuette of a Chinese fisherman have in common?" over a shot of his favorite animal washing itself. Medvedkine went on to direct short instructional films for the Soviet army, such as *For Your Health* (ca. 1921), which stresses the importance of personal hygiene. He creatively used the technique of dissolve in this film to eliminate members of a regiment several at a time as if from disease. As for the statuette of the Chinese fisherman, Marker observes that one was always kept on Medvedkine's bookshelf, perhaps as a figuration of the Chinese proverb "give a man a fish, you feed him for a day; teach him how to fish, and you feed him for life." Marker then says to the dead Medvedkine: "You wouldn't give people films—you would give them cinema." Here Marker draws a distinction between *films* made for mass entertainment and *cinema,* which he suggests has a more pedagogical, critical, and participatory component. Diomens, a former colleague of Medvedkine, recalls that the director cried when, for the first time, he put two images together and produced a third (dialectical montage), at once discovering cinematic illusion and manipulation.

At one moment, *The Last Bolshevik* focuses on a celebrated photograph of the storming of the Winter Palace in 1917. Marker shows that in 1920, on the third anniversary of that event, an enormous theatrical production of the revolutionary uprising was staged to re-create the upheaval. He then notes that the photograph to illustrate the actual historical event is in fact a document of the spectacle of its reenactment. For Marker, this substitution of art for history ushered in a half century of cinema in the service of propaganda, including Sergei Eisenstein's *Battleship Potemkin.* The Eisenstein film, Marker observes, was a commercial failure when it was initially released in the Soviet Union and only subsequently achieved its canonical status thanks largely to the propaganda machine it served. What people wanted most in the 1920s was entertainment. Marker links this insight to the present by citing from a 1992 *Time* magazine article that dismisses European cinema for its lack of entertainment value—a pronouncement that leads him to make an unusually bitter quip: "Morons of the world unite." Thus, if the first letter discusses collaboration in an upbeat way, the second letter takes up the hoary question of the power behind aesthetic production.

At this point Marker interviews Yacov Tolchan, Medvedkine's cameraman and one of the first to use a handheld camera in the 1920s. Marker lets him try out his Handycam, with the ironic comment that Tolchan's "last act of propaganda would be for Sony!" We catch a rare glimpse of Marker as he hands over the camera, intimating that perhaps his own political filmmaking in the past, carried out with enthusiasm, may have inadvertently served as propaganda. "You never know what you might be filming." A decade earlier in *Sunless,* Marker reassessed with embarrassment a type of image production "that makes one ashamed for having used lightly—even if inadvertently—the word *guerilla* to describe a certain breed of filmmaking." But what is the difference between making films for a cause one believes in and making propaganda? And when does propaganda become collaboration? And at what expense? These seem to be core questions posed by *The Last Bolshevik.*

The interview with Tolchan summons the ghost of Vesvelod Meyerhold, the theatrical genius who projected extracts of films by Dziga Vertov on the back of the stage. Like Babel, Meyerhold was executed during the Moscow trials, whereas Vertov got off relatively easily: he was stripped of all filmmaking possibilities and died a recluse. If Babel serves as a foil for Medvedkine in the first letter, that role is attributed to Vertov in the second letter. "Vertov, of all of them, he was certainly the closest to you in terms of ambition and sincerity. You would be endlessly compared to each other and sometimes opposed, *Isn't that so Mr. Godard?*" You fought on the same propaganda fronts, you had the same enemies, which should be a good bond, you even once lived in the same building. . . . And yet all testimonies confirm that in your whole lives you barely exchanged a few words." Marker's invocation of Godard is ambiguous; it might refer to Godard's participation in the establishment of the Dziga Vertov Group in the late 1960s—a group that was markedly in contrast to the Medvedkine Group of committed filmmakers in which Marker participated. Like Vertov and Medvedkine, Godard and Marker represented the two modes of alternative nonfiction filmmaking practices in France in the 1970s. Marker leaves the full extent of their relationship, and the particular role each played vis-à-vis the other, open.

What Marker does *not* leave open, however, is the role of Eisenstein. He makes Eisenstein's unabashed service to the state painfully evident when he notes that Eisenstein reedited his film *October* in order to eliminate all trace of the recently discredited figure of Trotsky. But Marker refuses to moralize about this issue. Rather than condemning Eisenstein, he gives a sense of the complexity of the situation by quoting a brief aside by the filmmaker Roman Karmen: "The world is an endless war. There are two camps. You have to choose your camp and do everything possible to make sure it will be victorious." These very words are echoed a couple of years later when Laura in *Level Five* pronounces, "You have to choose."

All of the figures whom Marker interviews in *The Last Bolshevik* agree on one thing: Medvedkine genuinely believed in communism. He made clear choices and never lied about his position. He was a true Bolshevik. Yet Marker detects contradictions between Medvedkine's beliefs and the way they were put into practice. The first signs that all was not right with Medvedkine's work emerged at the time of the ciné-train—a remarkable railroad caravan, complete with a film laboratory, that traveled throughout the Soviet Union in the early 1930s filming problem situations. The ciné-train's purpose was to help people resolve social conflicts through the means of film. Medvedkine's strategy, as the organizer of this project, was to engage the subjects of these films, who would also constitute their audience, in the production process. The films were then followed by worker's council discussions that sought to solve labor conflicts and collective farming disputes. Yet the project was undermined by a combination of inconsistencies and weaknesses in the policies of the Communist Party. As Medvedkine's daughter recalls, the party feared the activities of the ciné-train "because it showed that all was not well" in the factories and on the farms. As a result, "nothing was made of the train, nothing appeared in the press, as if it didn't exist. . . . The train was hushed up." All of the films produced by the ciné-train were believed to have been destroyed. Sixty years later, however, Marker discovered a few of these documents shelved in deep storage. Viewing them with the knowledge of all that transpired in the subsequent decades, he admits to "a pinch in his heart," for they represent the last images of reality in the Soviet Union before "life was completely made up."

Letters four and five in *The Last Bolshevik* address the Moscow trials and the State's ruthless extermination of numerous artists and intellectuals. Marker identifies this moment as pivotal, with "all the culture from the past meeting all the impatience of the future. Memory and madness." The generation of revolutionaries who believed in a utopian ideal was betrayed as that idealism was repeatedly abused. Records of Medvedkine's activities during this period are fuzzy. Marker searches in vain to fill the gap. Suddenly, after Medvedkine's death, Marker makes a discovery that throws his admiration for the Russian director into complete disarray. On the directorial credits to a 1939 May Day propaganda film entitled *Jeunesse Florissante* that is in full praise of the Soviet Union and its leadership, he finds Medvedkine's name. Was that the price his friend had to pay to remain productive, to continue to make films in the wake of the ciné-train and the Moscow trials? Was that the cost of avoiding the fate of Vertov or, even worse, of Babel or of Meyerhold? Marker is clearly disillusioned by the discovery. Yet he refrains from condemning his Russian friend. Rather, he gives him an out by dubbing an imaginary text onto a silent segment of documentary footage of Medvedkine receiving the Lenin Prize in 1971. There, before the enormous audience of Communist dignitaries, Medvedkine reflects on past events, referring to his life and that of his generation as a "black hole" in Soviet history (Marker, "Le tombeau d'Alexandre," 1993, 45).

The final moments of *The Last Bolshevik* are spent with the ninety-three-year-old Tolchan. Rather than continue the conversation, Tolchan insists on listening to his preferred music, his own version of a black hole, as his eyes well up with tears. Hence, a whole epoch is concentrated in one life and a whole life in a few notes. Marker refracts the often-heard claim that the generation of Medvedkine, Tolchan, and Vertov represents dinosaurs from a previous era. But look at what has happened with dinosaurs, he exclaims optimistically, "children love them." The film's final image focuses on a happy young girl, the future awaiting her, tightly hugging a stuffed green dinosaur. Marker's politics prompt him to end on a hopeful note. The future remains unwritten.

The Wolves: Political Filmmaking

After so many stories of men who had lost their memory, here is the story of one who has lost forgetting, and who—through some peculiarity of his nature—instead of drawing pride from the fact and scorning mankind of the past and its shadows, turned to it first with curiosity and then with compassion. In the world he comes from, to call forth a vision, to be moved by a portrait, to tremble at the sound of music can only be signs of a long and painful prehistory. He wants to understand. He feels these infirmities of time like an injustice, and he reacts to that injustice like Che Guevara, like the youth of the sixties, with indignation. He is a Third Worlder of time. The idea that unhappiness had existed in his planet's past is as unbearable to him as to them the existence of poverty in their present. Naturally he'll fail. The unhappiness he discovers is as inaccessible to him as the poverty of a poor country is unimaginable to the children of a rich one. He has chosen to give up his privileges, but he can do nothing about the privilege that has allowed him to choose.

—*Sunless*

Wolf being shot at
from a helicopter in
A Grin without a Cat

The film *Le fond de l'air est rouge/A Grin without a Cat* (1977) opens
with one of the most remarkable montage sequences of the second half
of the twentieth century. The voice-over (by Simone Signoret in the
original French-language version) addresses images from Eisenstein's
Potemkin: "I didn't see *Potemkin* when it first came out, I was too young.
I remember the shot of the meat—definitely—with the maggots, the
little tent where the dead man was laid out, and when the first person
stops in front of it, and the bit when the sailors take aim on the brink
of the battleship and just when the officer gives the order to fire, a
huge sailor with a big mustache shouts a word which spreads itself all
over the screen: 'Brothers!'" The beginning credits roll, and the musical composition "Musica notturna nelle strade di Madrid" (Nocturnal
Music in the Streets of Madrid) by Luciano Berio fills the sound track
as a rapid sequence of archival film clips and images are intercut with
scenes from *Potemkin.* The entire passage lasts only four minutes, yet
it spans a half century and five continents. The narrator immediately
problematizes that act of memory—"I did not see *Potemkin* when it
first came out"—but then recalls certain scenes. Further disorienting
the viewer is that the images from the film do not correspond to those
described by the narrator. Neither the dreadful meat sequence nor the
"little tent" one are replayed. Instead the image track begins with the
sailors taking aim to fire, the priest gently shaking his cross to signal

his full accordance with the forthcoming execution, and a close-up of a sailor raising his head. Thus a cognitive gap is created between what the spectator sees, what she hears, and what she remembers (if she is familiar with *Potemkin*) or imagines (if she can not recall the film). At the word *battleship,* however, the spoken text begins to correspond to the visual one, and the image and sound tracks converge as *Brothers!* fills the screen. The effect is similar to that of a ballet with two dancers; sound and image, in meticulous choreography, separate and joined together only to fall apart again.

Immediately after the word *Brothers!* the film cuts to a close-up in color of four hands raised in the air, making a peace sign. This is the first of many rapid cuts that follow one another in apparent disorder, though they are in fact linked in their message. The credits then announce, "Part One: Fragile Hands," which is followed by a shot from *Potemkin* of empty steps in the old city of Odessa. Through a series of dissolves, the steps fill with throngs of people, then the film cuts to a contemporary crowd winding their way through a narrow street. A clip from *Potemkin,* with people lining up to pay respects at the small tent for the slain sailor, Vakoulitchouk, is followed by one from the funeral procession in Paris on February 13, 1962, when five hundred thousand mourners took to the streets to honor the nine anti-OAS protesters (including a sixteen-year-old boy) slaughtered by the French police at the Charonne metro station. During this sequence the camera closes in on a woman wiping tears from her eyes, a gesture that is then visually rhymed with the same movement performed by a woman in *Potemkin.* Another flurry of shots: a cut back to the funerary procession for the victims killed at Charonne; an image of the dead Vakoulitchouk; the Charonne funeral again; a clip of a large crowd mourning Camilo Torres, the Colombian priest and sociologist turned guerilla who was killed in a revolutionary action in 1966; another shot from *Potemkin,* this time of two women lowering their heads in grief. The camera then pans up to focus on a funeral placard bearing the image of the seventeen-year-old student protester Gilles Tautin who was killed on June 10, 1968, by the Paris police; then to shots of men bearing the coffin of the French left-wing activist Pierre Overney, assassinated in April 1972. As if to signal that these and other deaths were not passively accepted, Marker inserts a series of clenched left fists raised in protest around the world, from

Potemkin to the Black Panthers. The consequences of resistance are evoked with the fictional sequence of the Tsarist army descending the Odessa steps and opening fire on the panicked crowd. This is coupled with recent real-life incidents when various armed services, claiming to act in defense of the state, brutally beat down young protestors. Images from Berkeley, India, Germany, Belgium, Japan, Washington, Paris, and Ireland follow one another in rapid succession, each one punctuated by visual correlation to *Potemkin*. Mark Rudd's bloody face after the student uprising at Columbia University in 1968 is juxtaposed with the bloodied face of a woman in *Potemkin;* the pathetic sequence of a mother with her dead child in her arms as she walks back up the Odessa steps is rhymed with the image of a protestor carrying an unidentified female corpse; a shot of the carnage in Odessa is visually correlated with the last gesture of a slain revolutionary in Cuba.

Thus opens *A Grin without a Cat,* a three-hour (four hours when it was initially released) film that in many ways stands as a watershed in Marker's filmic oeuvre. Completed in 1977, it can be read as a eulogy or funeral procession both for the revolutionary Left (or the communist movement that was widely taken, including by Marker, as its institutional manifestation) and for a certain type of committed film production with which Marker had long been involved. If he began his filmmaking career in the aftermath of the catastrophic World War II, when the reborn utopian possibility of building a new society arose, phoenix-like, from the ashes, by the end of the 1970s it had become clear that the revolutionary Left had lost the day, defeated not only by the Right but by betrayals and abuses within its own ranks. The French title, *Le fond de l'air est rouge* (The Base of Air Is Red), refers both to revolution and to blood. The English title comes directly from a line spoken in the film and evokes the decisive moment when the Communist Party ceased to represent the revolutionary avant-garde and began to be contested and superseded by smaller units and organizations. In the process, the guerilla fighter, once the bright figure of the fighting political Left, came to function as a spearhead without a spear, like the grin left behind by the vanishing Cheshire Cat in Lewis Carroll's *Alice's Adventures in Wonderland*. Marker locates the start of this rupture in Venezuela in the 1960s when the Communist Party betrayed the guerilla fighters (Douglas Bravo and others), no longer supporting their actions. Yet the film, although mourning at certain moments, does not indulge in self-pitying nostalgia. Rather, *A Grin without a Cat* only proposes to depict and explain what has happened. To that extent it follows the strict documentary tradition that draws on the etymological roots of the word *doc-ere*, meaning "to teach and to warn." And although Marker rejected the label of documentary filmmaker, finding the term too limiting ("I've always hated the word, but the fact is no one has come up with anything better, though the Germans are a little more elegant with their *Kulturfilm*"), much of his filmic work is characterized by efforts both to inform and instruct the public (interview with Walfisch).

Statues Also Die

Cinema, for Marker, extends beyond the making of films and encompasses a broad range of activities. His work is characterized by an artistic solitariness, but he has also been involved in a number of socially oriented collective enterprises over the years. To call Marker an auteur is thus fundamentally to contradict his working practice. One of his first films, *Statues Also Die* (1953), was made with Resnais, and his most recent release, *Remembrance of Things to Come* (2001), was codirected with Yannick Bellon. At various stages in his long career, Marker has used his well-established status as an important cultural figure to help draw attention to lesser-known or obscure filmmakers and screenwriters. In 1998, when the Fundacio Antoni Tàpies sought to present his work, he agreed but added the condition that they also screen the works of Spanish avant-garde filmmaker José Val del Omar (1904–82). Similarly, Marker used the occasion of his 2003 *Film Comment* interview to promote the deceased writer François Vernet. Thus, an important part of his intellectual project involves recuperating names, events, and individuals from the "dustbin of history," offering them a second chance in the world.

This generosity extends to the area of film education. In the 1950s and 1960s, Marker wrote cinema criticism for *Esprit, DOC, Cahiers du Cinéma, Cinéma,* and other similar publications. His short reviews helped to draw attention to interesting films made in foreign countries, to introduce new concepts and possibilities in the field of filmmaking, and to create a context for avant-garde filmmakers to discuss and situate their work. During that period, Marker attended many international

Leopard statues in
Statues Also Die

film festivals (e.g., Leipzig, Moscow, Berlin), granted interviews, and was generally quite active publicly. Within the frame of these activities, he was also involved with Bazin in organizing and conducting an annual series of film seminars in Germany.[27] Sponsored by Travail et Culture, beginning in 1949 these retreats were intended to help the nation's cultural redevelopment. (It is important to recall that film criticism had ceased to exist in Germany in 1933.) The seminars included film screenings, lectures, and discussions and were attended by future film critics such as Frieda Graf, Ulrich Gregor, and Enno Patalas as well as by filmmakers Wolfgang Staudte and Paul Rotha.[28] This cultural initiative was all the more significant because it provided an alternative to the Hollywood staple offered by the U.S. government's cultural affairs division. It may also explain why Marker has had and continues to have such a strong following in Germany. He also engaged in cultural education in a number of other countries and contexts. In 1949, he began to travel extensively throughout the world for UNESCO. His charge: "to place film in the service of education" (see interview with Dubreuilh).

The use of film to produce and disseminate knowledge is at the base of most of Marker's work. In *Olympia 52*, ostensibly a report on the 1952 Olympic Games in Helsinki, Marker focused on the political maneuvering behind the scenes and on the process of commodification of athletes that was taking place. Similarly, *Statues Also Die* is a "pamphlet film" that scathingly critiques the lingering effects of the colonialization of

Africa. The film opens on a dark screen and is followed by a series of still shots of African masks and statues. The opening commentary introduces several basic themes that will recur in many of Marker's texts: animism, history, culture, art, and preservation. As was the case with *Letter from Siberia,* one detects an ambivalent stance toward the process whereby everyday life becomes transformed into culture and thereby is "museified," or mummified. Cinema, by its very nature, participates in this process by documenting and recording events, people, objects, the past, and the present and freezing them in a two-dimensional audiovisual verisimilitude. Marker's films excel in calling attention to their own artifice and thereby encourage a self-reflexive questioning of what happens when life becomes celluloid. The act of filming does not discriminate between living beings and inanimate objects but rather freezes what is in front of the camera on the same representational plane and renders interchangeable all that it captures. To that extent Marker's camera treats all subjects in front of its lens without differentiating between humans, statues, animals, landscapes, architecture, or signs. The magic of cinema both imbues inanimate objects with life and carries out the mortification of living subjects. The resulting animism, based on the ancient belief that even inanimate objects are endowed with a soul, finds a striking illustration in Marker's cinema when images of objects return the gaze of the spectator. In *Statues Also Die,* Marker and Resnais film statues and masks as if they were alive. An unusually disturbing sequence, featuring the violent death of a disemboweled gorilla, appears toward the end of the film. These are not the only images of animals being hunted and killed in Marker's films. Indeed, a giraffe is slaughtered in *Sunless,* wolves are shot in *Grin without a Cat,* and whales are stalked in *Vive la baleine* (1972). To film the slaying of an animal doubles the mortification process. On the one hand there is the aesthetic and symbolic death that occurs when life is fixed in filmic images, and on the other there is the literal death captured, replayed, and relived filmically. These effects are only amplified by Marker's curious treatment of animals in his films—they function somewhere between humans and objects, animate and inanimate actors, agents of action and figures of contemplation.

Just as humans and animals die, so do civilizations and their artifacts. The commentary of *Statues Also Die* reminds us that the inanimate figures represented once had special practical or symbolic functions or roles: They served as tributes to fertility, to the health or beauty of children, to the gods, to the telling of stories—all features of a civilization that has been lost. With bitter irony the film notes that the history of Europe from the Middle Ages to the present is relatively well known, whereas that of Africa is an epistemological void. The process of disenchantment and demystification of African statues persists to the present day and is directly related to colonialism. Art and culture are promptly reified when money is introduced into an economy that had previously relied exclusively on barter for exchange. This point is underscored in the film by a clip depicting the factory production of African "objets d'art" in the Congo. The commentary continues: "And because the white man is the buyer, and the demand exceeds the offer, and one is in a hurry, African artists are turned into mere native craftsmen." *Statues Also Die* thereby illustrates the process whereby a religious fetish is transformed into a commodity fetish by Western civilization.

The film also tracks the instrumentalization of the African body by Western culture. It moves from a focus on inanimate statues to the consumption of African ritual performances and dances in the West where white audiences are often entertained by black performers. Meanwhile the commentary reminds us that the same blows that are applauded when delivered in the boxing ring are met by shots from policemen when they are given by protest marchers in the streets. Tellingly, Marker and Resnais' subversive critique of colonialism and its sequels was at the time in sharp contrast with the popular appeal of negritude, which promoted the unproblematized consumption of the culture and objects of the exotic Other. The film's final commentary, clearly a revolutionary statement in its original historical context, asserts: "There is no break between African and our civilization. Faces of the African art are shed by the same human faces, like snake's skins." No wonder then that the French Centre National de la Cinématographie censored *Statues Also Die* until 1963. Its committee claimed not to have problems with the first half of the film, which summarizes the religious and cultural history of African art. Inadmissible, however, was the film's second part, which critiques the practice of colonialism and implicates policies of contemporary France. The latter was fighting a colonial war in Indochina in the 1950s and was increasingly apprehensive of the possibility of a war of liberation in Algeria. Several of Marker's films would be censored for one reason or another during this period, even though the focus of his cinema shifted from France to the historical conditions of faraway countries such as China, the Soviet Union, Israel, and Cuba.

Description of a Struggle

Today, China, Russia, Israel, and Cuba seem totally distinct, yet, during the five years spanning 1956 to 1961, all four nations pursued utopian dreams of building a new society. Each seemed to represent an alternative to the capitalist economy. Of the corresponding four films, the one chronicling everyday life in Israel, *Description d'un combat* (Description of a Struggle, 1960), became for Marker the most problematic. Filmed in the early months of 1960, *Description of a Struggle* examines the "miraculous" survival of Israel twelve years after its founding. The film, however, prophetically warns that miracles die with those who witness them and that a second struggle (combat) was beginning. The title, with its allusion to Franz Kafka's eponymous short story about the complex relationship between a victim and a victimizer and the narrow boundary between the two roles, anticipates Israel's problematic future.[29] Following the Six-Day War, waged seven years after the release of *Description of a Struggle,* Marker pulled the film from distribution and refused to allow its screening. When the film was awarded the Berlin 1961 Golden Bear, Marker noted with irony: "It is somewhat comforting to see that even though in West Berlin one can't talk about China, nor about Siberia—and probably not about Cuba—at least for the moment, it is possible to talk about Jews" (Marker, *Commentaires,* 125).

Description of a Struggle opens with still shots of a depopulated landscape. The first word of the commentary (spoken in Hebrew) is "signs." It is followed by a series of static images of different sorts of signs and the corresponding words, "signs of the earth, signs of water, signs of man."[30] The camera then moves from the symbolic to the very concrete, fixing on a universal red, white, and black road sign indicating a rough and uneven surface. At this point the image begins to move as a camel passes behind the sign to cross the road. With the juxtaposition of the camel, a most ancient means of transportation, and a modern highway meant to carry trucks and cars, the sign becomes allegorical. Marker's focus on signs corresponds to the rise of structuralism as a methodological approach to understanding society and culture in the postwar era. Structuralists, among other things, emphasized signifying code systems and networks of signs over essential meanings and essences. The panoply of images captured by Marker's camera reveal that Israel is transforming quickly and that the visible traces of the past will soon disappear, preserved only in strips of celluloid. As the commentator observes: "Signs have but a short life, this tire dump no longer exists." Vast expanses of empty landscape, the narrator predicts, will soon be developed and turned into factories or settlements and, in the case of the Mediterranean coast, littered with hotels in an effort to create a new Miami Beach. Marker must have been struck by this ability of film to record a soon-to-be past because he echoed it two years later in *Le joli mai*, which also tracks twin urban development and destruction. But the central focus of *Description of a Struggle* is the study of Israel as a sign; indeed, the last words of the film are "like a sign," thus bracketing the motion picture between two semiological references. Throughout, Marker maintains this dual structure in dialectical tension: modernity and history, advances of capitalism and the Socialist utopia of the kibbutz, victims and victimizers, Jews and Arabs. The kibbutz in particular is idealized by the filmmaker. Yet during a lengthy sequence of this "world where money doesn't count" he wonders how long the "purity" of the kibbutzim will last, "isolated in their own country, isolated from the socialist states."

Other signs do not just represent the present or issue Cassandra-like prophecies into the future, they also revive the immediate and traumatic past. Marker observes that "war has marked this landscape, this climate heavy with murder" and that "war is embedded in all memories." The signs of war, persecution, and the Shoah are everywhere: in the multitude of languages that echo in the streets (German, French, Hungarian, Yiddish, and Arabic), in the "wonder" of the old people as they "search for a link between them [the youth] and the ghetto ghosts," and most directly in the numbers tattooed on the left forearms of the camp survivors. *Description of a Struggle* not only studies a nation as a complex system of signs, it also vibrates with the memory of the not-too-distant horror of the Holocaust. In that sense, the film can be viewed as a pendant to Resnais' *Night and Fog* (1955) for which Marker served as assistant director and aided Jean Cayrol in scripting.[31] The prolonged shots of barren landscape and the images of concentration camps evoke the earlier film, but if *Night and Fog* served as a record of past atrocities, without close relationship to the current reality, *Description of a Struggle* situates itself firmly in the present, at once positing the existence of Israel as a direct consequence of the Holocaust and the imminence of yet another conflict. As the commentary stresses: "Israel was born of war, of war through lack of foresight: Herzl didn't anticipate bloodshed; England didn't foresee this result of her promise of a homeland; the West didn't foresee that the Middle East would cease one day to serve as its gas station, and that its first inhabitants would want to be heard, that the U.S. and Russia would vote for the birth of Israel, even though they would turn their back on it later." Noting that the founding of this "promised land" had resulted in pain, dislocation, and death for significant numbers of the Arab minority, Marker reflects on the increasingly militarized Jewish youth, border skirmishes, and casualties and includes a sequence with a young and destitute Arab woman named Mouna whose father has gone mad from misery. The Israeli victims are shown in the process of becoming victimizers; nation building and chauvinistic nationalism are linked by Marker's observation that "to become a nation like the others means acquiring the right to national selfishness, national blindness, national pride." But *Description of a Struggle* is very clear about where the ultimate responsibility for the need of the State of Israel lies. A remarkable sequence of 1947 documentary footage featuring Jewish refugees (on a ship) who set out for Israel but were stopped by the British and returned to deportation camps is accompanied with the following voice-over: "This we have done, we old Europe who boast of our spiritual values, caused thousands to flee from us, camp survivors, camp orphans, born in camps, crushed by camps, they fled from us, Germany, with our crimes, France, with our indifference, and when they turned to England, they were dragged back to the camps."[32]

In *Description of a Struggle* Marker identifies Israel as both victim and victimizer. It remains unclear, however, why so many images in the film project an ambivalent portrait of youth. There already exists a generation in Israel for whom the narrator's question, "Why did you come to Israel?" does not apply. The question is followed by a still image of an adolescent boy, then by photographs of elderly men whose response is, "To forget." But "To forget what?" The final response, "I forget," is uttered as the moving image of a young boy eating an ice-cream cone fills the screen. Is it a matter of generations? The ambiguity remains puzzling. The boy speaks for the generation that has no direct memories of persecution. Do the young embody the hope of Israel, freed from its past? Not quite, because the consumption of ice cream leads to a rapid-fire sequence of images from cheap and conformist consumer culture: televisions, radios, posters, pervasive manifestations of dominant mass taste for which Marker makes clear he has no sympathy. Is, then, the future without hope? Not necessarily, for the film closes with a sequence filmed in a drawing class of children who have been "born without fear." The narrator optimistically remarks over the final shots of a striking-looking girl: "She will never be Anne Frank." This is followed by the concluding comments that state: "The most wondrous thing is that she exists, like a bird, *comme un chiffre*" (the English subtitle reads "like a sign," but the French text uses *chiffre*, meaning a number, evoking the concentration camps one final time). Finally, one is left wondering: Will Israel take the right turn?

As with *Sunday in Peking, Statues Also Die,* and *Letter from Siberia, Description of a Struggle* is dominated by a controlling voice-over that rules over a backdrop of images. The people are for the most part mute, which grants the filmmaker more control over the point of view or perspective of the film. As a rule, images do not contradict the sound track, and the commentary serves as a guide to understanding. There is one exception to this unanimity: the sequence of a kibbutz meeting that through the multiple voices recorded reveals sharply conflicting ideological positions. Marker's next film, *Cuba Si!*, develops this multiplicity of perspectives even further as it ushers in a new filmic practice and a technology that will permit live, synchronized sound to be recorded.

Cuba Si!

Writing in 1961, Marker states that *Cuba Si!* is "the film closest to my heart, and not only because it is the most recent" (Marker, *Commentaires,* 150). Filmed one year after *Description of a Struggle, Cuba Si!* celebrates the two-year anniversary of the Cuban revolution and attempts to "communicate, not quite the experience, but at least the shiver or rhythm of a revolution that will perhaps someday be viewed as the 'decisive moment' in a large part of contemporary history" (ibid.). The film, breaking with the more reserved tone dominating Marker's previous studies, demonstrates an open enthusiasm and admiration for the Cuban people and their revolutionary leaders. Not surprisingly, in June 1961 (two months after the failed Bay of Pigs invasion) the film was censored in France, where the authorities deemed it to be propagandistic. That the Cuban press and radio at the time made frequent attacks against French citizens and elected government officials in nearby Martinique and Guadeloupe did not help matters. When Marker published his first collection of screenplays in 1961 (*Commentaires*), both its opening text, *Statues Also Die,* and its closing one, *Cuba Si!,* had not been shown publicly. Their censure led him to describe these works as "two shadow zones, the infrared and the ultraviolet segments of the vision of a power with a decidedly narrow, very narrow, spectrum" (ibid., 155). Both films were eventually granted screening visas in 1963.

What the French officials referred to as "propaganda" may have been the result of Marker's strategy of using the film to check the growing tide of "misinformation" about Cuba disseminated by the international press. *Cuba Si!* thus initiates a production period when Marker's work would serve the express purpose of providing oppositional or counterinformation to that distributed by dominant media sources. This strategy included mastering new media technology as a means to democratize and make generally available the processes needed to produce information. Thus in *Cuba Si!* Marker included remarkable footage of a guerrilla camp in the Sierra Maestra, filmed during winter 1958, where the revolutionaries produced their own television transmissions to undermine the power of the Batista dictatorship.

More than thirty years later, in 1993, Marker similarly helped Bosnian refugees in Slovenia create their own media stations (*Prime Time in the Camps*). During the three decades in between, several times he attempted to produce alternative television programs: for his documentary series *On vous parle de . . .* in the late 1960s and early '70s; for his thirteen-part cultural documentary *L'Héritage de la chouette* (The Legacy of the Owl) in 1989; and for his 1991 installation *Zapping Zone: Proposals for an Imaginary Television*. In *On vous parle de Paris: Les mots ont un sens* (1970), Marker focused on François Maspero, the owner of the Left Bank bookstore La Joie de Lire and the editor of the literary series Editions Maspero.[33] La Joie de Lire prospered from 1956 to 1975, during which time the "periphery became the center of interest to European, and particularly French, intellectuals" (Ross, 2002, 82). Maspero published writers who were reputed revolutionaries or just beginning to fight against oppression, such as Frantz Fanon, Che Guevara, and Malcolm X. Part of his strategy was to allow the reading public direct access to the voices of these revolutionaries in order to combat the distortions and misinformation circulated in the bourgeois media, a strategy in the literary world that paralleled Marker's attempts to produce a countercinema.

Both as a whole as well as in its separate segments, *Cuba Si!* launches a systematic attack against the myths and outright lies disseminated by the mainstream press in order to diminish the significance of the Cuban revolution and minimize its effect. One such myth, perpetuated with the blessings of the United States government in order to explain and undermine what happened in Cuba, portrays (and thereby infantilizes) Castro as a modern-day Robin Hood who steals from the rich and gives to the poor. Marker intercuts clips of Castro and the revolutionaries with the 1938 *The Adventures of Robin Hood,* the voice-over explaining that today's Robin Hood has read Marx and is carrying out sweeping reforms in order to create a new and just society. The myth of Robin Hood is thus expanded beyond the bogs of Sherwood Forest to encompass a world-wide revolutionary movement. In another sequence Marker replays a globally televised broadcast of the execution of one of Batista's military henchmen by the revolutionaries. Along with this clip he also shows an array of horrible crimes committed by the Batista regime, including twenty thousand killings during the six years leading up to the revolution. In yet another instance, he introduces a newspaper headline that reads "Miracle needed Archbishop says . . .," followed by an interview with a member of the clergy who praises Castro and concludes that the revolution is perhaps the closest thing to true Christian Socialism.

This strategy of shot followed by countershot (misinformation/information) structures the entire film project up to the very end. Three months after the compilation of footage for *Cuba Si!* was completed, Cuba was threatened with an invasion by the United States. Marker quickly added to his film the way these events were reported in the Western press during April 1961. The misleading reports included headlines such as "Havana Is Being Bombed," or "A Counter-Revolution Is Taking Over!" The new sequence begins with a tracking shot into the darkness of a tunnel with the voice-over saying: "But for us, 8,000 kilometers away, we have behind us only memories and confidence, and ahead of us only spurious news." This is followed by a fast montage sequence of Cubans resisting the invasion and shouting their triumphant jubilation. To underline the highly ideological reporting of the Western news media, which projected that counterrevolutionaries with the assistance of U.S. forces would defeat Castro, Marker quotes from the coarse voice of the people in the form of graffiti that reads "Patria o Muerte!" (Homeland or Death!). The final words of the narration are, "But it would seem that we only believe those witnesses who had their throat slit. And, if necessary, we are ready to slit their throats in order to believe them."

Although it sharpens Marker's political commitment, *Cuba Si!* initiates a significant shift in his geographical focus; his camera, which had previously moved eastward (from France), now moved westward, to the Americas. *Cuba Si!* was the first in a series of films and television programs that discussed revolutionary politics in Latin America up to 1977; Chile, Brazil, Argentina, and Bolivia were all featured in other productions. Marker's politics now became firmly located in Third World struggles against capitalist imperialism. His identification as a *troisième mondiste* [Third Worlder] led him beyond Latin America to focus on other geopolitical sites of injustice such as Vietnam. In that sense, despite his self-cultivated image as a maverick, his interests were very much symptomatic of their time. The "Third Worldism" and solidarity with the colonial "Other" that seduced many members of the French intellectual Left paralleled the trauma of, and enthusiasm for, decolonization in the 1950s and early '60s, especially in Algeria.[34] Marker's filmmaking thus began with an exposure of the disastrous effects of colonialism in Africa and subsequently turned to a region where a revolutionary popular movement had toppled a regime propped up by a superpower.

If, in Israel, Marker was looking for a "David," in Cuba he found many "Davids" in the figures of Guevara, Torres, Raul Castro, Fidel Castro, and other heroes of the Cuban revolution. Yet the absence of strong references to Algeria, perhaps the issue closest at that time, is particularly puzzling in Marker's oeuvre. The same year that the filmmaker turned his attention to Cuba, one of the most violent acts of police brutality against Algerians took place in Paris, where hundreds of peaceful demonstrators were beaten to death by the police and summarily dumped into the river Seine in October 1961. The closest that Marker comes to addressing the Algerian conflict in his films is through indirect questions in *Le joli mai* and, fleetingly, in a quick montage sequence in *Cuba Si!* that begins: "What were people talking about at that time? About people, strange animals, Algeria, France, America, space, time (or weather), Congo, Laos, Africa." Marker's silence on Algeria is perplexing.

This silence at any rate may explain why *Cuba Si!* is so full of energy and optimism. In a particularly charming sequence, Marker's camera captures the spontaneous transformation of an orderly military march celebrating the revolution into a lively street dance in which the distinction between the soldiers and the crowd is blurred. The portrayal of Cuba thus stands in sharp contrast to that of Israel, which, with the exception of the kibbutz community, seems doomed from the onset. In Israel, Marker's camera captured the militarization of the youth; in Cuba the opposite takes place as the military becomes youthlike. The film's Cuba of 1961 tells the story of success: the revolution combats malnutrition, illiteracy, disease, and assures the population housing, schools, and equality. Above all, education is exalted. But Marker also foreshadows what will become the main source of problems for Cuba in the future: the uneasy relationship with the United States and the resulting dependence on the Soviet Union. As he observed, the economic embargo of Cuba by the United States forced Castro to seek another market for the island nation's sugar production, which he found in Russia. Yet this in turn prompted the United States to become even more paranoid about Cuba and to retaliate in various ways. Several subsequent developments come to mind: the flight of the middle class to Florida, the Russian missile crisis, the aging of the dictatorship, and the extended economic embargo following the collapse of the Soviet Union.

Cuba Si! is primarily about a left-wing political revolution. But the film also signals a revolution in Marker's filmic practice as he uses—for the first time—a camera that records synchronized sound. Thus, along with the voice of the narrator, the camera captures live voices, music, and the noises of the Cuban population. Popularized by Jean Rouch and Mario Ruspoli in their 1961 *Chronique d'été*, this practice of recording live heightened the veracity (or illusion) of that which was being filmed. Indeed, it led to the inauguration of the cinema verité documentary movement. Although in *Cuba Si!* Marker resorts to voice-over commentary and only uses synch sound for selected scenes, *Le joli mai* of the following year would be filmed entirely with a handheld synch camera. This in turn allows the political messages to emerge directly from the filmed sequences and not just from the filmmaker's comments, now reduced to a minimum.

When Marker returned to Cuba in 1969–70, he found that the jubilation that he captured in *Cuba Si!* had largely been tempered by a number of factors, including the failure of a ten-million-dollar sugar harvest. The compilation film that he made at this time, *La bataille des dix millions* (The Battle of the Ten Million, 1970), reveals his continued allegiance to Cuba. He does acknowledge, however, that the Cuban cause is no longer fashionable, for "just as aging actresses marry younger men, so we marry new movements." Furthermore, although still filled with admiration for Castro, *The Battle of the Ten Million* is more dialectical than its predecessor and more about international politics. It shows Cuba positioned between the United States and the Soviet Union. In many ways, the former is easier to deal with for Cuba because its function as the enemy is unambiguous; it is with the latter, in principle friendly, that careful negotiations need to take place. Cuba wants to ally itself with the USSR yet at the same time retain its independence and not become a mere satellite of the superpower. The film coincided with the centennial of the birth of Lenin, and Marker used the occasion to include a montage sequence of Castro engaged in an imaginary debate with the Bolshevik leader about the ideals of a Communist state. Marker questions some aspects of the industrialization of Cuba, such as the cost to the environment and the impact of the embargo on the economy. But this criticism is compensated by his inclusion of a disarming and self-critical speech by Castro. Seven years later, in *A Grin without a Cat*, Marker would revise his portrait of Castro, tracing the slow corruption of ideals and the dissolution of the dream.

A Grin without a Cat

By 1977, important events had altered both the course of revolutionary politics in Latin America and the evolution of Western left-wing parties. For instance, the attempt on Rudi Dutschke's life in 1968 marked a watershed in the thinking of many Germans. In *A Grin without a Cat*,

Marker underscored the suddenness of that dramatic shift by showing the white chalked outline of Dutschke's body on the Berlin sidewalk and following it with a cut to *Potemkin's* first victims fired upon and dying on the Odessa steps. Dutschke had penned one of the key slogans of the late 1960s: "It is necessary to revolutionize the revolutionaries!"—an idea no doubt particularly appealing to Marker. The voice-over then notes that a similar shock occurred for the French Left one year earlier in 1967 with the arrest and trial in Bolivia of Regis Debray, author of *Révolution dans la révolution?* Indeed, in *A Grin without a Cat,* Marker casts 1967 as a pivotal year in shaping the landscape of world politics. He recalls that "In La Paz, I saw on the walls 'Viva Fidel!' as well as posters demanding the death penalty for that young philosopher who had published with Maspero." That same year, the narrator observes, also marked the rise of the French Nouvelle Droite (New Right) and the first political successes of Valéry Giscard d'Estaing.

For Marker the event with the greatest significance in 1967 was the capture and execution of Guevara by the Bolivian military. The filmmaker weaves the biography of Guevara with the politics of liberation movements in Latin America. He begins with footage of a 1963 speech by Castro condemning betrayals of the revolution by members of the party. Castro's specific reference here is to the Venezuelan Communist Party's split from the guerilla movement, which in turn made it possible for a right-wing government to come into power. In an interview conducted shortly before the Venezuelan elections of 1963, the guerrilla fighter Douglas Bravo underscores that the revolution is a struggle of the poor against the rich and not between an opposition party and the government. Bravo's betrayal by the Communist Party foreshadows for Marker the fate of Guevara four years later, when U.S.-trained Bolivian military forces, in collusion with the CIA, captured, tortured, and executed the revolutionary. Through a series of interviews with Pentagon officials or high-ranking U.S. military personnel, Marker reconstructs the ambush and addresses the decision to kill Guevara instead of imprisoning and trying him in a court of law. He concludes that to keep a personality with the vast popular support of Guevara in prison would have been unwieldy for the Bolivians at the time, especially because the country's dictatorship had little popular support. Furthermore, the execution of Guevara was in accord with U.S. determination never again to lose control of spheres of influence in Latin America. As a Pentagon official remarks during an interview: "Those *miracles* won't happen anymore because the countries are prepared."

In *A Grin without a Cat,* Marker includes an important speech delivered by Castro during which the latter, discussing the fate of Guevara, reiterates his fallen comrade's call for the support of the Vietnamese in their battle against U.S. imperialism and for the "creation of two, three, many Vietnams." That speech seemed to reaffirm that neither sidestepping nor compromise was acceptable in the revolutionary struggle, yet Marker also hints that Castro's public praise for Guevara was not without hyperbole. As the commentator sanguinely notes in an important aside, after Guevara's death, "Alongside all the parades praising Che, there was also a sigh of relief." Guevara, Marker implies, had clearly become so popular that his strict adherence to revolutionary politics threatened the Cuban leader, who was by then already beginning to waffle. The manner in which Guevara is set up as a foil for Castro recalls the way Marker judges Babel in relation to Medvedkine in *The Last Bolshevik.* Marker points to future compromises that Castro and others on the left would make throughout the 1970s and to the growing lack of ease that afflicted many while Guevara was still alive. Later in the film, he signals these contradictions through a peculiar technique, by trembling the image. For instance, one hour into *A Grin without a Cat,* a rapid succession of images depicting clashes between police and demonstrators employs the quivering technique, intercut with white intertitles on a black screen featuring the words "Pourquoi?" (Why?), "Quelquefois" (Sometimes), "les images" (images), "Se mettent-elles" (do they begin), "à trembler?" (to tremble?). The voice-over eventually specifies that the images began to shake in May 1968 on the Boulevard Saint-Michel (in Paris) and continued in Prague that same summer, as well as in Santiago, Chile. The agitated hand holding the camera, the commentary explains, unconsciously indicates that something is not right, "You never know what you may be filming." The optical unconscious of the camera lens thus captures and communicates the political unconscious of a population or movement.

Marker goes on to suggest that the events in Czechoslovakia during summer 1968, when the Communist Party declared independence from the Soviet Union and was promptly invaded by the latter, were made even more harsh by the response (or lack thereof) of the international Left. In a particularly shocking speech of August 23, 1968, Castro excused the Soviet Union's heavy-handed reaction and thereby condemned the revolutionary struggle in Czechoslovakia. Castro's conclusion is as follows: "But the main issue like it or not is this: can the Socialist camp allow the development of a political situation that would mean the isolation of a Socialist country forcing it into the arms of imperialism? In our opinion it cannot allow it. And the Socialist camp has every right to prevent this." Marker's indignation at the bad faith reflected in Castro's speech is indicated not only by the quivering image but also by the growing interference and distortion of the audio track and the layering of cacophonous electronic music. The filmmaker's disillusionment with Castro also has its lighter moments as he derides the Cuban leader's habit of constantly adjusting the microphones before him when he speaks. Marker finds it revealing that the only time Castro's play with the microphones does *not* work is in Moscow, where they are fixed, cannot be manipulated, and remain unmoved by his rhetorical style and performance.

The final speech by Castro included in *A Grin without a Cat* is the address he gave at the first congress of the Cuban Communist Party in 1975. In this talk, Castro reaffirms that the party "synthesizes revolutionary dreams throughout history" and "gives concrete form to the ideas and forces of the revolution." The next part of the film turns to Chile, focusing on Allende's rise to power, the tragic coup, and his assassination on September 11, 1973. Marker includes several speeches by Allende (the new foil for Castro) addressing workers and expressing his solidarity. The film returns to Cuba for a final time when Beatriz, Allende's daughter, delivers her father's final message to Castro: "Tell Fidel, I will do my duty." At the end of her speech the synthesized music distorts, and a clapping echoes eerily as the camera focuses in on her face blinking away tears. The voice-over then informs that on October 12, 1977, she committed suicide in Havana.[35] The last message in this sequence is again in Allende's voice as he proclaims his admiration for Chou En-Lai and Che Guevara, both of whom had an "inner force" and "resolution." There is a heartfelt pathos here but unrelated to Castro, whose voice has been muted. Even more telling is Castro's absence from Marker's 1997 CD-ROM *Immemory*, in which only one clip of him (taken during his 1961 speech against illiteracy) is shown; the remaining images in the film are of the Cuban people.

The coup in Chile closes Marker's Latin American cycle. Immediately following the events, Marker made a short film that brought the coup back to Paris, *L'Ambassade* (The Embassy, 1973) and another, *La Solitude du chanteur de fond* (The Loneliness of the Long-Distance Singer, 1974), that doubled as a portrait of his longtime friend Yves Montand and an excursus on the plight of Chilean refugees. Marker also collaborated with Armand Mattelard, Jacqueline Meppiel, and Valerie Mayoux on *La Spirale* (The Spiral, 1975), a documentary detailing the rise of Chile's Popular Unity government and the direct U.S. assistance to Augusto Pinochet's coup d'état.[36] Viewed together in a study of contrasts, Fidel's Cuban revolution and the democratic election of Allende provided Marker with two successful models of left-wing intellectuals coming to power (although only briefly in one case): the first through armed struggle, the second through peaceful democratic process. The Pentagon official interviewed in *A Grin without a Cat* might have been correct when he pronounced that Latin American countries have learned how to get rid of guerillas. It is obvious, however, that he did not anticipate Allende's popular support, which necessitated a CIA-assisted coup and ushered in a Fascist dictatorship. No wonder, then, that Marker in *A Grin without a Cat* ominously predicts, after reporting the 1968 murder of the student Luis Edson by the Brazilian police, that a whole generation of political fighters in Latin America would end up under Fascist regimes.

Far from Vietnam

The Cuban revolution advanced a model of political transformation with proven success. Yet the Vietnam War was closer to the European psyche than was the Cuban revolution and certainly resonated strongly in France because of the country's recent military engagement in that part of the world. Thus, when Marker observes, toward the beginning of *A Grin without a Cat*, that Western standards of civilization peaked in the early 1960s—"then everything collapsed . . . in Cuba, in China"—he feels compelled to add: "But if it had to be summed up in one word, that would be 'Vietnam.'" The collapse refers to the end of both the American dream and the relatively unchallenged postwar European belief in the superiority of the combination of imperialism and consumerism. Immediately after World War II, the United States was viewed by the majority of Europeans as "liberators." U.S. military operations in Korea in the 1950s were virtually ignored or applauded, but with the Vietnam War the tide of popularity receded as the United States came to be increasingly criticized. The French themselves either forgot their own atrocities in Vietnam and their defeat by the Vietcong at Dien Bien Phu or sought to redeem their reasons to feel guilt. For the West, the Vietnam War became an exemplary sign of an imperial war waged by a superior military power against a relatively weak Third World country, with large numbers of civilians killed by napalm, saturation bombs, Agent Orange, and the like. Even in the United States a vast movement emerged to protest and condemn the war. Eventually, under the sustained pressure of Vietcong forces abroad and civil unrest at home, the U.S. military withdrew.

Marker directly addresses the Vietnam War in two films: *Loin du Vietnam* (Far from Vietnam, 1967) and *A Grin without a Cat*. He organized *Far from Vietnam* with other committed filmmakers who, as announced at the beginning of the film, wanted "to affirm, by making a film, their solidarity with the people of Vietnam in their resistance against aggression." Resnais, William Klein, Varda, Ivens, Godard, Claude Lelouch, and Marker contributed sequences to the 115–minute film. The final editing and mixing was done by Marker. The film represents a true collective endeavor, presented as a whole without singling out individual contributions. The credits list all the directors without assigning a particular scene to any of them. In that sense, it departs from the auteurist tradition, proposing a new kind of filmmaking. In fact, on a self-reflexive level *Far from Vietnam* draws a parallel between U.S. military global power and U.S. cinematographic global domination, presenting itself as a cinema of poverty opposed to a cinema of riches. By the same token it also promotes the idea of guerilla filmmaking. More generally, *Far from Vietnam* manifests the will to produce a film that cuts through the sensationalized media reports on Vietnam—the misinformation—while simultaneously joining the growing protest against the war.

Far from Vietnam was made during the height of the war, when the outcome was not yet clear. The film records the demonstrations both for and against the war in the United States and in France and clearly sympathizes with the protesters. It also includes several remarkable sequences of everyday life in North Vietnam and the effects of the carpet bombing on civilians. One part of the film, generally attributed to Godard, expresses the frustration of not being able to film in situ and of instead having to come up with alternative techniques and strategies that work in absentia. Politically, the film encourages its audiences to continue to protest and thereby hasten the war's end. A particularly effective passage, eschewing the technical problem of distance, centers on an interview with the widow of Norman Morrison, the U.S. Quaker who immolated himself on the steps of the Pentagon. This sequence calls for direct action and must be seen in the context of Marker's earlier condemnation, in both *Night and Fog* and *Description of a Struggle,* of European passivity when faced with massive injustices. Indeed, Marker links the atrocities of the extermination camps and those taking place in Vietnam by including parts of Hanns Eisler's composition for the sound track of *Night and Fog* in *Far from Vietnam.* Eisler's haunting music thus forges a sound bridge between the atrocities in Europe in the 1930s and 1940s and in Vietnam in the 1950s and 1960s. Yet *Far from Vietnam* was made during a period of optimism and hope: the antiwar protest movement was growing; Guevara had not yet been hunted down and executed; and May 1968, the Prague Spring, and many of the other significant events of that year were still months away.

A decade later the situation, as reflected in *A Grin without a Cat,* was quite different. Although the Vietcong had been victorious in their underdog battle against the United States, by 1977 all the left-wing global protests and massive French demonstrations had been unable to prevent a new Right from coming into power. If *Far from Vietnam* was a spontaneous response to military events as they were unfolding, *A Grin without a Cat* carefully wove Vietnam into the larger political fabric of the film. An interview with a bomber pilot conducted during a napalm bombing mission opens the Southeast Asia segment. The sadistic pilot can barely contain his excitement as he observes the effects of his napalm bombs on the civilians: "We can see people running everywhere, it is fantastic, outstanding," he exclaims gleefully. "We really hosed them down, great fun!" His only regret is to be sky-bound and not on a ground-level search-and-destroy mission that would have allowed him to observe the anguished looks on the people's faces as they were incinerated. The camera then cuts to images of Vietnamese victims of napalm: adults with their faces melted away, children with unrecognizably burned bodies. Another sequence includes the air broadcast of screams and wails of dying North Vietnamese who are tortured by U.S. troops. That broadcast, we are told, was meant to inspire terror as a part of psychological warfare to frighten the Vietnamese. Still other clips show the training of torturers by the United States intercut with documentary footage of actual torment. In the more optimistic moment of 1967, Marker held back from showing the cruel side of the U.S. military, but in 1977 no holds were barred.

A Grin without a Cat also includes footage from a military antisub-versive training camp in the U.S. South. We learn that the camp, which used to prepare forces for Vietnam, receives high-ranking official visitors from many countries, especially from Latin America, who seek training in how to wage war against guerilla insurrection. In the relatively hope-ful *Far from Vietnam,* a link was forged between war protestors around the world and the struggling Vietnamese people. *A Grin without a Cat,* however, is a much more pessimistic film, at once stressing the solidarity of leftist movements and demonstrating how that solidarity prompted the consolidation of the right.

Le Joli Mai

Marker's filmic practice realized the wish of the "troisièmes mondistes" "to create two, three or more Vietnams, to bring Vietnam home to France." Indeed, if during the 1950s and 1960s he spent much time focusing on the forms and fate of dissent abroad, his perspective was always dialectically related to the situation in France. His first film to focus directly on France, and more specifically on Paris, was the 1962 *Le joli mai* (The Merry Month of May; the English translation fails to convey the ironic intimacy of the French original that I shall use from now on). This cinematographic pilgrimage "home" is not a matter of simple nostalgia; rather, it seems to Marker to satisfy his ambivalent longing for the familiar as well as a desire to discover the unexpected after all memories of the old Paris are erased. To quote him: "Paris is the city that one wishes to see without any memories, where one wishes to return after a very long absence in order to find out whether the same keys still open the same locks, whether it still displays the same blend of light and fog, dryness and tenderness, whether an owl still calls at dusk, whether a cat still lives on the island." It may be significant that *Le joli mai* was filmed one year after Rouch and Morin produced *Chronique d'un été* (Chronicle of a Summer, 1961), a film about everyday life in Paris. *Chronique d'un été* constituted a significant cinematic event for a number of reasons: it featured Paris as a topic, it dealt with the Algerian war, and technological advances made it possible to make the film with handheld, synch-sound cameras (cinéma synchroné) that allowed the simultaneous recording of acting and talking subjects.[37] With *Le joli mai* Marker attempted to dialog (or compete) with *Chronique d'un d'été* in all three of these areas, which culminated in the development of the documentary genre known as cinema verité.

   Le joli mai opens with a disorienting low-angle shot of a figure scaling the wall of a building. The visual effect, clearly derived from early-twentieth-century Constructivist experiments with vision (the 1920s photographs of Alexander Rodchenko come immediately to mind here), evokes the beginning of *Sunday in Peking*. As the figure reaches the top of the wall, the sound of church bells and wailing sirens suddenly prevail, and the building dissolves into a shot of the Eiffel Tower shrouded in mist (again mirroring *Sunday in Peking*). Simone Signoret's voice announces: "It is the most beautiful city in the world, one would like to see it for the first time at dawn, without having seen it before, without memories, without habits, one would like to track it like a detective, with a telescope and a microphone." The defamiliarizing strategy puts the viewer off guard, however briefly. As the film progresses, an image of Paris is presented in which the past unrelentingly inhabits the present. Along with the Eiffel Tower, the camera films other clearly recognizable landmarks: the Church of Madeleine, the Odéon Theater, the river Seine. The sound track plays back various recorded voices, radio broadcasts, and ambient city noises that are disjunct from the images. The narrator of this sequence concludes that Paris, with its old buildings and monuments, "is the most beautiful set in the world"—a film set whose charm peaks in the month of May, with its clichéd springtime made famous by Montand's eponymous song heard during the interlude.

   Le joli mai has its evident parallels with Marker's *Sunday in Peking*, though only one day is depicted in the latter, whereas the Paris film covers a whole month. Just as Marker's choice of Sunday was not arbitrary, his decision to film Paris in May was also overdetermined. Indeed, May

1962 was heralded as the "first spring of peace," following eight years of war in Algeria. The Evian peace accord had been signed by de Gaulle on March 18, and a provisional government had been put in place in Algeria on April 7. Of course, violence against Algerians, both in Paris and in North Africa, continued throughout the "joli" month of May. Marker alludes to that violence by referring obliquely to the "Semaine Sanglante," when the Communards were brutally massacred in May 1871. He also warns that the end of colonialism will bring about a problematic new order that will continue to exploit the underprivileged in France and abroad: "In the month of May 1962, during the euphoria of the Evian Agreement, we tend a bit to forget that the poorest worker in a colonizing country always has a poorer subworker in the colonized country and that this aspect of reality survives colonization and its end."

Le joli mai is divided into two parts: "Prière sur la Tour Eiffel (Prayer on the Eiffel Tower)" and "Le retour de Fantômas (The Return of Fantômas)." The title of part one was inspired by a passage from a Giraudoux novel that is spoken on the commentary as images of the city roll on the screen:

> On May 1, 1923, Jean Giraudoux climbed the Eiffel tower and wrote: "Thus I am looking down on the five thousand hectares of this world where the greatest number of ideas have been born, the greatest number of words have been spoken, the greatest number of writing has been done, the planetary crossroads that was the most free, the most elegant, and the least hypocritical. This air so light, this void beneath me are made of many layered strata of spirit, of reasoning, of taste. All work accidents here are accidents of thinking. There are more chances here than elsewhere that the ailing backs, the wrinkles of its bourgeois and its craftsmen have been suffered while reading, printing, and binding Descartes and Pascal. This is the hectare where walking to the post office to mail the plays of Corneille, Racine, and Hugo caused the greatest number of varicose veins. Here on the corner of the Voltaire Quai is the small surface where the largest number of body blows had been received when fighting against despotism, and the square decimeter where, on the day of his death, Molière spilled his blood."

The second part of *Le joli mai* refers to Fantômas, the criminal antihero of thirty-two pre–World War I French thrillers written by Pierre

Souvestre and Marcel Allain. Fantômas also inspired the production of five serial films directed by Louis Feuillade for the Gaumont studios in 1913–14. The character was cast as an elusive figure, a type of early urban guerilla who relied on his intimate knowledge of Paris to outwit the law.[38] The figure scaling the building's exterior represents Fantômas, but it also doubles as Marker, who, armed with his discrete camera, stealthy journeys through the streets of Paris, bagging an assortment of images, words, and sounds of a city undergoing a profound transformation.

The first part of *Le joli mai* features a series of interviews with people in the street interspersed with a commentary that imparts information, ranging from the hours of sunshine thus far in May to the amount of potatoes and meat consumed in Paris that month. Marker's reference here is Alfred Döblin's remarkable modernist novel *Berlin Alexanderplatz* (1927), which seeks through a mixture of a fictional narrative and documentary facts to paint a portrait of Berlin. Just as Döblin sought to represent the spectrum of political parties in Berlin, so, too, Marker gives voice to a multiplicity of political positions through his interviews. The first, for instance, introduces a shopkeeper who works long hours to make as much money as possible. At the end of the day, he comes home and he immerses himself in television so as not to have to talk to his wife. The second interview is with an unemployed middle-aged woman who spends her time cultivating her garden; we learn at the end of the conversation that many of her flowers are made out of plastic and that she is waiting for the real ones to sprout. Yet another interview involves two adolescent boys who declare that they want to become wealthy businessmen when they grow up. When asked what they would rather have, money or power, they answer that they want both. World events for them are only relevant in terms of their impact on the stock market—a sentiment echoed by a stockbroker who, when asked about Algeria, complains that the war has caused a 10 percent fall in the market. Other interviewees include an inventor whose primary objective is to get rich, a tire repairman who paints in his spare time, and a young couple who give the appearance of being in love and truly "happy." This interview, the last in part one, seems lighthearted and affectionate; however, toward the end, when questioned about politics, the couple's response is sobering: they simply do not like to think about it. Strikingly, the man reveals that he is leaving for Algeria in ten days.

Yet the only thing that matters to the couple is their domestic world and happiness. When pressed to conjecture whether other people think as they do, they state that their motto is let other people think and do as they please. The young man's final words close part one: he believes in eternal happiness. One wonders, where are the thinking individuals praised by Giraudoux? Perhaps they are to be found in the small group of Marker's friends who have cameo appearances in the film: Montand, Signoret, Varda, Gatti, Resnais, Rivette.

Part two of *Le joli mai,* with its guiding trope of the return of Fantô-mas, offers a more active debate about contemporary politics and its links to the past. Marker includes footage of police violence at Charonne in February and the enormous funeral procession that followed. Then the commentator observes, "For the first time, at midday one could hear a bird singing at the Place de la République." The funeral, which doubled as a mass popular protest against the state, signals the growing possibility of political action, meaning, an end to passivity. Marker thus increases the political register of a guilty past. One of his interviewees recalls that Jews have been deported during the war, another—a young Algerian adolescent—speaks about his and his family's daily persecution, humiliation, and beatings by the French police. This is contrasted with the contentment of three sisters who only discuss their interest in fashion and dancing. One of the most provocative interviews in this section is with a former Catholic priest who explains the sense of outrage that led him to convert to Marxism-Leninism.

Parallel to Marker's attempt to capture a certain esprit de corps of Paris, a second narrative thread running through the film focuses on urban renewal and reconstruction. The beginning of the 1960s ushered in a period of radical architectural transformation in the city: The large municipal central market (les Halles) was torn down, blocks of tene-ment buildings were leveled, new modern apartment complexes built (HLMs), and suburbia sprawled in several directions. The commentary prophesies: "In ten years, these images will look stranger to us than today do the images of Paris in 1900." The awareness of the ephemerality of the present that was already noticeable in Marker's report on Israel reappears in *Le joli mai,* although without the same optimism of the former. Traces of an earlier Paris found in old photographs can also be seen in the Fantômas films of the 1910s; in a similar way, Marker's film may in the future stand as the record of a different but not necessarily more pleasant Paris. The future, with its promise of a better life, is presented at best ambivalently. The advantages of modernization are undermined by the image of an advertisement in twelve points that makes fun of an elevator. But here again Marker's approach is dialectical. For instance, although he criticizes television's promotion of a fantasy life that withdraws from the world, he points out in a sequence filmed in a one-room apartment of a poor immigrant that "for many Parisians television is the only window open on the world, and this window is all the more needed when the room is small."

Le joli mai is also a film about filmmaking and the technical possibilities offered by the lightweight, handheld camera. One cannot overestimate the freedom that this apparatus brought with it and how much it revolutionized filmmaking. It allowed Marker to record hitherto unattainable images, including those yielded by clandestine filming. The new mobile camera could go anywhere. Marker even includes, inspired no doubt by Vertov, a shot that shows how the new camera looks. It is significant that the reliability of the camera's images as a record of reality became one of the issues in the debate, fittingly opened by Le joli mai, about the relationship between politics and cinema. Whether Marker's film was really only recording the objective facts and therefore deserved to be praised as cinéma vérité, or whether his editing and montage actually produced a subjective film that could more accurately be called cinéma engagé, was called into question.[39] As if to undermine both positions, Marker includes several poetic and artistic interludes that take the form of time-lapse photography of traffic patterns that turn into geometric abstract images. Yet the film also includes an explicit statement about the role that politics could play in modern cinema. The issue is raised in the form of a rhetorical question directed toward the audience: "So, what do you say? You are in Paris, the capital of a rich country. You are hearing a secret voice that tells you that as long as poverty exists you cannot be rich, as long as people are in distress you cannot be happy, as long as there are prisons you cannot be free." This passage, in turn, evokes the dedication at the beginning of the film: "To the happy many." What could Marker have meant by these words? Was he being ironic? Here it is worth recalling that, for the most part, the Parisians that Marker interviews seem happy or claim to be happy. But that happiness stems largely from their ignorance about society.

Be Seeing You

If the question of whether Marker was engaged in producing cinema verité or *cinéma engagé* was left open in *Le joli mai,* by 1967 his work had become decidedly committed. While making *Far from Vietnam,* Marker also became involved in another film project that concerned the dangers facing the working class in France. Vietnam and Latin America were the main objectives of the campaign waged by Third Worlders, but the polemics about the worsening plight of French workers were equally important. Marker, like some of his colleagues, wanted to unify the two groups by advocating for social justice. As was the case with so many other issues in France and elsewhere during that time, the roots of the pursuit of solidarity were located in what was happening in Southeast Asia. Thus Pol Cèbe, a worker who is also a member of the French Communist Party, explains in *A Grin without a Cat* that it was as a young soldier fighting against a peasant population in Indochina that he realized that he was on the wrong side. His experience in Indochina directly led him to a greater social awareness and to a sense of commitment in the international struggle of the poor against the rich. Upon his return to France, Cèbe became a union activist at the Rhodiaceta factory in Besançon. Marker met him there while making the film *A bientôt j'espère* (Be Seeing You, 1967).[40] The film includes a passage in which Cèbe eloquently defends the importance of culture for the workers' struggle: "For us culture is a struggle, a claim. Just as with the right to have bread and lodgings, we claim access to culture. We lead the same fight for culture as for the union or in the political field." *Be Seeing You* covers the workers' strike at Rhodiaceta during Christmas 1967. In its brief thirty-nine minutes, the film depicts not only the brutality of the conflict and the reasons behind the strike (proposed new working conditions and cutbacks in the labor force) but also the self-identification of the workers with their class. As part of their individual speeches, many of those Marker interviews reveal that they come from a family of laborers who worked in the same town. Yet the interviews make clear that the life of a worker during the previous generation was qualitatively different.

By the 1960s, modern business strategies, Fordist production methods, and the round-the-clock factory operations made working life barely tolerable. Marker speaks to several families who reveal that because of scheduling conflicts—typically, one member of a family works the night shift—they rarely see one another, and when they do they are exhausted. One worker recalls how a colleague's wife had a nervous breakdown, another complains that his job is "meaningless" ("it just brings in the pay"), and a third that his previous year's production of 188 spools a day has now climbed to 244 spools. In one of the film's most poignant moments, the third worker challenges Marker (and thus the audience) to think about what it means to perform the same gesture 244 times a day. When Marker asks the workers their age, they reveal that they are only in their late thirties, which is shocking because they appear to be ten to twenty years older. Downtrodden as they are, they have the energy and willingness to go on strike in solidarity with other workers in France. Although this strike at Rhodiaceta eventually fails, the film ends on a note of optimism, with the young activist YoYo anticipating success in future struggles.

Be Seeing You, which belongs to the French tradition of worker's cinema (cinéma ouvrier), revived Marker's interest in the political role of the workers that led him already in 1952 to cowrite Regards sur le mouvement ouvrier. Be Seeing You initiated a decade when the workers became the central focus of Marker's properly cinematic oeuvre. The reception of these films had a mixed response. When Be Seeing You was first screened for the workers at the Rhodiaceta plant, Cèbe and other radicals expressed their disappointment. They were critical of the distance they sensed between the filmmaker and his subject, the working class. This prompted Marker to encourage workers to make their own films, to represent their issues themselves. With his technical and financial assistance, a group composed of Cèbe, Henri Traforetti, and Georges Binetruy made Classe de lutte (Class of Struggle) in 1968. They became part of a worker's filmmaking collective, the Medvedkine Group, that eventually produced twelve films. The latter were funded by SLON (Société pour le Lancement d'Oeuvres Nouvelles [Company for the Launching of New Work]), a militant production company that Marker founded during the making of Far from Vietnam (the first film that the company produced). SLON was active between 1967 and 1976.

By 1972 it had produced fifty titles. SLON did not follow any particular party line; it was only important that the films be political in theme, non-fictional in content, and collective in production. To get around the type of censorship that had plagued Marker and other political filmmakers in France in the previous years, the company was initially registered in Belgium. In 1974, however, the SLON collective transferred its operations to France under the new name ISKRA (Images, Son, Kinescope, Réalisation Audiovisuelle). Not coincidentally, ISKRA had been the name of Lenin's newspaper. Marker was directly involved in at least a dozen SLON productions, including *La sixième face du Pentagone* (The Sixth Face of the Pentagon, 1968), a documentary about the 1967 protest march on the Pentagon; the *On vous parle . . .* series; *The Battle of the Ten Million; Le Train en marche* (The Train Rolls On, 1971); and *Puisque l'on vous dit que c'est possible* (Because We Say It Is Possible, 1974).[41] Among these films, *The Train Rolls On* is particularly significant because it indirectly explains the basic structuring principle and the modus operandi of SLON.

The Train Rolls On

The word *SLON,* in addition to being the Russian term for elephant, was also the nickname of a Soviet cinematographer named Slonmouski. The latter was one of thirty-two filmmakers who participated in Medvedkine's ciné-train. In January 1971, while Medvedkine was in Paris, Marker conducted an interview with him at the locomotive depot at Noisy-le-Sec.[42] On the basis of this interview, found footage from Soviet cinema of the 1920s, as well as photographs and other documentation, Marker made the short essay film *The Train Rolls On.* At the time, it was believed that all films made by the ciné-train had been destroyed or lost. *The Train Rolls On* was initially intended as a preview film *(préface cinématographique)* to be shown before Medvedkine's *Happiness* (1934), which had recently been rediscovered and reedited with the assistance of SLON. *The Train Rolls On* opens with the words "First the eye, then the camera, which is the printer of the eye," immediately followed by Lenin's proclamation that of "all the arts, cinema is the most important." The passage at once summarizes Marker's assessment of cinema—a mechanical means of recording vision as well as an art form—and his overall approach to film—neither purely documentary nor purely aesthetic but

Archival photograph
of the ciné-train
production team in
The Train Rolls On

a mixture of the two. As he states later in the film, "Imagination is no longer an enemy of reality nor art an enemy of life."

The Train Rolls On traces the history of a mode of filmmaking that threw "art out of the museums" and brought "it to the streets," thereby making culture accessible and a right for all. During the 1920s in the Soviet Union cinema was considered an art form, yet it was an art form for the people, like novels and the press. As Marker explains, *litiera-tioura* ("literature" in Russian) means all things printed, including films. To illustrate the everyday nature of cinema, he tells a story that blends the humorous and banal with the serious: "One day an elephant came to Moscow, then a duck (we forgot to tell you how). The cinema saw it all. The civil war was still close. Mikhail Kaufmann saw it all. Dziga Vertov saw it all. Eisenstein saw it all. . . . Medvedkine saw it all." The humorous aside "we forgot to tell you how" betrays Marker's inclination for playfulness—a playfulness otherwise kept in check during most of the films he made during this period of active political engagement. In the case of *The Train Rolls On*, the story's comic relief may have been inspired by Medvedkine's own recourse to humor because, as he recalls, "laughter was the principal weapon of the train." In theory "cinema was not just a means of entertainment but a powerful weapon in the hands of the people," and, therefore, it was in the people's interest to become involved in cinema's interactive magic. In fact, during its travels across the Soviet Union, the ciné-train managed to carry out the production of seventy films. Marker warmly praised the rail caravan's potential to radically transform cinema. He also insisted that the ciné-train odyssey was still very much alive and not just bound to the limits of its time period: "The ciné-train is somewhat of a myth for us—train of revolution, train of history—but the biggest mistake would be to believe that it had come to a halt." Indeed, as the formation of Groupe Medvedkine attests, the process of putting the means of cultural production into the hands of the people continued. It was no longer a train but a new technological device, the video portapak (*unité portable,* available in France after 1968), that carried the promise of facilitating audiovisual production and radically democratizing the process of film distribution.

Marker welcomed such advances in technology as the video portapak because he foresaw in them powerful tools accessible to those who had previously been oppressed by the dominant mass media. The relationship between technology and the dissemination of information forms a central theme in *A Grin without a Cat.* In the written preface, Marker reminisces that he "tried for once (having in my time often made an abusive use of the power of the guiding commentary) to give back to the spectator, through the means of montage, 'his' own commentary, i.e., his own power" (Marker, *Le fond de l'air est rouge,* 7). The film was meant to be shown on television in four sixty-minute segments. Each opened a space for direct intervention through added counterexamples or alternatives. Hence, Marker, like Marshall McLuhan, saw that the mode in which the information is presented forms an inseparable part of that information, one that is full of possibilities:

> The mode in which information is presented forms a part of that information and enriches it. It was one of the principles followed in the choice of documents when a choice was possible (television screens, lines of kinescopes, newsreel quotes, letters recorded on "minicassettes," wobbly images, radio voices, first-person commentaries on images by those who recorded them, recalls of filming conditions, clandestine cameras, *ciné-tracts*); other principles were: relating documents to the concrete circumstances of their formulation and proceeding in such a way that the information would not appear as a *cosa mentale*—a mental object—but

as a material object, with its grain, its spots of irregular surface, sometimes even its splinters. (Marker, *Le fond de l'air est rouge*, 10)

Thus, throughout *A Grin without a Cat* Marker highlights the media that impart the information; in one instance it is a cassette tape with the voice of a worker remembering a deceased comrade, in another a Super 8 camera brought undetected into a jail cell in Mexico. At other times the images are taken with a video recorder or copied directly from television. The film thereby provides not only a sociohistorical portrait of the Left from the period after World War II until 1992 but also a chronicle of the history of contemporary recording technologies.

For Marker, the necessity to coalesce the history of the Left in the postwar period with that of the development of recording devices was motivated to a considerable degree by his belief that those in power have buttressed their position through their savvy manipulation and control of the media. This point is emphasized on several occasions in *A Grin without a Cat.* In one instance the filmmaker recalls that although only four or five cars were actually burned in Paris during the May 1968 upheavals, footage of these cars was replayed on television several nights in succession in order to give the false appearance of wanton destruction. This impression effectively turned the middle class against the protestors. As one woman notes in the film, the upheavals are "an outrage, not even the Germans burned Paris!" But Marker's optimism that the Left, with the aid of the media, would transform the structure of power, was short lived. Georges Pompidou died in 1974, and Giscard d'Estaing was elected, ushering in a new era of conformist broadcasting. As Marker pessimistically notes about the election of d'Estaing: "Ten years of continuous advertising had finally sold the product."

A large part of *A Grin without a Cat* seeks to comprehend the fate of the optimism captured just ten years earlier in *Be Seeing You*. Then, with the Cuban revolution and the worldwide protest against the Vietnam War, everything seemed possible; for a brief moment forces of dissent seemed united. In *A Grin without a Cat,* Marker returns to Cèbe's recollection of his political awakening in Indochina, where he was sent by the French military to fight the communist forces. The film then cuts to May 1, 1967, on the final day of a long but successful strike of workers at Saint Nazaire shipyards. The workers are optimistic and recall the strikes initiated by the Popular Front in 1936: "1936 was something else, 1967 won't be bad either." But with the death one month later of a student, Benno Ohnesorg, at the hands of the police in a peaceful demonstration against a state visit to West Berlin by the shah of Iran, Europe entered a period of violent upheaval. Marker believes that the workers' strike in France inspired protests elsewhere and produced a new type of collective action. Demonstrations became more aggressive and often sought retaliation instead of discussion. And as the number of protest marches increased, the "state was forced to reveal its repressive side, the one that is more or less diluted in everyday life."

A Grin without a Cat captures the growing tensions between the workers and the more radical student groups. It also documents the increased presence of police. Marker observes, however, that alliances of students and workers still function and tracks the impressive wave of strikes that hit France one week after the Sorbonne barricades in May 1968. The narrator predicts that "the workers will take the flag from the fragile hands of the students." Yet the coalition would not last. Marker shows that by 1968 it had already begun to unravel and detects the early manifestations of the fissure that would eventually rip the leftist movement asunder. Maspero, in an astute analysis of the spatial manifestations of the struggle, observed how important it was to master the space between the police line and the workers. This prompted Marker to film the distance between a line of police and one of strikers from a bird's-eye perspective and to locate the students in that ever-decreasing space. Indeed, by 1972 that space within which the avant-garde functioned was closed, and two years later all semblance of worker-student solidarity had evaporated. As the Left split into factions of Trotskyites, Maoists, Stalinists, and Leninists, with each group dismissing the others as "Fascists," a whole range of possibilities disappeared.

Marker indicates that he is fully aware of the complex array of reasons that led to this dissolution. He lays one factor in this process at the feet of the labor movement, suggesting that when the unions joined the political struggle of the students, they pressed too much to lead that struggle. Yet he also points to some of the fundamental ideological changes produced by France's postwar transformation into a consumer society. As an articulate manager for Citroën, whom Marker interviews, observes, even the Soviet Union was at the time undergoing a shift in economic policy, marked by a rise in domestic competition and the growing popularity of consumer goods and leisure activities (captured by Marker with images of a Russian man waterskiing). This begins to explain why workers still followed the direction of the union in 1967, but barely two years later they were willing to defy the union and return to work should they be offered a significant pay raise. The students also became less sure about goals and means. To make this point, Marker includes an early sequence from July 1968 during which student protesters shout down theater director Jean Vilar, whose commitment to the student movement the filmmaker believes to be unquestionable. Marker focuses the camera on the angry faces and brutish expressions of the students haranguing Vilar and shows them to resemble those of pro–Vietnam War demonstrators.

The sequence of funeral processions of slain leftist heroes that opened *A Grin without a Cat* is repeated later in the film, though new names are highlighted: "Ulrike, Tania, Sarita, Nguyen Van Troi, Javier Héraud, Malcom X, Camilo Torres, Txiki, Victor Jara, Julian Grimau, George Jackson, Carlos Marighela, Roque Dalton, and Pierre Overney." At this point the narrator ends his litany for the dead and explains that Overney, who was killed by a Renault security guard, was nastily denounced by both the Communist Party and the Confédération Générale du Travail (CGT, a labor union) for being a "provocateur" because he was a Maoist. This leads Marker to note that "for all those who were part of the '6os, this was the last parade." Just as the Venezuelan guerilla fighters were abandoned a few years earlier by the Communist Party to become a spearhead without a spear, a grin without a cat, so too by extension one can see the fate of the nonparliamentary Left in France: the spearhead detached from the spear.

The 1977 version of *A Grin without a Cat* ends with scenes from Portugal in which people flash the "V" for victory sign, crying out triumphantly: "A united people will never be vanquished!" This fragment is followed by a television broadcast about an explosion of armaments and a sequence with wolves being hunted and shot by men in helicopters. The 1992 version of this film adds new commentary and footage. The narrator explains that transformations that took place during the past fifteen years have introduced idioms that had no meaning in the 1960s: boat people, AIDS, Reaganism, with perhaps the most remarkable being

Commonwealth of Independent States. By contrast, the Soviet Union no longer exists. Marker observes with a tone of lament that capitalism has won a major battle against communism, if not the war itself, and that terrorism has now replaced communism as the public embodiment of evil. This prompts him to reflect on the wiliness of history: "So our editor would marvel at the ingenuity of history that always seems to have more imagination than we do." The final shot of the film focuses on the wolf hunt. Over gruesome footage of the animals in their death throes, Marker has the narrator note that although their population has been greatly diminished, fifteen years later "some wolves still remain." Cold comfort, perhaps, but from Marker's perspective it is very cold outside.

The Wise Owl: Questioning/Expanding Form

> Gone and never to return
> and being for myself alone
> a remembrance of things to come
> who fancied being a human.
>
> —Claude Roy, as cited in *Remembrance of Things to Come*

Marker's *Remembrance of Things to Come* (2001) bears a close formal and thematic resemblance to his best-known film, *La jetée* (1962). Both productions investigate the nature of the relationship between static pictures and moving images and propose a paradoxical, seemingly unrealistic, theory of memory that extends beyond the past into the future. In describing the photographs used in *Remembrance of Things to Come*, Marker notes that they "show a past, yet decipher the future." Photographs, he continues, capture not one but multiple representations of what the lens sees when the shutter momentarily snaps open. The images immediately fall into the past while concomitantly providing an intangible glimpse of the future. That glimpse can only be discerned with the passage of time, as what was in the future reaches the viewer's present. In the process, the eye of the camera, in indiscriminately registering what lies before it, captures the shapes of the future. As Marker repeatedly observes, "You never know what you are filming."

O.W.L. (Optional World Link) in *Level Five*

The passage of time and the manner in which it is stored and transformed into memory are, for Marker, intimately connected to the medium through which the past is represented. Like the taste of Marcel Proust's madeleine that unwittingly releases a flow of memories, so images and sounds in Marker's films evoke the past, each in their own way according to their particular form. The filmmaker's attentiveness to both the concrete visual and the more ephemeral sound medium characterizes his entire oeuvre. In fact, a basic part of his project has been to challenge the parameters of both media to provoke a reflection on (and reconsideration of) traditional forms, leading to neologisms and the invention of new formulas. Thus he refers to *Statues Also Die* as a "pamphlet film," to *L'Amérique rêve* and *Soy Mexico* as "imaginary films," and to his photo-journal, *Coréennes*, as a "short film." All of Marker's texts, whether filmic, photographic, or verbal, are in this sense highly experimental.

More generally, and in a sustained way, his audiovisual works all testify to his fascination with new technological inventions and their possibilities. Resnais recalls that Marker was one of the first to adopt and use a 16 mm camera after the war. As we have seen, *Le joli mai* relied heavily on the new technology of the handheld synch-sound camera. More than a decade later, *L'Ambassade* (The Embassy, 1973) was one of the first films to be shot in Super 8. Easy to use and producing high quality images, the Super 8 camera was rapidly employed by filmmakers around the world involved in politically committed cinema. Marker's work in the 1990s continued to engage with emergent technology such as the Internet and CD-ROMs. His appropriation of new media is never banal or fashionable. Rather, in the spirit of Brecht and Walter Benjamin, it is always politically and socially committed, seeking novel means of transforming habitual vision and breaking through calcified ideological structures.

La Jetée

While working on *Le joli mai,* Marker contemplated adapting one of his science fiction radio scripts to cinema. True to form, he kept his project secret; when questioned during the 1961 Leipzig film festival about his plans, he responded enigmatically that he would like to make "a futuristic film." The high costs of a science fiction film rendered it impossible, however. (For additional background, see Marker's interview with Gersch.) But Marker soon found a strategy that enabled him to produce a low-budget, quasi-science fiction film that was ultimately highly successful. Titled *La jetée,* the work is composed almost entirely of black-and-white still photographs edited together on 35 mm film. The sound track offers an overarching commentary or voice-over as well as various diegetic background noises. Although the audio flows uninterruptedly and advances the narrative, the image track is punctuated by the sequence of photographs. Their combination resembles a slide show or illustrated lecture in which each transparency supplements a different segment of the spoken text, establishing a direct relationship between word and image. *La jetée* is subtitled "ciné-roman," and it is one of three photo-based films that Marker has made to date—the others being *If I Had Four Camels* and *Remembrance of Things to Come.* In each, he uses still photographs to different effect.

La jetée has generated the greatest amount of critical attention of all of Marker's films and has achieved the status of a cult classic, largely because of the theoretical discussions it has provoked.[43] The latter have tended to focus on the film's multilayered formal and thematic problems, though these have often been kept distinct and separate. In this respect, *La jetée* is at one and the same time a film theorist's film, a philosopher's film, and a cultural critic's film.[44] Yet its appeal also derives from the fact that it is the only work of narrative fiction in Marker's oeuvre thus far.

Woman's face in *La jetée*. Courtesy of
Filmmuseum Berlin—Deutsche Kinemathek

This filmic genre addresses a much broader audience than the others within which Marker operates, which perhaps explains why Terry Gilliam adapted *La jetée*'s plotline as a base for his feature film *12 Monkeys*.

La jetée is set in an imaginary, subterranean, post–World War III Paris, which has been devastated by a nuclear catastrophe. Although the film is evidently a product of the cold war raging in the early 1960s, the scientists of the future communicate in German, evoking the previous World War. Further, the still photos of a bomb-devastated cityscape bear an uncanny resemblance to the immediate postwar imagery of Germany, especially Berlin, as captured in films by Wolfgang Staudte, Günther Lamprecht, and Roberto Rosselini.[45] The story line of *La jetée* revolves around a prisoner who has exceptional memory associations and capabilities. He is "marked by an image from his childhood" in the prewar past that revolves around a "violent scene" on the observation platform *(jetée)* of the Orly airport. The memory, whose context he does not fully understand, is that of the horrified expression on a woman's face as she watches a man crumple and fall. Already from the onset of the film the prisoner is cast as suffering from the symptoms of trauma. The trauma appears uncontrollably and irrationally in image flashes, defying linguistic order. As the commentary notes, "Nothing sorts out memories from ordinary moments. Later on they do claim remembrance when they show their scars." Marker's recourse to the cicatrix underscores the often physical and woundlike nature of the past-witnessed scene that generates the present trauma. A parallel is constructed between the act of memory and that of filming or photography, namely that the significance of what is captured by the camera's eye or the image lodged in one's memory is often not readily apparent for years to come.

The postwar setting and subtle evocation of Germany is significant because it points to the traumatic rupture of World War II and the Holocaust in the history of the twentieth century. The scientists examining the prisoner manage, after a series of experiments, to send him back in time to this prewar period in the hopes that he will be able to alter the course of history and thereby prevent the subsequent nuclear holocaust from occurring. Their only hope for survival lies in a "loophole in time." Hence, the protagonist is returned a number of times to the past world, where he encounters images from times of peace such as a bedroom, a cat, a child's face, a graveyard, as well as the woman that haunts his dreams and memory. Each return is longer in duration as the man and woman engage in a classical courtship ritual, visiting the Jardin des Plantes, the Museum of Natural History, and other sites where history and culture are preserved. Several shots are of "timeless animals" such as manatees, hippopotamuses, and manta rays. Their preserved, taxidermic state recalls Marker's earlier musings on the wooly mammoth in *Letter from Siberia*. Indeed, the cadavers of animals are often displayed for exhibition and future contemplation in museums (not to mention as trophies in private settings). By contrast, the "museum of man" focuses on the cultural artifacts produced by humans and not on their corpses. A series of images of classical statues of the human body (mainly female and headless) is included in the protagonist's journey into the past. Not only do these maimed statues of Western civilization evoke Marker's earlier meditations on the fate of non-Western art in *Statues Also Die,* but they also serve to underscore the role that representation plays in the crystallization of human memory. Yet there is still another space where history and memory are preserved, one that is less ordered and noninstitutional, namely in the mind. As the commentary observes: "Other images appear, merge, in that museum, which is perhaps that of his memory." The idea of each individual's memory housing its own museum of images resurfaces as a formal project thirty-five years later with Marker's CD-ROM *Immemory*. But it was with *La jetée* that Marker first imagined a highly personalized virtual museum without a physical site or walls.

The entire narrative of *La jetée* is communicated visually, via snap-shotlike photographs that freeze the two characters at telling moments of action. The voice-over commentary fills in the narrative gaps. Only at one point in the main body of the film does movement occur: what seems to be a still photograph of the woman sleeping in bed is suddenly transformed as her eyes flutter open. Yet more important than this often-commented-upon moment are the final shots of *La jetée* when the protagonist arrives back at the initial site of his memory, the platform at Orly. That primal scene is repeated, but with a twist: at the last instant he realizes (as does the spectator) that he is in fact the man who is falling, having just been shot by the scientists from the future. Thus, all along, his memory was that of his own death.

This seemingly impossible memory and the corresponding play with time can also be related to the ongoing intratextual dialogue Marker engages in with Alfred Hitchcock's *Vertigo* (1958). The film classic finds its way into several of Marker's works, including his CD-ROM *Immemory*. In *La jetée*, *Vertigo* is evoked in one of the encounters between the protagonist and the young woman as they examine the growth rings and historical markings on a giant sequoia in the Jardin des Plantes. Whereas in *Vertigo* it is Madeleine (played by Kim Novak) who goes back in time to show Scotty (Jimmy Stewart) her era, in Marker's film it is the man who gestures to a point outside of the trunk in the future stating, "This is where I come from."[46] This mirror effect is further enhanced by the fact that the unknown woman in *La jetée* "pronounces an English name" and has her hair set in a spiraled bun similar to Novak's. The spiral, of course, also evokes vertiginous experience. Marker's fascination with *Vertigo* returns twenty years later in *Sunless*, which includes a detailed sequence centered on Hitchcock's classic. In *Sunless*, Sandor Krasna writes to the narrator that *Vertigo* is the only film "capable of portraying impossible memory—insane memory." He also writes that "power and freedom" and "melancholy and dazzlement," were "carefully coded within the spiral so that you could miss it and not discover immediately that this vertigo of space in reality stands for a vertigo of time."[47] Marker intercuts shots from the original *Vertigo* with his own shots of the same locations in San Francisco years later. Some places have changed, whereas others remain the same. And in a stunning passage in front of the giant sequoia at Muir Woods, Krasna remarks: "He remembered another film in which this passage was quoted. The sequoia was the one in the Jardin des Plantes in Paris, and the hand pointed to a place outside the tree, outside of time."

Marker's tale thus proposes a rationally impossible scenario that defies the usual logics of memory and undermines the accepted concepts of time. His narrative is reminiscent of the novels of Philip K. Dick and other authors whose science fiction is set in what has been coined the "bad new future." The plot adopts the trope of time travel in which a voyage to the past is used to change the course of history. The film plays on the idea that memory is not structured as a continuous narrative flow but as a series of discontinuous snapshots, an approach that recalls the *bande dessinée,* or cartoon strip, which was quite popular in France at the time. The rapid succession of images breaks the mirror of verisimilitude. In order for the relationship between the fragments—each cartoon frame or each photograph—and the whole story to be understood, the viewer must reconstitute the narrative. In this way, Marker underscores the artificial nature of film as well as that of history.

If I Had Four Camels, The Embassy, Remembrance of Things to Come

La jetée is a fictional work that encourages avant-garde reflection on the place and function of still photographs in cinema. By contrast, *If I Had Four Camels* meditates much more directly on the general nature and possibilities of photography. Marker describes the subject of the film as follows: "An amateur photographer and his two friends comment on images taken a little bit from all over the world." In this case "all over the world" refers to twenty-six countries, including the Soviet Union, Cuba, China, North Korea, Japan, and Israel. The focus on these sites is not entirely surprising given Marker's cinematographic oeuvre to this point. Yet there are some unexpected choices, including extensive shots of Iceland (some of which will return as the first and last images in *Sunless*) as well as pictures from Berlin and Stockholm. Against the backdrop of these images, a running commentary and dialogue between three voices identified as P, C (a woman), and N, discuss what is shown on the screen and reflect on the ontological nature of photography. The film begins with a programmatic statement by P: "The photograph, it is the hunt, it is the instinct to hunt without the desire to kill. It is the hunt of angels. . . . One tracks, one aims, one pulls the trigger and clack! Though, instead of killing, one makes something eternal." What follows are examples of the photographer's efforts to preserve and hence immortalize subjects throughout the world. A case in point is a picture taken by Marker of a crude mosaiclike heart inlaid in the pavement of a parking lot in Paris. Yet, as the commentator reveals, this pavement with its embedded whimsical heart had been removed by the time the film was completed. As N notes, "Happily, our photographer was there!" One is here reminded of Benjamin's observations on Proust's theory of *mémoire involontaire,* in which the former concludes that "the past" is "somewhere beyond the reach of the intellect and unmistakably present in some material object (or in the sensation which such an object arouses in us)" (Benjamin 158). Objects, animals, humans, architectural structures, all bear witness to events from the past and to the passing of time. The photograph has the capacity to "capture" this past, but only through a flash or glimpse whose comprehension is fleeting.

In *If I Had Four Camels,* Marker posits a direct and unproblematic relationship between photographic representation and empirical fact. The photographs in the film function as truthful documents or records of that which they represent. Yet Marker's understanding of photography changed substantially over the years. By the time he made *Level Five* (1996), his primary concern had become that of exposing how the photographic image is both contrived and manipulated. This skepticism reaches its apogee halfway through *Level Five* when the camera turns to the image of the U.S. flag being raised atop Mount Suribachi on Iwo Jima near the end of World War II. As the commentator observes, the event, presented as if caught spontaneously, has actually been carefully restaged (like the storming of the Winter Palace); because the original marines were not available for the photo session, the U.S. military found substitutes.

In 1973, Marker foregrounded the duplicitous nature of the cinematic medium in his film *The Embassy.*[48] Filmed in Super 8 with a handheld camera in the style of cinéma vérité, the film is narrated by an anonymous cameraman who records images and sounds in an unidentified embassy two days after a coup d'état. *The Embassy* takes place over five days (Wednesday to Monday), during which period a number of political refugees manage to enter the diplomatic building and tell their stories to the ambassador and his wife. The images and dialogue are presented by the narrator as spontaneous, unedited, raw footage. But Marker in fact employed nonprofessional actors to play various roles. The characters include a student, Marco; a militant anarchist, Tsikos; his wife, Carole; and a lawyer, Volodia. The sound track is punctuated by street noises such as police sirens and gunshots. On the fourth day in the embassy a lively political debate breaks out among the asylum seekers. The narrator states: "It is impossible for me to reread my notes from this time, the camera has become witness." The film concludes with the political refugees leaving the embassy assured of safe passage to a country of exile. The voice-over recalls: "From the widow of our room, I shot my last images: the small truck that carried the refugees into exile and of this city where we once knew liberty." The camera then pans down a typical Parisian street and upward into the sky in which the Eiffel Tower is clearly recognizable. The entire production is thereby revealed to be an oblique critique of contemporary French society. *The Embassy*'s elusive opening words, "Ceci n'est pas un film" (This is not a film), with their explicit allusion to Magritte's painting *The Treason of Images* (1928), are suddenly filled with meaning, and in the spirit of a mockumentary the myth of a cinematic reality or truth is debunked.

By contrast, Marker's approach to the veracity of cinema and of the photographic negative in his earlier *If I Had Four Camels* is that of "truth twenty-four times a second." Here truth means that the photograph *has* a referent (even if it is only fragmentary) and that the image is a record or document of something located in a precise historical moment. Marker's photographs often reveal that which is least expected, the unfamiliar, alongside scenes from everyday life. *If I Had Four Camels* incorporates several different photographic genres, including portraiture. Some images depict anonymous individuals who will never be known, captured unaware in brief and fleeting instants. P declares that these are his favorites: "I prefer best those of unknown people. Especially when they are not aware that you have taken their image. . . . It gives one a strange sense of possession, the fact that they are unaware that their image exists and that you are the only one that knows it." A flow of candid shots follows. Figures from different cultural locations are shown repeating the same gesture, creating visual echoes that cross spatial and temporal borders. Thus a young, dark-haired woman sits in an interior and rests her chin on her left hand, as does a young blonde child sitting outside with a dog. Marker also includes photographs of intimates, friends and family such as Agnès Varda standing on the steps of the Kolomenskié Church in Moscow.

At this point in the film the photographic themes decidedly shift abruptly from personal to collective memories. The voice-over notes that the Moscow church is the same one that Ivan the Terrible frequented long ago. There are also shots of flora and fauna, notably that of a rare white rose, and of a series of exotic animals (including an elephant) in Moscow. Here Marker mentions self-reflexively that the word for elephant in Russian is *slon*, a gesture toward the SLON production company that he was in the process of forming during the filming of *If I Had Four Camels*. In yet another self-referential gesture or playful wink, Marker includes a photograph from *La jetée*. This is followed by pictures of modern architectural structures that the three friends (P, C, and N) do not immediately recognize, giving rise to a guessing game about their geographical location: all three guess incorrectly that all of the structures are located in New York, when in actuality they are in Paris, Brussels, Moscow, and Havana. These inanimate edifices are as significant for Marker as are humans and animals in imparting history and culture. In one sequence, the camera tracks a number of walls in Jordan, China, and Berlin as the narrator comments: "It is the petrified form of a dialogue of deaf people. At Berlin, everyone thinks they are right." In addition to walls, Marker also includes a collection of photographs taken of dogs in Paris and Moscow and another of sets of lottery machines in Cuba, Portugal, and Japan. Marker thus establishes a parallelism of forms while simultaneously underscoring their differences because of their particular context. Multiple shots of children from all over the globe reveal that differences between those who come from privileged groups and those who do not begin very early: "There are no united children, just as there are no united nations at the United Nations. Children are primarily that which they eat, and believe what they are taught."

For the most part, however, the photographs assembled and re-produced seem to be portraits of people caught spontaneously by the camera. The emotions conveyed by the expressions of those depicted are sometimes as fleeting as the historical events that have inspired them. One is struck, for instance, by the sense of sheer joy that lights up the face of a smiling young boy in Nanterre, a Paris suburb, on the first day of Algerian independence. C comments and judges in an aside: "They were happy. One instant of happiness paid for by seven years of war and one million dead. And the following day the castle was there again. And the poor people are still there, day after day. And day after day, we continue to betray them." The *castle* refers here to a dominant trope running through the film, which is divided into two parts: the "castle" and the "garden." The former stands for those structures of power that exclude the disenfranchised poor; the latter represents the utopian space where various possibilities of social justice can be imagined.

Although many of the subjects of the camera seem to be caught unaware, several of them directly face the apparatus, returning the look of the photographer. Theorizing the gaze, or *le regard*, with its more active meaning in French, is important for Marker as both filmmaker and writer and continues to preoccupy him. In his films, the *regard* can be returned by animals and even by inanimate objects such as statues. The commentary in *If I Had Four Camels* notes: "There is life and there is its double, and the photograph is part of the world of the double. . . . When you approach these faces, you have the impression that you participate in their life and in the death of live faces, of human faces. But this is not true: if you participate in anything, it is in their life and in the death of images." The concept of the double articulated in this passage, based as it is on the writings of the theater theorist Antonin Artaud, refers to the staged representation of life through performance or, by extension, through photography. In short, Marker underscores that although film and photography may have a high degree of verisimilitude, under no circumstances are they to be taken as anything other than what they are—signs and representations. Their meaning can never be stable; it is constantly changing. As the narrator observes regarding photos of smiling Soviet citizens: "I am not naive. I know that these people whom I have photographed during a moment of happiness or in a good humor are the same as those who applaud when a writer is condemned for seven years in a cell because he has used a couple dozen old poetic forms. . . . The same people!" If the photograph "captures" anything, then, it is a fleeting instant of truth that is no longer there except as an image the moment the shutter snaps shut.

Thirty-five years later, Marker returned to the meditation on the nature of the photographic image in *Remembrance of Things to Come*. The film starts with a series of pictures of the 1938 surrealist exhibition in Paris. The voice-over comments that it is thanks to photographer Denise Bellon that a record of the show exists and that her "perfect" images illustrate "the unique moment in time when postwar was becoming prewar."[49] It concludes with the enigmatic phrase that "each of her photographs shows a past yet deciphers the future." Through a series of examples drawn from Bellon's oeuvre, the rest of the film explicates what it means for the past to decipher the future. In one example, Marker shows us a photograph of a parachutist. Yet he warns that in memory there will be no parachutists but only paratroopers, and he superimposes over the still image moving footage of paratroopers jumping out of a military plane during World War II. In another instance, a photo of a nude woman sunbathing on a riverbank is accompanied by the spoken observation that "the sight of an outstretched body close to a river will inevitably evoke the sight of other bodies stretched on the road after Stukas have flown over" and followed by images of 1940 bomber planes. The initial "meaning" of each photo is thus transmogrified by the war that followed only a few years later. The photographs have an uncanny, prescient content that demonstrates that they, like some works of fiction, possess a "political unconscious" that unwittingly points to the future. Commenting on the prophetic vision of the architects who placed the German and Soviet pavilions facing each other at the 1937 World's Fair in Paris, Marker notes that they saw "further than the politicians." But he suggests that there is no logical or rational explanation for these premonitions; the photographs merely bear witness to events that become acknowledged only decades later.

As a narrative, *Remembrance of Things to Come* is mired in a nostalgia for the past. In this film about memory, Marker pays tribute to French cultural figures of the early twentieth century. Theorists of surrealism such as André Breton, who according to Marker "has the perfect eye the way some people have the perfect pitch," are held up as models. Similarly, Marcel Duchamp is positioned as the artist whose "regard" "has changed ours the most." Equally important, however, are filmmakers of the Golden Age of French film during the prewar era. The masterworks of this "cinema never to be found again" included *La règle du jeu* (1939), *Quai des Brumes* (1938), and *La belle equipe* (1936). These films were preserved during World War II thanks in part to the efforts of Henri Langlois, who secreted them away in different locations throughout France. There were myths, recalls Marker, that Langlois used to hide canisters in his bathtub and transport them from one location to another in a baby carriage. Marker substantiates these rumors by means of Bellon's photographs, which, here as elsewhere, provide the documentary evidence that transforms myth into reality. In another instance, Bellon's camera records the 1944 failed Republican attempt to recapture Spain at Val' d'arran. Often unbeknownst to the photographer, the eye of the camera assembles shards of history—"You never know what you are filming"—offering an optical unconscious, as it were. Photographs make up part of a visual archive, and the importance or relevance of past original events is determined by present-day circumstances. The question arises as to the difference between the *photo-roman,* which also offers archival interest, and the photo-film. There are obviously many. But the most striking is the photo-film's sound track, which provides not only the simultaneity of audial and visual commentary—far more effective than a written text following or preceding the printed photographs—but also music to affect the work's meaning. In a photo-film the tension between the still image—snapshot—and the moving image—film—parallels the relationship between the instantaneous truth of the present and the lesson of historical continuity. The photo may be viewed as a sign of the process whereby memory is summoned—a trigger or flash that unleashes a successive narrative flow.

Remembrance of Things to Come ends as it begins, with a photograph of a group of surrealists. Reassembled in 1947, all of the surrealists now wear white masks as they pose for a portrait. Marker declares this image to be "prophetic" because "the history of the century's end will be that of its masks."

Sunless

> I remember that month of January in Tokyo, or rather I remember the
> images I filmed of the month of January in Tokyo. They have substi-
> tuted themselves for my memory. They are my memory. I wonder how
> people remember things, [people] who don't film, don't photograph,
> don't tape.
>
> —*Sunless*

Second only to *La jetée, Sans soleil* (Sunless, 1982) is one of Marker's
best-known films. The title refers to the cycle of Mussorgsky songs of
the same name. The film, one hundred minutes in length, constitutes
a tightly woven audiovisual meditation on the relationship between
memory and the technologies that record and mediate it. The voice-
over commentary is spoken by an unidentified woman who reads and
paraphrases letters written by the fictional character Sandor Krasna. The
latter is endowed with traits that identify him as a fictional stand-in for
Marker. Krasna, a filmmaker, at one point describes an idea for a project
that closely resembles *Sunless*. Yet he immediately dismisses this idea in
an offhand way: "Of course I'll never make that film. Nonetheless I'm
collecting the sets, inventing the twists, putting in my favorite creatures.
I've even given it a title of those Mussorgsky songs: Sunless."[50] He writes
the woman a series of letters from faraway places, most located in Asia
and Africa, commenting on local patterns of everyday life. Ultimately,

"An image of happi-
ness" in *Sunless*

he concludes: "I've been 'round the world several times and now only banality still interests me."

The film is composed of several sequences shot in different locales: Japan, the Cape Verde Islands, the Isle of Sal, Iceland, and the Ile de France. With the exception of the latter, all are real islands, indicating Marker's fascination with the dual literal and figurative meaning of *island* as an isolated monad separated from the mainland and operating according to its own, relatively autonomous flow of time.[51] The populations of islands exist both as part of and yet removed from continental civilization. At the beginning of the film, the female commentator announces that her correspondent, Krasna, once noted that "in the nineteenth century mankind had come to terms with space, and the great question of the twentieth was the coexistence of different concepts of time." As the film explores the interface of the issues of time and space through various cuts back and forth from one location to another, it creates a disjointed montage that prompts the viewer to remember a myriad of narrative threads simultaneously.

Just as *Le joli mai* opens with an evocation of a feeling of happiness—dedicated, as the film is, to the happy many—with the first image of *Sunless,* Marker offers what he describes as Krasna's "image of happiness." This image consists of a short clip set off from the rest of the film with a black leader. The clip depicts three children on a road in Iceland in 1965. The voice-over informs us that Krasna had tried to link this image to others several times but had been ultimately unsuccessful. The clip is repeated toward the end of the film, but this time with more information as Marker's stand-in adds: "I picked up the whole shot again, adding the somewhat hazy end, the frame trembling under the force of the wind beating us down on the cliff: everything I had cut in order to tidy up, and that said it better than all the rest." By this point in the film, the viewer has been reminded of the volcanic eruption that in 1965 covered in black ash the entire village in Iceland from which the children came. Marker includes footage of the natural disaster shot by filmmaker Haroun Tazieff. In a formal sense, the burial of the town's architecture under mounds of black ash recalls the black leader that follows the initial clip of the three children. At the same time, the haze of volcanic ash that blocks the sun evokes the title of the film.

In recorded visual memory, the clip of the children comes to be replaced by images of destruction, stressing once again the impermanence of things. The ostensible function of the film, however, is to capture a glimpse of the happiness of that sunny day and to transform it into a renewable memory. Years later the protagonist in *Sunless* films a purification ritual on the island of Okinawa. He indicates his awareness that, as he did earlier in Siberia, in Okinawa he is witnessing "the end of something": "Magical cultures that disappear leave traces to those who succeed them. This one will leave none." Marker thus anticipates that a pervasive amnesia in the future will erase and obliterate these ancient ceremonies. The Okinawa purification ritual is but one of several rites that Marker's camera in *Sunless* records in contemporary Japan. Others include visitations to cat temples, fertility temples, coming-of-age celebrations, and other events such as the communal mourning of animals and the annual burning of dolls.

The greater part of the film takes place in Japan and is structured as a return or homecoming for Marker. Yet much has changed in the almost two decades that have passed since his last Japan foray, *The Koumiko Mystery*. Whereas the country was undergoing rapid modernization in the 1960s, by 1982 this process was complete. From this perspective, the title also refers to an apocalyptic moment in modern Japanese history when a black rain fell in 1945, causing the imperial sun to set in defeat. *Sunless* thus evokes the new Japanese society, based on democracy, although with vestiges of the past occasionally shining through.

Krasna's return to Tokyo recalls the opening commentary of *Le joli mai* in which the narrator describes his wish to revisit cities such as Paris to verify the validity of memories. Krasna compares "his reunion with Tokyo" to the experience of "a cat who has come home from vacation in his basket and immediately starts to inspect familiar places": "He ran off to see if everything was where it should be: the Ginza owl, the Shimbashi locomotive, the temple of the fox at the top of the Mitsukoshosi department store. . . . These simple joys he had never felt: of returning to a country, a house, a family home. But twelve million anonymous inhabitants could supply him with them." The Japan that Krasna encounters now is very different from the country that hosted the Olympic Games in 1964. Marker's filmic approach is also significantly different. Whereas *The Koumiko Mystery* centered on an intimate portrait of a young Japanese woman, *Sunless* focuses instead on a phalanx of "anonymous inhabitants."

There is one exception to that anonymity: Hayao Yamaneko, a computer technician with wizardlike skills who generates synthesized images in what he calls the Zone. Yamaneko's Zone is based on the space of the same name theorized by Tarkovsky in *Stalker*. In his Zone, Yamaneko manipulates images drawn from a variety of sources, both historical and imaginary. Five different concrete Zones are presented within the film. The first starts with documentary footage of past events. Yamaneko transforms this footage with the aid of a digital synthesizer. "If the images of the present don't change, then change the images of the past," he states in an effort to explain his motives. These synthesized images, Yamaneko continues, are "less deceptive than those you see on television. At least they proclaim themselves to be what they are: images, not the portable and compact form of an already inaccessible reality." The second Zone is devoted to the manufacture of video games. Krasna's (and Marker's) most beloved animals, the cat and the owl, find a home in this Zone together with distorted images of a class of Japanese people, the *burakim,* whose existence continues to be socially denied in Japan today: "They are non-persons. How can they be shown, except as non-images?" Zone 3 is devoted to signs that function in memory, and Zone 4 recreates images of kamikaze pilots from World War II. The last Zone, presented at the end of the film, is the most self-reflexive within the framework of Marker's

An emu on the Ile de
France in *Sunless*

An emu from the Zone in *Sunless*. Courtesy of
Filmmuseum Berlin—Deutsche Kinemathek

work: it reproduces, albeit in a highly distorted form, key images that
have composed *Sunless*. We recognize among others the emus from the
Ile de France, the dogs playing in the surf on Sal, and a woman whose
return of the camera's gaze at the market in Praia "had lasted 1/24th of
a second or the length of a film frame." The Zone thus freezes what was
initially intended to be fleeting and barely perceptible. The technology
that enabled the manipulations and transformations that constitute the
Zone is based on a crude computer synthesizer that Marker used in
his dual monitor installation, *Quand le siècle a pris formes* (When the
Century Assumed Form, 1978). With *Sunless* four years later, however,
he makes it a point to show how that equipment functions and thereby
demystifies the means of production.

Yamaneko declares midway through the film that only "electronic
texture" can adequately "deal with sentiment, memory, and imagination."
Hence, the problem of the relationship between human emotions, remembering, and creative thought as they are expressed through mediating apparatuses is introduced. A significant leitmotif of *Sunless* concerns

the translation of emotions—or, as is stated on more than one occasion, "things that quicken the heart"—into systems of representation. Toward the beginning of the film, the letter writer tells the story of a man who, upon the death of his beloved, plunged himself into his work. Yet we learn that the man ended up taking his own life in the month of May because, having lost his love, he could no longer bear to hear the word *spring*. Hence, language is posited as the mediating agency, one capable of conveying unbearable grief. Writing, too, insofar as it functions to record memory, serves to transform the past: "We do not remember, we rewrite memory, much as history is rewritten." Here the narrator also addresses the pivotal role of the broadcast medium of television, which is referred to as a "memory box." Much of life experience is thus advanced as a mediated memory, not based on solid ground. The term *sunless* thereby assumes another meaning, one that evokes a world in which the direct vision under the sun has been replaced by a variety of mediated representations, including film.

Marker presents Japanese society as one that epitomizes mediation. Japan is figured as a "world of appearances" in which even manufactured sound plays a crucial role. Speaking of Tokyo, the narrator notes "that this city ought to be deciphered like a musical score; one could get lost in the great orchestral masses and the accumulation of details." Indeed, canned sounds are pervasive in the film, from crosswalk indicators to the background noise of telephones and video games. Marker thus shows the extent to which the environment is not only controlled visually but is also managed acoustically. Westerners in this context are shown to be handicapped by their inability to "hear" adequately and thus to navigate the city successfully. As Krasna observes, "There is in the score that is Tokyo a particular staff, whose rarity in Europe condemns me to a real acoustic exile."

Even the animals in Japan function as ciphers of mediation. A case in point is a sequence that features the ritualistic mourning of the death of a panda. Instead of genuine sorrow, the narrator sees only curiosity in the eyes of the children. Death has become abstract. By way of contrast, Marker then inserts, without commentary, a graphic and drawn-out film clip depicting the shooting of a giraffe. This image of slaughter is immediately followed by a strand of the second main leitmotif running through *Sunless*, namely the successful revolution in the 1970s against the Portuguese led by Amilcar Cabral in Guinea-Bissau.[52] The narrator rhetorically asks: "Why should so small a country—and one so poor—interest the world?" and then provides the answer: "They did what they could, they freed themselves, they chased out the Portuguese. They traumatized the Portuguese army to such an extent that it gave rise to a movement that overthrew the dictatorship and led one for a moment to believe in a new revolution in Europe. Who remembers all that? History throws its empty bottles out the window." Thus the theme of revolutionary politics reemerges like a message in a bottle. Despite Krasna's claims at the beginning of *Sunless* that only "banality still interests" him, this scene reflects a return to the construction of history and a commitment to recording stories/histories that might otherwise be forgotten or thrown out. Thus, embedded in a film about the predominance of superficial features in contemporary Japanese society is a contrasting story about the promise of liberation and its subsequent disappointments. As the narrator asserts, "rumor has it that every Third World leader coined the same phrase the morning after independence: 'Now the real problems start.'" Amilcar Cabral never had the chance to say it himself; he was promptly assassinated. Marker inserts a film clip dated February 17, 1980, showing Luiz Cabral, the half brother of Amilcar, decorating a Major Nino, who seems to be moved to tears. The voice-over cautions us that in order to understand this clip properly one must move forward in time: "In a year, Luiz Cabral, the president, will be in prison, and the weeping man he has just decorated, Major Nino, will have taken power. . . . And beneath each of these faces a memory. And in place of what we were told had been forged into a collective memory, a thousand memories of men who parade their personal laceration in the great wound of history." The impermanence of images merely mirrors the impermanence of history. They are constantly shifting, fleeting, being rewritten and re-remembered. As for Krasna, he is plagued by the condition *not* of losing his memory but of losing the ability to forget. Such handicaps stall what is called the movement of history. Just as repression is an important function for maintaining a healthy psyche, so too, Marker paradoxically suggests, is it beneficial when "history advances, plugging its memory as one plugs one's ears."

From this perspective *Sunless* concerns the processes of remembering and forgetting. The role that individual storytelling plays in constructing history is capital, especially when there are no visual records. In Japan, where "the world of appearances" is ruled by audiovisual stimuli, there are big gaps in the archives, especially in the representation of World War II. Thus it is the duty of our traveler/guide Krasna to tell the story of Okinawa's desperate resistance for more than a month before final capitulation to the U.S. infantry in June 1945. Okinawa, Marker reminds us, had a separate identity (Ryukyu) from the rest of Japan and was a matriarchal society. The narrator recounts how at the end of the battle against U.S. troops, two hundred local girls used grenades to commit suicide rather than be captured alive. This event is memorialized by a tourist site where "souvenir lighters are sold" in the shape of grenades. History is here, as in so many other sites in the modern world, mediated through kitsch merchandise. The oral narrative of historical events on Okinawa works to counter the way in which memory has become a tourist commodity and "small fragments of war [become] enshrined in everyday life."

Level Five

Level Five is Marker's fourth film about Japan. Similar to both *The Koumiko Mystery* and *Sunless, Level Five* filters its representation of Japan through the figure of a woman, Laura, played by the actress Catherine Belkhodja. Yet if in *The Koumiko Mystery* Marker actively followed his protagonist through the streets of Tokyo in an attempt to discover the way in which she directly experienced the city, thirty years later he presented the experiences of both Laura and Japan as heavily mediated.

Throughout *Level Five,* Laura addresses a video camera from behind a desk in a small office space. Her face, cropped in a giant close-up, fills the entire screen as she is surrounded by bookshelves, computers, and video monitors that combine to form a prisonlike cell. She is thereby effectively reduced to a bewitching image, recalling her namesake in Otto Preminger's *Laura* (1944). Her only apparent links to the exterior world in *Level Five* operate through contacts made via the World Wide Web and by speaking into the video camera. Japan is represented exclusively by found footage: old film stock, clips from television, or images snared off of the Internet. If Marker's filmic style during the 1960s, especially in its use of a lightweight synch camera to directly, quasi-spontaneously shoot street scenes, resembled cinéma vérité, his work of the

1990s represented a counterpart to that technique. With the exception of one short sequence when the camera depicts Laura in a park, the audiovisual material of *Level Five* has been carefully assembled from recorded footage in the filmmaker's studio. The work thus constitutes a type of filmmaking in which it is no longer necessary physically to travel to remote regions or to go on location. Everything can now be captured from stored film tape. Of course, this technique would not be possible without the technological innovations of the past decade. Advances in image production and editing have radically transformed the way in which cinema can be made. There is now an enormous audiovisual archive or databank that can be readily accessed. In a spirit antithetical to that which generated and animated auteur cinema, a basic question may be raised: Why make new images when there are so many stills and clips already in circulation? Would not it be more efficient and yet just as aesthetically effective to snare, appropriate, and montage some of those ready-made images? Marker, whom Laura calls the "ace of montage," demonstrates his awareness of the vast range of these new filmic possibilities in *Level Five*.

The opening shot of *Level Five* features a close-up of a gnarled male hand (presumably Marker's) gliding a computer mouse across a pad. A graphic design of an owl appears on the computer monitor as, simultaneously, a computer-generated image of a head emerges against an urban landscape on the electronic screen. A disembodied female voice asks: "What can these be but the playthings of a mad God, who made us build them for him?" The images on the monitor are easily decipherable by the contemporary viewer, though, as the voice points out, they would be unrecognizable to someone—a "Neanderthal"—whose vision was still completely unmediated. Laura's face gradually fills the screen as she directly addresses an imaginary "you." As the film progresses, it becomes apparent that the latter is a former lover with whom she has engaged in a lengthy e-mail exchange. Marker brings the epistolary trope that structured *Letter from Siberia* and *Sunless* technologically up to speed in response to the advent of digital communication. Laura informs us that "he" was working on the design of a computer game while she was pursuing the more old-fashioned activity of writing a book. The "he" to whom she refers seems to have disappeared or died, and she has subsequently assumed the task of completing the game. The game entails an intricate reconstruction of the battle of Okinawa. Laura's unsuccessful attempts to change the program result invariably in the reappearance of Error #14 on her screen. In a self-reflexive gesture on Marker's part, when she appeals to "Chris" for help, an elderly man's voice announces: "That's when I came in. I was reader now for other people's images, instead of my own." The man admits that although he is very familiar with the nation, the war game will provide him with a new *clé* (key) to unlock Japan—a madeleine as it were. Thus begins the virtual voyage to Tokyo and the investigation of the details surrounding the battle of Okinawa.

In *Level Five* the autobiographical elements that were present to some degree in Marker's previous films, particularly those that involve journeys and explorations—*Sunday in Peking, Letter from Siberia, If I Had Four Camels, The Koumiko Mystery, Sunless*—achieve greater density and beg for identification. The office space in which most of the recording takes place displays several clues that make it recognizable as Marker's studio—a Steiff owl present in *Letter from Siberia* now sits on a bookshelf, photographs of the beloved Guillaume-en-Egypte, now deceased, grace the computer, and various books from Marker's oeuvre are prominently visible. Despite these autobiographical elements and the obvious correspondence between the disembodied man's voice and that of the filmmaker, it is important to remember that, at least in this film, Marker casts himself as a fictional character. Indeed, it is as a fictional character that one must consider him if one seeks to understand the complex operation of *Level Five*.[53]

The references to the battle of Okinawa recall a theme touched upon at the end of *Sunless*. Why are these historical events so important? The voice of the character Chris remarks at the beginning his commentary: "I'd become so Japanese that I shared in their collective amnesia." In sharp contrast to the Krasna figure, who had lost the capacity to forget, our new protagonist cannot remember. Okinawa thus becomes a cipher that triggers the process of remembering and, at the same time, a sign for the role that technology plays in reconstructing the past. Although framed as a fictional film, *Level Five* is still essentially an essay, that is, a postdocumentary demonstration of a new way of accessing audiovisual archives and performing research. We are led to believe that all of the information on the battle of Okinawa that appears in *Level Five* can be obtained through online sources with the magical click of a mouse. At the beginning of the Okinawa game, a menu with items such as Witnesses, Japanese Military, and U.S. Forces flashes on the screen. Depending on where one clicks, different windows open on various still and moving images. There are interviews with survivors who recall the Okinawan resistance to U.S. forces and the ensuing ritual mass suicide. An old man speaks of how the men killed all the elderly, women, and children before turning their weapons on themselves. Another story focuses on the visit to a cave in which hundreds of schoolgirls hid among maimed, dead, and rotting bodies before finally committing suicide. Yet another documentary film clip records how women jumped off the cliffs of the island, ending their lives in the sea below. Although such testimonies and documents are readily available, Marker suggests that the events are still shrouded in an embarrassed silence because, according to recent Japanese military history, Okinawa was coldly sacrificed in the mistaken belief that this would stall U.S. forces moving to reach the rest of Japan. The resistance of Okinawans thus represents blind mass obeisance by a people to a government that has already given them up—a complete waste of human lives, many of which were women and children. One film clip in particular encapsulates this ideology of ruthless sacrifice: A small girl emerges from the countryside, waving a white flag—she has been sent forth by the troops in order to protect the rest of the Japanese army.

Multifaceted perspectives of the battle of Okinawa are provided by advances in interactive media. These perspectives are available and now easily accessible to historians and interested parties throughout the networked world. Although much is captured, stored, and archived by the new technology, Marker reminds us that there are still limits to this dissemination of knowledge. The same limits hamper mediated attempts to represent war because all of the books and films of combat fail to adequately convey the odor of the battlefield. Marker assures the spectator that if the rotten, unbearable smell of putrification and death was replicated in the cinema, there would be no more war films because there would no longer be an audience. In the meantime one must face the distortions effected by such aestheticism, or more properly, anesthesia, whereby history is mystified as it is transformed into culture or art in order to make it more palatable for general (commercial) consumption.

On several occasions, however, Marker does try to impart the full horror of war. In *Sunless*, speaking of the revolutionaries in the Cape Verde Islands, he states: "She [history] doesn't care, she understands nothing, she has only one friend, the one that Brando spoke of in *Apocalypse Now:* horror." He then cuts to a color close-up of a maimed leg, wounds infested with maggots. Marker is aware that one can always close one's eyes when viewing a film and rationalize that what is on the screen is not real, but merely an effect of the deliberate manipulation of a strip of celluloid. Supporting and illustrating this view, in *Level Five* Laura discovers a secret about a soldier, Gustave, who was filmed as he was burned alive. Gustave is presented as a "gift of war documentaries," a "real unknown soldier" consumed by flames and suitable to serve as an icon of horror in different war zones around the world. Indeed the same clip is reused in the Philippines, Okinawa, and Vietnam. This periodic resuscitation or rehabilitation by the media inspires Laura to track down the original sequence filmed in Borneo. What she discovers is that the initial clip was much longer than that which is repeatedly shown and that the original Gustave gets up and is given a chance to survive. This last part of the clip, however, has subsequently been cut by those who have employed the image of the burning man, lest the scene of Gustav's possible recovery detract from the clip's (morbidly) spectacular appeal.

The problem of the photograph as spectacle is even more complicated. This is because the camera often overdetermines what it represents before the shutter is even closed. Events unfold differently if there is a camera trained on them. In *Level Five* Marker includes two examples of such influence. In one of the clips from Okinawa a woman runs across a field toward a precipice from which her compatriots are leaping. A close examination of the clip in slow motion reveals that she momentarily hesitates and begins to turn back. Yet the woman recovers her resolve upon meeting the camera eye and takes the plunge. Marker then shows the same clip again, only this time he superimposes onto it images taken in 1900 from the first floor of the Eiffel Tower, where an inventor demonstrates a new personal flying device. The filmmaker shows that at the last moment the inventor realizes that his new contraption will not fly, but because he is being filmed, he is still compelled to jump, like the unknown woman in Okinawa, to his death. Thus the very act of tracking a film camera on an event is shown to produce actions and, hence, to have the potential to affect and steer the course of history. In *Level Five*, even more than in his previous films, Marker problematizes the relationship between historical events and their mediated representations. The power of the media is that it grants those in control of the technological apparatus the ability to determine what will be remembered. Those who program the game, as it were, establish the limits of the playing field.

Zapping Zone, Silent Movie

Marker's concern with the interrelation of history and media is closely linked to his awareness of the importance that form plays in structuring both concrete representation and its historical reception. His experiments began in the 1940s with the possibilities offered by television, culminating in the production of several television broadcasts in the 1960s and 1970s that were meant to serve as noncommercial counterexamples for what was becoming increasingly standardized TV fare. Television, because of its ability to reach mass audiences, held a potential for social education and reform that it has yet to realize. Marker observed that rather than provide real information about the world and coalesce communities around topical issues, commercial television disseminated misleading constructions of news and information and constructed publics that were passive in everything but the pursuit of commodities (Marker, *Commentaires II*, 90). Yet, as the *On parle de . . .* broadcasts reveal, Marker was not willing to give up entirely on that medium. In 1989 he made a thirteen-part series for the Société Nationale de Programmes France-régions on FR3 entitled *L'Héritage de la chouette* (Legacy of the Owl). The series consisted of twenty-six-minute segments on topics such as "Démocratie ou la cité des songes" (Democracy, or the City of Dreams), "Nostalgie ou le retour impossible" (Nostalgia, or the Impossible Return), "Tragédie ou l'illusion de la mort" (Tragedy, or the Illusion of Death), and "Philosophie ou le triomphe de la chouette" (Philosophy, or the Triumph of the Owl). The broadcast covered Greek antiquity to the present day and included interviews with contemporary philosophers such as Manuela Smith and Cornelius Castoriadis. By offering alternative programs, Marker, like the German filmmaker and media theorist Alexander Kluge, actively sought to use television as a means by which to create an oppositional public sphere.

Marker's *Les 20 heures dans les camps* (Prime Time in the Camps, 1993) follows the same principles. This twenty-seven-minute documentary, shot in video and Super 8, demonstrates how alternative television broadcasts can use satellite and radio signals to snare, produce, and transmit rogue programs. Marker visited a refugee camp outside of Ljubljana, where he instructed and assisted the residents in creating a studio capable of producing their own pirated television programs. The programs would focus on the specific concerns and interests of the refugees and thus disseminate more than just the official newspeak. Echoes of Medvedkine's ciné-train and of the SLON productions are evident in these experiments with television. Throughout, Marker remains aware that the members of the public addressed by all of these television programs are significantly different from the ones addressed by his cinematic productions. To that extent, his television forays are in line with his other attempts to explore the possibilities of communicating with mass audiences—members of the public who do not or can not attend films.

But film and/or television spectators are not the only audiences that Marker evidently wanted to reach. Since the late 1970s, he increasingly explored the possibilities opened up by museum exhibitions. In 1978 he installed *When the Century Assumed Form* in the Paris-Berlin exhibit at the Centre Pompidou in Paris.[54] The relatively simple installation consisted of two small video monitors, each projecting the same images, albeit with a programmed three-second delay between them. Accompanied by a Hanns Eisler–composed sound track, the images depicted devastated cities and other catastrophic scenes from World War I and the Russian Revolution.

Marker's next installation, at the Centre Pompidou twelve years later, was more complex and ambitious. Entitled *Zapping Zone: Proposals for an Imaginary Television* (1991), the installation comprised an assembly of twenty video and computer monitors, various photographs, and several sound stations. *Zapping Zone* was part of the traveling exhibition *Passage de l'image,* which is now included in the museum's permanent collection. The monitors play animation clips, documentaries, and newly produced short videos, as well as sequences from Marker's *La solitude d'un chanteur de fond* and *Le fond de l'air est rouge.* Many of these components, ranging in length from a few minutes to half an hour, were also distributed as separate works.[55] They include video portraits of fellow filmmakers and artists: *Matta* (1985), *Christo* (1985), *Tarkovsky* (1986); animal features: *Chat écoutant musique* (Cat Listening to Music, 1990), *An Owl Is an Owl Is an Owl* (1990), *Zoo Piece* (1990), *Théorie des ensembles* (1990); and sociopolitical studies on videotape: *Détour Ceausescu* (1990) and *Berlin '90* (1990). *Détour Ceausescu* studies the television coverage of the execution of the former Romanian dictator, which many believe was staged for cameras; *Berlin '90* is a short report about the state of the post-Wall city in March 1990 when the former East Germany held its first free elections. *Berlin '90* was initially part of a longer made-for-television program entitled *Berliner Ballade* (1990), broadcast on French television as a segment of *Envoyé Spécial*. Asked to contribute despite his controversial reputation, Marker acknowledged the risk taken by the sponsors and produced a benign work consisting of interviews, shots of everyday life, and personal observations. The television station found the result acceptable, though in the end Marker remained somewhat disappointed. This prompted him to reedit the video footage for his subsequent project, *Zapping Zone*, which offered a more personal montage of his impressions of Berlin as a city in transition.[56] Thus if *Berliner Ballade* conformed to the rules and parameters of what was acceptable on standard television, *Berlin '90*, in contrast, displays the forms and ideas that an ideal broadcast might inspire on a utopian imaginary television suggested by the ironically critical subtitle.

As an installation, *Zapping Zone* requires monitors of different sizes, shapes, and forms, some set up on the floor, others on a crude metal platform with an intricate antenna in the background. The overall effect is intended to overwhelm the spectator with multiple sources of information. Marker initially thought of titling the project "logiciel/catacombes" (software program/catacombs), given that the logic informing the installation is more cybernetic than cinematic. The structure of *Zapping Zone* served as a crude architectural model for the future program of Marker's CD-ROM, *Immemory*. The *Zapping Zone* installation establishes a more complex viewing experience than does a single-channel cinema, video, or even television. This is due to a number of factors. First, by offering several different viewing options simultaneously, the work invites the spectator to partake in the decision-making process about what to look at. Second, in contrast to the set starting times and schedules of cinema and television broadcasts, the *Zapping Zone* installation does not control when and how a viewer enters into the space of the work. Rather, the images are projected as loops, and the viewer engages with the material on his or her own schedule. Third, the conditions of viewing are different: Instead of a seat at home or in a darkened theater, *Zapping Zone* is installed in a public space, usually without available seating. Fourth, the videos that make up *Zapping Zone* are not meant to be viewed in their entirety. Indeed, their mode of presentation parallels their fragmentary nature, consisting as they are of snippets and digressions. Finally, the potential for distraction with the installation is great, especially because sounds and images from competing monitors bleed into one another, making discrete viewing impossible. To a certain extent, the effect is like "zapping" television programs, switching between different channels or sequences that bear little in common with one another. The installation thus blasts apart the concept of an aesthetic whole or *Gesamtkunstwerk*. Though the medium may be the same as that used by Marker the film-maker, the final product is entirely different. And by placing the installations in museums of contemporary art, Marker prompts his audience to consider these works as art. The expansion of cinema into an art form would probably not be possible without the concomitant expansion of the field of art in the latter part of the twentieth century to include film and video installations. But in this new context, art museums as well as more traditional screening venues have increasingly featured Marker's work during the past decade.[57]

In 1995 William Horrigan, the new media curator at the Wexner Center for the Arts in Columbus, Ohio, invited Marker to organize a project commemorating the centennial of cinema. The resulting installation, *Silent Movie,* featured five video monitors inserted in a metal tower. Next to the tower were eighteen enlarged, framed images selected from the videotapes playing on the monitors as well as ten posters for imaginary films. Throughout the exhibition space, viewers could not escape close-up images of actress Belkhodja, whose enlarged and cropped face was featured on a number of large photographs placed on the walls throughout the space. Marker was at the time working with Belkhodja on *Level Five,* and her appearance can be considered a calculated preview of coming attractions. The five monitors were arranged in a vertical column. Each played a twenty-minute video loop composed of images edited by Marker to illustrate the following themes: the top monitor, "The Journey," projected travel images; the second focused on the face; the fourth was called "The Gesture;" and the bottom one "The Waltz." The third and middle monitor featured a collage of eyes intercut with ninety-four silent film–style intertitles. The images were predominantly excerpted from pre-1940 black-and-white films. Although the title, *Silent Movie*, suggested that the emphasis was to be placed on films prior to the advent of sound in cinema (1927), this was a misnomer. Marker explains in "The Rest Is Silent," his introduction to the catalog accompanying the exhibition, that even silent films were never entirely soundless. The films were always accompanied by music or lecturers as well as by the sounds of the audience, which by today's standards would be considered loud. More significant than silence for Marker was "the muffling of another kind of signal, much more meaningful than the words: the erasing of colors, the black-and-white" (17). He considered black-and-white film as a form of resistance against the dangerously seductive qualities of color film, thus he worked in black and white to underscore the artificiality of the image and to emphasize its function as representation.

To enrich the visual dimension of the project, Marker selected a complex music track that included eighteen piano pieces by Scott Joplin, Duke Ellington, and Peter I. Tchaikovsky, among others. The notable presence of the piano recalls once again the early years of film, when it was the usual form of film accompaniment. It also indicates that although *Silent Movie* was clearly a tribute to cinema, the project is also aimed at creating a bridge between film, music, and the visual arts and at breaking down the institutional barriers between the three. Unlike Marker's earlier productions, *Silent Movie* was to disappear at the end of the exhibition, leaving no trace except for the catalog. Indeed it ceased to exist as such, for the individual twenty-minute video segments are not available separately. *Silent Movie* is the most ephemeral of all of Marker's projects to date. Intended to be a study of cinematic memory, it exists today only as a memory.

Immemory One

> I think that any reasonably long memory (like every collection) is more
> structured than it seems at first sight. For example, in some images ap-
> parently taken at random, on postcards bought without thinking, we
> can recognize the first steps of a road on which we can draw a map of
> that particularly imaginary landscape. I am sure that if I study my docu-
> ments systematically, I shall find, hidden in that disorder, a secret map,
> like the map of the treasure in a tale of pirates.
>
> —*Immemory One*

Marker's obsession with memory reached its zenith with *Immemory*.[58]
This CD-ROM project, produced in collaboration with the Centre Pompidou, has been exhibited in various museums and is widely available
for private purchase. (Titled *Immemory One* in its exhibition form, the
CD-ROM is known simply as *Imemmory*.) Needless to say, the effect
of the work on the viewer is different if one views the CD-ROM in a
public space with limited time and access or on a personal computer
where hours can be spent navigating through all of the channels and
paths. Projected in a public space, the CD-ROM is more conventionally cinematic. Although the work itself may promote interactivity, the
conditions of public viewing encourage a passive spectator. By contrast,
the experience of viewing the CD-ROM installed on a private computer
is closer to that of reading a book, with the spectator in control of the
viewing conditions. Furthermore, if the publicly installed CD-ROM
project functions as a repository of culture, fulfilling a role in the construction of collective cultural memory, a CD-ROM in a private context
offers a more personal encounter. The latter produces a more focused
and concentrated experience than does the open exhibition. In addition,
the CD-ROM can be programmed to incorporate viewers' input. For
example, at the Antoni Tapies Foundation in Barcelona in 1998, Marker
collaborated with Laurence Rassel to extend the concept of *Immemory*
to the general public, transforming the project in a way that enabled the
participants to substitute their own images and memories. The result was
Roseware, an interactive installation in which visitors were encouraged
to add new information, culminating in a dynamic and continuously
changing project.[59]

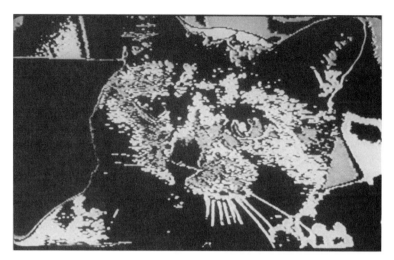

A cat from the Zone in *Sunless*. Courtesy of
Filmmuseum Berlin—Deutsche Kinemathek

As a CD-ROM, *Immemory* is designed to allow the user to follow a seemingly infinite number of divergent viewing paths. There is no preestablished sequential logic. The route chosen by the viewer dramatically transforms him or her from the role of being a mere witness of Marker's memory and lived history to that of a coproducer of histories and memories in the twentieth century. Marker recorded and selected the bits of information in advance. Yet the order in which the information is processed is left to an active spectator. Marker's CD-ROM thus places viewers as coorganizers of history. Comprehension or knowledge of the past is no longer imparted according to a preordained linear arrangement such as that found in the traditional book form. Rather, historical constellations appear simultaneously, irrespective of their temporal or geographical location. Therefore, *Immemory* cannot be taken as a pure autobiographical essay. Although it communicates Marker's personal archive, the narrative that it weaves, the paths it follows, and the amount of time it requires to process are all up to the viewer. Throughout the CD-ROM, the viewer can freely decide where to click and what routes to follow. For example, the first menu screen presents eight possibilities: War, Film, Memory, Museums, Photography, Poésie, Voyages, and

Xplugs. If one chooses Photography, several options are in turn offered: China, Korea, Vietnam, Cuba, Bosnia, World War II. Each of these windows opens onto a multitude of images, some of which are new, others old, and many recognizable from Marker's past photo essays and photo films. A click on Cuba unfolds (at a speed determined by the viewer) a series of images of the country from the 1930s to the present. Musical and film extracts can also be accessed, and images are often accompanied by written texts. Some of the latter come from literary sources, others reproduce telegrams and postcards addressed to Marker. The section on Film includes sequences from *Wings* (1927), *Vertigo* (1958), and *Aelita* (1924). The site devoted to War predictably features a large detour to the battle of Okinawa, and Voyages takes the viewer to Japan with the possibility of crossing over or entering into the Okinawa space. Thus the CD-ROM evokes—and is structured like—the house described in *One Day in the Life of Andrei Arsenevich:* a large space of interconnected films in which characters pass at random from one set into another. The Museums section yields a playful superimposition of Duchamp's *Nude Descending a Staircase* (1912) on Eisenstein's *Battleship Potemkin*—the stairs of Odessa providing the décor. Semiautobiographical characters are evoked: Uncle Anton, who went to China to photograph the guardians of the tomb of the Mings and later accompanied his nephew to Cuba; an Aunt Edith; and a Krasna branch of the family. Indeed the entire CD-ROM is peppered with allusions to elements from Marker's oeuvre and life.

To navigate through *Immemory* takes hours, and a different voyage occurs each time. The story/history changes depending on the whim of the viewer. As with a deck of cards, once the play is over the archive is reshuffled and nothing remains of the past game save for the participant's memory of the experience. Popping up periodically is the cartoon image of Guillaume-en-Egypte, who prompts the spectator onward through the digital archive. Each click produces a Proustian recreation of the past that sends the viewer into another long series of meditations. As Marker stated in his initial proposal for *Immemory:* "I claim, for the image, the humility and the powers of a madeleine" (*Silent Movie* 9).

The possibilities produced by Marker's digitalized audiovisual montage are infinite. Yet choices do have to be made (e.g., what window to

Temple honoring cats
in *Sunless*

open and when), resulting in a work in which the spectator codirects, edits, and arranges the heterogeneous text.[60] *Immemory* will thus always remain an open text. In typical essayistic fashion, the viewer's role is to complete the work, perpetually constructing new narrative trajectories and creative possibilities. In a way, the ideal viewer of Marker's CD-ROM stands obliquely for Marker himself: always constructing new architectures with whatever building blocks are at hand.

With *Immemory*, then, Marker not only expands the parameters of image production, memory, and the way of creating history, he also propels the essay into another dimension. Fifty years ago, he experimented with the possibilities of the written essay and explored the ways that that genre could be pushed beyond its literary roots into cinema. One of the central aims of his installations in the past quarter-century has been to conceptualize the essay as a three-dimensional form. With his more recent discovery of the CD-ROM and the technology that enables this medium to produce rich anecdotal digressions, palimpsests, contrapuntal images, and sounds, Marker has found a contemporary form for the classical essay. *Immemory* is more than just a journey into the director's past, it is a testimony of Marker's commitment to the exploration of the most recent technological discoveries in the field of audiovisual production and to the memory of a social and cultural history that today is all too often forgotten.

Notes

1. Throughout this book, the French title will be used when referring to the original 1977 film and the English title when referring to the 1993 version.

2. Chris Marker, "Le chat est aussi une personne," *Esprit* 186 (January 1952): 78–79.

3. There is considerable ambiguity concerning the exact date of Marker's birth. It has been cited as July 21, 22, or 29, 1921.

4. Raymond Bellour observes that in Alain Resnais' 1956 film *Toute la mémoire du monde*, the credits read "Chris and Magic Marker." See Bellour, "The Book, Back and Forth," in *Qu'est-ce qu'une Madeleine?* For further meditations on Marker's name, see Ross Gibson, "Letters from Far-off Lands: Two Studies of Writing in Exile," in *South of the West: Postcolonialism and the Narrative Construction of Australia.*

5. For more on the complexities of auteur theory, see Lanzoni, *French Cinema.*

6. For a valiant attempt to trace a clear trajectory of the early part of Marker's biography, see Tode, "Phantom Marker: Inventur vor dem Film," in *Chris Marker: Filmessayist.* More recently, see Pourvali, *Chris Marker.*

7. Gérard Lorin in Kämper and Tode, *Chris Marker: Filmessayist,* 202.

8. Remo Florani in Kämper and Tode, *Chris Marker: Filmessayist,* 204.

9. Resnais recalls when he first met Marker, he was told that the latter was rich and could help finance his film because "there was a rumor that his father was a wealthy property owner in South America." In the same interview Resnais goes on to mention that Marker was a translator for the U.S. Army. Ibid., 206.

10. For an overview of Marker's writings, see Chaiken and DiIorio, "The Author behind the Auteur."

11. In Volumes 0 and 1, the editor is listed as Chris Villeneuve and in Volume 2/3 as C. B. Villeneuve.

12. Letter from Marker to Bill Horrigan, March 31, 1994. That Frank himself went on to make films is as interesting as it is revealing, for it indicates the limits of photography in the later twentieth century. See *Silent Movie* (Columbus, Wexner Center for the Arts, 1995).

13. See Ray, "The Automatic *Auteur*," 62–66.

14. As Richard Neupert (*A History of the French New Wave,* 20) observes, "Cultural figures, from Sartre and Picasso to Sagan and the anthropologist Claude Lévi-Strauss, saw unprecedented wealth and celebrity heaped upon them as they became part of the new 'culture industry,' which carried them far beyond the traditional intellectual circles more common to 1930s and 1940s artists and academics." Concomitant with this new type of intellectual was an emphasis on "culture as a serious category," and the "job of the critic was to decode modern culture in all of its forms" (Neupert, *A History of the French New Wave,* 24).

15. For details on the legislative act related to cultural policy and cinema, see Lanzoni, *French Cinema*.

16. Bazin, "Chris Marker, *Lettre de Sibérie*." Although a translation of this text has recently been published in *Film Comment*, it fails to capture some of the nuance of Bazin's writing style. I will therefore use my own.

17. As Gibson notes, "Montaigne's famous motto, 'que-sais-je' (What do I know?), which he had inscribed on his family medallion, was an attempt to sum up his belief that the investigation of the world and its meaning is inevitably an investigation of one's own subjectivity and intelligence" (Gibson, "What Do I Know?" 49).

18. See appendix to Marker, *Commentaires*, which lists five phrases in particular that were held objectionable, including one in which Marker is greeted joyously as "Bienvenue, oncle soviétique!" (Welcome, Soviet Uncle!).

19. For a discussion of the use of the epistolary form in Marker's films, see Naficy, "Epistolarity and Epistolary Narratives," 146–51.

20. See Porcile, "Chris. Marker, à la poursuite des signes du temps."

21. In France, animators were considered to be experimenters rather than auteurs. See Porcile, *Defense du court metrage français*, 173.

22. Richard Neupert observes "that the mid-1950s was indeed a challenging new era where new detergents were needed for new washing machines, new shopping routines were determined by new cars and new refrigerators and a new generation was reading new novels and watching new, sexier films" (*A History of the French New Wave*, 15). For a detailed analysis of the new consumer culture, see Ross, *Fast Cars, Clean Bodies:Decolonization and Reordering of French Culture*.

23. The allusion is to the 1962 film *The Loneliness of the Long-Distance Runner*, directed by Tony Richardson.

24. For an insightful essay on Marker's relationship with Tarkovsky, see Howe, "Sorting Facts."

25. Marker includes a video address made in 1988 by Medvedkine, shortly before his death, in which Medvedkine pays homage to Tarkovsky.

26. The French title, *Le Tombeau D'Alexandre* (Alexander's Tomb), is significantly different from the politically explicit English version. My references will be to the official English version of the text. References will at times also be made to the French script reprinted in Marker's "Le tombeau d'Alexandre" and will be indicated as such.

27. In his 1951 essay "Croix de bois et chemin de fer," Marker recalls a conversation with a former Nazi train conductor: "My best friend died in a concentration camp, and I have been active in education for the people in Germany for the last five years—because I harbor no hatred for the German people. But it is precisely by not forgetting anything, by recalling together the concentration camps, that we shall perhaps succeed to work together on a world without concentration camps."

28. The first seminar took place in the Black Forest, then at Titisee (1949), Schluchsee (1950), Bacharach am Rhein (1951), Lindau am Bodensee (1952), and Bad Ems (1953). For a more detailed account, see Andrew, *André Bazin*, 95, and Marker, "Adieu au cinéma allemand?"

29. Kafka's story was written sometime around 1904. The Hebrew title of Marker's film is *Hatsad hashlishi Shel Hamatbea* (The Third Side of the Coin).

30. It is interesting to note that this is one of Marker's few films that has a foreign voice-over.

31. As Resnais recalls, "There was an art of fusion between Marker and Cayrol, and in the end, I would be hard put to decide which sentence came from Marker and which from Cayrol" (Resnais, "Rendez-vous des amis," 212).

32. During the immediate postwar period, the British government sought to restrict immigration to Palestine and refused many Jews passage.

33. Maspero's significance in the 1960s cannot be underestimated. He was a politically engaged publisher and often sold and published works that otherwise would never have appeared in print.

34. For an excellent account of the French Left in the 1960s, see Ross, *May '68 and Its Afterlives.*

35. In his section, entitled "Repères" (Landmarks), Marker reprinted, under the category "Femmes" (Women), the following quotation from Carmen Castillo on October 15, 1977: "It is not only she [Beatriz Allende] who killed herself. Her act involves all the women who survive at the limit of action and death. Because a woman in the middle of men cannot speak, because this solitude of women, this daily self-destruction is also a form of suicide. . . . True politics must involve the existence of people. One only fights for others if one fights for oneself" (Marker, *Le fond de l'air est rouge*, 12).

36. Marker also provided invaluable assistance, especially in the editing stage, for Patricio Guzman's *The Battle of Chile* (1975).

37. In general the introduction of new and advanced lightweight camera equipment had a significant impact on French New Wave directors. "In 1959, the Swiss Nagra III, a new fourteen-pound version of earlier models, became available; it caused an immediate sensation within the cinema verité community and was adapted right away by some New Wave directors. Recorders such as Nagra simply used standard quarter-inch magnetic tape, unlike studio machines, which used 16 mm- or 35 mm-wide tapes. . . . These young French directors also used newer, and more portable, 35 mm and 16 mm cameras such as Auricon and Eclair's Cameflex and NPR, which allowed then more handheld options and freedom of avoiding standard, heavy camera mounts such as dollies and tracks" (Neupert, *A History of the French New Wave*, 40).

38. Fantômas was painted by both René Magritte and Juan Gris and memorialized in a poem by Robert Desnos.

39. When the film was screened at the Cannes Film Festival, *Le joli mai*

was the center of a lively debate entitled "Autour du 'Joli Mai': cinéma-vérité ou cinéma engagé?" (Combat, 16 May 1963, n.p.). For a summary of relevant points, see Gauthier, Chris Marker, 111.

40. The official English title is a bit misleading because it does not quite capture the note of hope and the quiver of uncertainty of the French, better rendered with something like "hope to see you soon."

41. For a detailed account of the founding of SLON and Marker's association with it, see Lee, "Joining Forces with the Militant Collective Slon."

42. Pol Cèbe was also present during the meetings with Medvedkine; see Cèbe, "Rencontre avec Medvedkine."

43. See Cohen, "12 Monkeys, Vertigo, and La jetée."

44. See the range of essays from such diverse writers as Bensmaïa, Dubois, Gregor, Rancière, and Ropars.

45. These films were also known as "rubble films" because of their location shots in war-devastated Berlin. Examples include Staudte's Murderers Are among Us (1946), Lamprecht's Somewhere in Berlin (1946), and Rossellini's Germany, Year Zero (1947).

46. Further, the name Madeleine resonates for Marker because of its association as the involuntary memory trigger in Marcel Proust's Remembrance of Things Past.

47. La Spirale is the title of the 1975 film about Chile produced by SLON.

48. For a detailed treatment of The Embassy as well as a transcription of the screenplay, see Gauthier, Chris Marker, 139–50.

49. All English citations are from the official English-language version of the film.

50. All citations from Sunless are from the official English-language version of the film.

51. On Marker and islands see Wolfgang Bongers, "Inseln."

52. Independence was finally granted in September 1974, a year after the death of the revolutionary leader Amilcar Cabral.

53. For a discussion of the use of the authorial "I" in Marker's films, see Naficy, "Epistolarity and Epistolary Narratives," 146–51.

54. The exhibit's alternative title was Guerre et Révolution (War and Revolution).

55. Subsequent to Zapping Zone's initial exhibition, four videos have been added: Azulmoon (1992), Coin fenêtre (1992), Slon Tango (1993), and Bullfight/Okinawa (1994).

56. Letter from Marker to Tode, in Kämper and Tode, Chris Marker: Filmessayist, 307.

57. It is important to note that Marker only exhibits in museums and other public spaces that are relatively independent of the art market.

58. A second version of the CD-ROM is under way. Currently, a French version of Immemory exists designed for PC and an English version for Macintosh.

For two insightful treatments of *Immemory*, see Roth, "A Yakut Afflicted with Strabismus," and Bellour, "The Book, Back and Forth."

59. Marker continues, "Roseware extends the concept of *Immemory*, a memory structured by the relationships between images and sounds. It is conceived as a blank book in which everyone has a chance to write a chapter." *Roseware* was also installed in Graz, Austria.

60. This methodology is entirely in keeping with Marker's tendency to credit himself merely as editor and not as director.

Chris Marker Interviews and Writings 1962–98

An Interview with Chris Marker (1962)

H. H., "Chris Marker: Ich werde bestimmt wiederkommen" [I Certainly Will Return], *Deutsche Filmkunst* I (1962), 26–27. (Translated from the German. The identity of "HH" is not known.)

HH: There is much wisdom in Chris Marker's films; however as clever and witty as they are, they never impose that knowledge on the spectator. For example he reports about Siberia's primordial history. It is frightening to think of the type of professional documentary film this could have been and how witty and refreshing this *Letter from Siberia* turned out to be. The title by the way was well chosen, for it always is Chris Marker who does the writing, filming, reporting—he sees a foreign country and shares his feelings with the audience. In France, Chris Marker is an established concept. As Chris Marker was guest at the IV International Documentary and Short-film week [Leipzig], we took the opportunity to address a few questions to him.

HH: Mr. Marker, you wanted to show us your film about Cuba. Is it true that you had trouble with the French censorship?

CHRIS MARKER: Yes, the film was prohibited in France. There is no possibility to show it in France or abroad. Of course we are still trying everything to have the film released.

HH: You already had the same problems with your first film: *Statues Also Die,* the film of Alain Resnais for which you wrote the commentary?

CM: Yes this film was forbidden for a long time and then could be only shown in a mutilated version.

HH: When did you make your first film?

CM: At the same time when I was working on *Statues.* This work [*Statues*] dragged on for a long time. In between I did a film about the Olympics in Helsinki. However, another French producer had procured the sole distribution rights, so my film was never shown commercially only in film clubs—by the way rather successfully.

HH: And then followed your *Sunday in Peking,* and *Description of a Struggle.* And now Cuba. What are your plans now?

CM: First of all I would like to get my film released from the French censorship. And then? Perhaps back to Cuba. Yes, I would like to go there again.

HH: Are there films of which you dream that you would like to make?

CM: Yes a futuristic film. But that costs too much and would hardly be possible.

HH: Which type of futuristic movie would interest you most, along the lines of Bradbury, van Vogt, or Asimov?

CM: No, more as a moralist in the French meaning like Voltaire, for example. That is to say, problems of living together in the universe according to definite principles. I would like very much to make a film of *Aelita* by Tolstoy. I have seen the old film by Protasanov in Moscow. It was wonderful. But you see at that time one did not believe that much in the future, one let the hero dream, wake up, tear up his plans, and follow his daily work. What kind of film would that be today?

HH: What do you think of the films here in Leipzig?

CM: Well, I was astonished about the technical mastery in the Soviet film *Menschen der blauen Flamme* [People of the Blue Flame] and about the ability of the Algerian director Grigrew's *Yasmina*—a heartrending film. The Cuban selection I partly was familiar with already. Especially, *Tod der Invasoren* [Death of the Invaders], which I consider to be an excellent work. By the way I incorporated some aspects from this film it my own.

HH: And *The General Assembly?* We, for example, never thought that one could film such an assembly and make it so interesting.

CM: Yes, it really is an extraordinary film. The director, Tomas Gutieres Alea, is still very young. I believe he will not only be the best film director of Cuba but of the world.

HH: How do you judge the French entry?

CM: I don't consider the French choice good. Nevertheless, we do have a number of documentary film directors that produce excellent work and who have developed new methods, new styles, without which the rest of contemporary documentary filmmakers could not function. At any rate I am very happy that Jean Herman could present his film *Actual Tilt* to the Leipzig audience. I find this film excellent, even though I consider Herman's second film, *La Quille,* better.

HH: We thank you for this interview and hope to be able to welcome you to Leipzig again next year.

CM: Oh, I will certainly come to Leipzig again.

An Interview with Chris Marker (1964)

WOLFGANG GERSCH, "Der Schöne Mai" [*Le joli mai*], *Filmwissenschaftliche Mitteilungen* I (1964): 194–98. (Translated from the German.)

WOLFGANG GERSCH: If one turns to the decisive standpoint of your film [*Le joli mai*], which in my view determines its great success, it is the total reflection of reality and its interpretation. Was this preceded by a cross section of this totality during the initial phases of the film's development?

CHRIS MARKER: The fifty-five hours that I shot the film were a cross-section. I tried to select in such a way that a totality emerges from this cross section.

wg: Would you please discuss in more detail this process, your ordering principle? How did you achieve out of 55 hours of shooting a totality of Paris in May 1962?

cm: In the beginning a plan developed with themes according to which the interviews would be conducted, then during the editing process, it was revealed that on certain occasions a theme yielded something completely different and that the linking of these themes was different than what I had envisioned abstractly. In life new connections turned up, sometimes due to an image. The film began to have a life of its own, and suddenly it had rules of its own. My work now consisted in curbing these self-imposed rules. The unexpected alluded [subject] that emerged in reality, in the interviews, had to be put into order according to the laws that arose out of the material. What probably captivated people here, and elsewhere, is the synthesis of the two ways of behavior in the documentary film—on the one hand the film predetermines how reality should be, and if it is not this way it is wrong—on the other hand, one has a modest attitude toward reality, one accepts it as it is. The synthesis of these two attitudes make up my film. Not too long ago, in France, I spoke with Pierre Schaeffer, the initiator of concrete music. He sees his task in developing sounds that he encounters in reality. I, too, started from the precept of what I found in thoughts, words, and pictures in reality and assembled it according to the laws that I perceived and heard. This procedure took place in three stages: facts that I encountered, their selection, and an editing together that expresses a certain meaning that extends it beyond the immediate time that I wanted to represent. But the starting point was the independence of these facts. This ordering principle divided my film into two parts, and I do hope that the viewer of my film understands that the first part reflects the presentation of space and the second the movement of time. The first is more a realization of the condition of objects and problems arising out of this given position, the second part represents the movement of time at a certain moment.

wg: In spite of the fundamentality of reality, it seems to me that the first part also possesses interpretative qualities, above all in the way questions were posed during the individual interviews.

cm: Yes, of course, only the questions had not been predetermined. The way and means are naturally determined by a certain spontaneity. It does not appear constructed, and it is not constructed, after all. The spontaneity develops from the relationship of question to answer. Beyond that it is natural that the interviewer wants to reach certain points. An example from our work: the entire group was in a working-class neighborhood of Paris, and walking by we heard a little girl say, "These walls are ancient [*vorsintflutlich*—before the great flood]." We reacted immediately and asked the girl, "What kind of word have you just said?" "Before the great [biblical] flood!" "What is before the great flood?" "The walls." "The walls?" End.

WG: Did you always meet your interview partners accidentally, or did you choose some of them with a goal in mind?

CM: Some I only met on the street and saw them for the first time, others I had known for years and chose them. Combined together it resulted in the possibility to be able to reflect all of the nuances.

WG: How did you achieve the naturalness of people in front of the camera, a rare occurrence in a documentary film.

CM: I do not know. Probably because we inspired confidence. The material that we used also did not intimidate them, because it was very discreet. There was lighting, the cameras were not very large, and we did not make much noise. The people have seen and heard little of it. They always participated immediately and forgot that they were being recorded during the conversation. Besides, the questions were of interest, and they reacted to them. Naturally, the art of questioning and speaking to people is also important.

WG: The press writes that there are 127 interviews . . .

CM: I do not know who has said this, I have never counted them.

WG: Beyond the critical ideological dialogue, the interview with the couple in love is poetic.

CM: It was like this: From a distance I saw on the bridge of Neuvilly a couple embracing. May, Paris, love, and I thought, "nothing will emerge from that." If I were caught in such a way, there would not be much to be seen. But to my great surprise they were happy that they could make the world witness their love, because they were so happy.

WG: Are you not of the opinion that naturalness in front of the camera is bound to a certain mentality?

CM: No I don't believe that this film is only possible in Paris. I even assume that it is more difficult in France than in Italy, where people are more communicative and like to play a bit of theater themselves. It is not a question of mentality, I think the film is possible almost everywhere, but it is a question of general atmosphere. People must not have the notion that it is somehow disrupting to voice their opinion.

WG: If a film wants to achieve this greatness, this totality, it must encompass multiple complicated contradictions.

CM: This is the decisive supposition. I believe, it is in general the tendency of the development of the documentary film, to grasp reality on the whole and not make a choice according to one's own wishes and concepts. With that I do not mean that one should keep out of contradictions and should represent them only contemplatively, as if saying to the viewer: Now do with it what you want. Of course one has to have a viewpoint. I think that the task of the documentary filmmaker consists of knowing and relating what is progressive, the meaning of the development, and to mediate the total truth, to uncover it with its contradictions and not to limit it to a chosen part of reality.

WG: At the Freien Forum in Leipzig it was said that modern documentary film suffers of an overabundance of material. Examples were drawn from *The Russian Miracle* and your film. I don't believe any further cuts on *Le joli mai* could have been undertaken without damaging the overall composition.

CM: Documentary films of this kind can only be considered long in comparison to the lengths of the usual films. Two hours are a minimum if one wants to give the viewer the possibility to really observe, think along, and participate. The interviews are all shortened. But one has to give the viewer time to recognize all the tics and individualities of the people, to penetrate intimately into their psyches. In order to show people's hesitations, to really experience different types of reactions, there needs to exist a certain quiet rhythm. And if one wants all that—one really has to want it badly—then it would have to last at least two hours. The length is, of course, a very complicated problem; if one worked for eight hours, it is certainly hard to watch and to think along for three hours. Because the film requires that. But it won't work in a shorter period of time. From the given material I first created a six-hour version that then I reduced to five and finally to three hours. In Leipzig, I showed a shorter version.

WG: Did you have difficulty in your country with censorship?

CM: Planning and execution were accomplished without thinking of censorship. When the film was done, I had to shorten it to three hours by one-and-a-half minutes. So I got off very lightly.

WG: Was it a matter of essential cuts?

CM: Not essential ones. Some things around De Gaulle at the military deployment were rather nice.

WG: In your film, a Communist is interviewed who was formerly a priest. Did you find him by chance?

CM: No, I have known him for a long time. Because of him I was able to realize my intention of showing a Communist on-screen, something that does not often happen in France. People can better understand him because they see a development and because they themselves often have to travel a long way.

WG: Do you have a special reason to place this interview in the second part?

CM: The golden cut. The essential turning point of the film.

WG: Is it your intention to make a symbolic statement with the final picture of the jail?

CM: I detest everything symbolic. I am concrete and want to be understood as such. After the statistics of general numbers, with which I didn't want to conclude, this complex image appears in order to remind and make clear that it exists as well.

Let Us Praise Dziga Vertov (1967)

Let us praise Dziga Vertov
for if I had to choose the Ten Best Documentaries of All Time
i'd call it preposterous
but if there's ONE to choose:
"A SIXTH OF THE WORLD"
Because this moment of our history, this palingenesis,
this dawn, this birth of our memory,
this first draft of what was due to be our world,
    good and bad,
    Paustovsky made us think of it

Eisenstein made us dream of it
but only one man made us SEE it
DZIGA VERTOV
KINO GLAZ Film Eye   Eye First
Camera Eye But Man's Eye (you SEE what I MEAN)
Camera, machine, montage, eyes, like hounds at Harry's heels
(O for a Muse of light . . .)
but the Eye über alles, the Eye leading the pack
seeing—donner à voir
and not only the faces, the gestures, the segments of life
but words also, words suddenly alive
by filling the whole screen, heavy words, real words,
(and the magic of the cyrillic, of course, but who's
    complainin'?)
Words coming to a new stage of perception
owing to these large, big BLOCKletters,

> words achieving equality with images
> ideas achieving equality with facts
> art achieving equality with life

How d'you say that in Russian?

DZIGA VERTOV

An Interview with Chris Marker (1968)

R. RITTERBUSCH, "Entretien vec Chris Marker," *Image et Son* 213
(February 1968). (Translated from the French.)

R. RITTERBUSCH: I read that Godard had said that you and Resnais had asked him to collaborate on the *Far from Vietnam* film. Can
one say that Resnais and you are the initiators of that film?

CHRIS MARKER: We belong to the initial group. I want to stress
that fact which is extremely important. Our film is the result of a truly
collective work, especially when compared to films where the collective
aspect developed only later. Here we have a collective with a continuous
collaboration although each one of us obviously is responsible for only

one part of the work. And this collaboration has increased our strength many times. One must not believe that the very well-known members of the collective had a proportionally larger input. All of us contributed to the common task as much as they could. Two of my montage assistants joined the delegation together with me. There was no hierarchy within the team. At the beginning, there were several persons with Resnais and me. But there were also people who collaborated and whose names were not well known, such as Jacqueline Meppiel and some others who joined the group.

RR: What reasons moved you to chose this collective work form?

CM. If we want to explain how we ended up with this collective work, I believe one must first note that no one among us was feeling able alone to solve the problem at issue. Since the Vietnam problem is an extremely urgent problem, we did not want the isolated work of a single person to distort that problem. Our attitude toward the Vietnam problem resulted from continuous discussions and continuous research. The Vietnam problem possessed us indeed, and all who collaborated on it drew a tremendous enrichment from this work.

RR: Could you tell us something about your procedures? What scenes, for example, were shot in France?

CM: This was mainly the responsibility of Resnais and Godard. For example, we reported on Vice President Humphrey's visit to Paris. Some bitter demonstrations were organized against him. We immediately decided to film them. Seven camera operators, three photographs, and various technicians were placed all along Humphrey's announced itinerary so as to get an overall view of that demonstration. Now, Resnais prefers to deal with monologues, and he decided to do a monologue in the perspective of a left-wing intellectual. In order to offer an integral view of that intellectual, and to focus on his particularities, he asked an actor to deliver a written text instead of using, as one could expect, a recorded interview. It was the only instance in the film when we chose the form of fiction. For Godard, for example, this film constituted a sort of self-analysis of one's conscience, and he jumped into it with great enthusiasm. But he was lucid enough to provide a commentary of this self-analysis. At the same time this served as an incitement [to action], and that part of the film has been attacked the most. The more he was sincere and modest while describing his interior conflicts, the more he was accused to be vain. In my opinion, he reached in that film a high degree of frankness and open-mindedness. He says, "Here I am," and he submits to his own judgment like few artists do. When you see that part, you can appreciate it yourself. For me that is the best part of what was shot in Paris. A large part of the film was shot in Vietnam, and other important parts in the United States and in Cuba where an interview with Fidel Castro was recorded.

RR: What part of the work did you carry out within this production frame?

CM: I must clarify one point in that respect. I did come to Leipzig a few times as an author and film director. I had the honor to receive a grand prize. But this year I am in Leipzig as someone who originated the whole thing, i.e., I did not shoot any part of the film, but I participated in its organization. I am very happy to have accomplished this organizational work.

RR: Could you tell me how the people have received the film?

CM: Up until now people have barely seen this film because it has not yet been shown to the public [at large]. It was shown in three places: Montreal, New York, and Besançon—a small town in France with which our group has a special relationship because it is the site of a factory owned by one of the largest French corporations and a very famous strike took place in that factory. We went there and we filmed it. From that time on, this film was made with the workers, I do not mean about the workers but with them. This is why we did not want the first showing of the film to take place in a Champs-Elysées theater or in another large movie theatre of the same type; we wanted it to be shown to the people for whom it was intended. It is a film made by militants speaking to militants and intended to be shown to them. The reception of the film was extraordinary. Many have received it with enthusiasm, but some workers found it too difficult to understand. After the showing, a long discussion took place between Resnais and Klein. During that discussion, the film received a critique, and its ideas took shape, which means that our film became alive. For the makers of the film, this outcome was of course more important than if all the spectators had been simply enthusiastic. This film has been made to trigger discussion.

RR: Did you have the opportunity to show the film on television?

CM: Yes, we also do work with television. When the film was finished, it was shown during a twenty-five-minute program that was generally received positively. Such a program has an average of about three million viewers. Personally, I have certain reservations about television methods, but television does exist, and hence one must collaborate with it, coexist with it in order to succeed to transform it.

RR: Could you clarify this idea? In our country, for example, some people claim that cinema has no more room for the documentary film.

CM: They say that everywhere, but it is a mistake; however, the reception of a film on television and in a movie theatre is quite different. The difference is more or less the same as between thinking and dreaming. In that sense, I compare dreaming to cinema and thinking to television. A well-known American sociologist [McLuhan] divided information media into two types: the "cold" media and the "hot" media. "Cold" media, according to him, do not demand a very active participation, and "hot" media demand an intensive participation. News on television does not move us much. In that sense, television is cold, and radio as well as cinema are hot. In a movie theatre, we feel more personally involved in a problem. De Antonio once said something quite interesting. He said that if television had not been there at the time of Kennedy's assassination, some sort of riot might have taken place. A news broadcast on radio leaves some void that must be filled, whereas on television, we learn definitive facts, already assimilated so to speak. On television we see so much circumstantial evidence that surrounds the shown events that the facts, as such, no longer move us in the same manner. In that sense, television declaws the facts. And the question is not whether the information is true or false; this is not as important for the problem with which we have been dealing.

RR: I thank you for this interview.

An Interview with Chris Marker (1971)

ANNE PHILIPE, "Medvedkine, tu connais? Interview avec Slon et Chris Marker," *Le Monde*, (2 December, 1971): 17. (Translated from the French.)

ANNE PHILIPE: Chris Marker, when and how did you discover Alexandre Medvedkine?

CHRIS MARKER: Ten years ago. At the Brussels Cinémathèque. As a part of a retrospective of Soviet cinema ranging from October to Barnet's works, they showed an unknown film, shot by an unknown director—a superb film as beautiful as Eisenstein's, as popular as Mussorgsky's music, deeply moving: *Le bonheur* [Happiness] by Alexandre Medvedkine. Where was the author? Dead? Alive? "Medvedkine, have you heard of him?" I asked Ledoux, director of the Belgian Cinémathèque. He answered: "I must have him in my files." I found a few lines on him in Georges Sadoul's *L'histoire du cinéma* [History of Cinema], and finally I found the information I was looking for in a history of Russian cinema (truly remarkable but not translated into French). The author, Jay Leyda, discusses *Happiness,* then another later film, but mainly narrates the full story of the "ciné-train." But I still didn't know what happened to Medvedkine, whether he was alive or not. Then a small miracle happened at the Leipzig Festival in 1967: I ran into Jay Leyda who told me, "There is someone with the Soviet delegation whom you absolutely must meet, a fantastic guy, Alexandre Medvedkine." It was love at first sight. Of course we kept in touch. Then some time elapsed. The production cooperative SLON, where I am a member, was founded in 1968, and, at the Rhodiaceta plant in Besançon, a group of workers took on the name of Medvedkine. We wrote to him. It made him happy. We wanted, and we hoped, one day to be able to rescue *Happiness* from oblivion. But all that was still rather vague. And then it became concrete early this year when Medvedkine arrived in France to make a film about pollution.

AP: Was it at that time that you filmed the discussion with Medvedkine that forms the core of the introductory film *The Train Rolls On?*

CM: Yes, in the Noisy-le-Sec train station. Finally we could hear from the mouth of the man called "the red horseman" the unique story of the ciné-train. One could listen to it for hours and hours, couldn't one?

AP: Did the idea of making a film about him become more precise?

CM: Yes, because we did realize that this man who was no longer a stranger to us was still a stranger to everybody else. Hence, we wanted to "put a spotlight" on him. We needed documents on the train, on life at that stage of the revolution. We looked for them a little bit all over, in France, Belgium, the USSR, the Scandinavian countries. And we did find them. They became *The Train Rolls On,* an introduction with Medvedkine as its center and its soul. On the other hand, we secured the distribution rights for *Happiness.* We still had to find a movie theater. Line Peillon liked the film, and she booked it for the Alpha studio.

AP: And this famous story of the train?

CM: The train . . . it has been a universal cinematographic theme from Buster Keaton's *The General* up to Abel Gance. . . . Cinema and railroads were born almost at the same time. But over there, in the USSR, trains were imposed by geography.

AP: It could have been a truck.

CM: No, in some remote parts of the country there were more railroad tracks than roads. Besides, there was a truck, carried on the train, and when necessary it was unloaded and used for exploring the surrounding region. And the space on the train that was thus vacated was used to work the miniprinting plant that published the train logbook.

AP: How long did the ciné-train survive?

CM: Exactly 294 days. Medvedkine's account is very precise: 70 films, 9 reels, 24,565 meters of edited and reviewed film. It happened in 1932. The train left Moscow on the 25th of January. It represented, no doubt, a legacy of the "agitprop" trains that used to crisscross the Soviet Union in the '20s. But in this case the train was not bringing art to the people; its function was to incite the people to intervene in matters with which they were concerned. The train: three passenger cars transformed into a laboratory, an editing room, and a viewing room. The team: thirty-two people (cameramen, editors, technicians, actors) who were sharing the rest of the space—a square meter for each. This experience remains unique. The Medvedkine team is alone to have achieved this type of instantaneous invention of a film, with people associated with its creation and interested in its immediate utilization because it was dealing with problems that had to be solved immediately.

AP: How were the destinations of the ciné-train chosen? Did the Communist Party intervene in that choice?

CM: Obviously this entire activity was relying on the party. The program was formulated on the basis of real problems selected by the following criterion: "Where did things go wrong, where can one be useful?" The program was developed in Moscow; it also could have been set in response to actual needs. For example, the trip to Krivoi-Rog, narrated by Medvedkine, had been requested by the Donbass authorities. Ordjonikidzé was then in charge of that region, and as he was concerned by the decrease in steel production at Krivoi-Rog, he wanted to find the reasons for it, uncover mistakes, abuses, and errors. It is always difficult to obtain the cooperation of various services, but, in his manuscript, Medvedkine states that actual conflicts always opposed party activists who, with him, urged the people to solve their problems themselves, and the local directors who were against any changes and wondered who were these nuisances, filmmakers, and activists who wanted to consult the rank and file about the ways to solve problems that were none of their business.

AP: What sort of problems were they?

CM: They were very specific. Medvedkine offers the example of blacksmiths in a Krivoi-Rog mine who would saw hooks off their carts and replace them with locally made hooks. Why? Because the carts, despite repeated requests and complaints, were delivered with hooks that would open when they were in motion. Medvedkine made a film of that, and then, with that document and a workers' delegation, he went to the plant, asked for a meeting of engineers and workers, and showed them the film. Reality was there, on the image, and it was persuasive. They won their case. Medvedkine also tells the story of a canteen in the same region of Krivoi-Rog where the food was not fit to be eaten. The workers suspected a large-scale pilfering but were not able to prove it. It was outrageous. Medvedkine's team made a film about it, having the miners act out some scenes because, let us not forget, it was the time of silent movies. Medvedkine stresses that feature a lot: he loved silence, which encouraged the spectator, from the very onset of the show, to address the screen with aggressiveness: "Just look at that bastard, that moron, that drunkard!"

AP: Yes, but were the local peasants and workers obliged to play their roles?

CM: Of course. But Medvedkine's team also included actors who, coincidentally or not—because there is a logic to everything and people of the same kind know each other—were part of the Meyerhold theater company. When it was necessary to show a character so negative that he would refuse to participate in the film, then an actor had to act out his role, and the film would become a fiction. Sometimes the actors acted out allegorical roles: one can imagine images of cold, progress, food supplies. . . . I mentioned to you the story of the canteen; another was found in the same region and its food supply was quite similar, and yet the food was acceptable. They made a film about it and showed that film to the first canteen in order to demonstrate how people with a revolutionary consciousness managed to offer correct food even under difficult conditions. The "troublemakers," the dishonest dealers, were unmasked and fired.

AP: Thus on that level the party did intervene?

CM: Yes, but it did not intervene in filmmaking at all. It only intervened in decisions made necessary by the reality revealed in the film. It was really a fantastic and unique experience. Just imagine a mobile laboratory that could operate while the train was moving with a water-tank system on the roof and technicians who were able to produce up to 2,000 meters of film per day. It was a forerunner of television (in fact the first experimental television broadcast took place in 1932). For example, for the inauguration of the giant Dniepropetrovsk dam, Medvedkine in a single day shot, processed, and "viewed" the film then sent a copy to Moscow where it was shown the next day.

AP: *Happiness* was filmed after the experience of the train?

CM: Yes, in 1934, and yet it was shot as a silent movie. While we were filming the French version, we viewed it hundreds of times, we memorized it, and, with each new viewing, we discovered new manifestations of beauty: the composition of images, the boldness of montage, the use of ellipses. . . . It is at the same time both a political and a poetic film. It is tied to a specific time in history. It is intended to convey a revolutionary message, but it has no usual shortcomings of a didactic film; I mean it is neither heavy nor boring. It is a funny film, full of humor and tenderness. When, at the end, Khymr—the hero whom we never saw laughing before—does begin to laugh, his laughter is explosive like that of a man who emerges from prehistory and notices two miserable thieves who are still immerged in it and who fight over a pathetic booty.

AP: Did he make other films after that one?

CM: In 1936, *La Fabuleuse*. Jay Leyda who saw it claims that it is even more beautiful than *Happiness*. When one knows nothing about a film, one always tends to judge it even more beautiful than the film one knows. I hope to see it. It can be found at the Moscow Cinémathèque.

AP: What is Medvedkine's opinion?

CM: He says that it is not bad. . . . He has always had a slightly ironic attitude: "Really? You are really interested. But who can still be interested in an old comedy like *Happiness* unless he is a Romantic like you. . . . We are like Don Quixote. . . ." At the same time, he is moved, he sees us as a reflection of his own "crazy" times. He let me read an unpublished scenario that he wrote in 1936, *Cette sacrée force* [This Sacred Force]. It is a terrific scenario and we would love him to make a film out of it. It would be marvelous.

AP: What do you mean when you mention Medvedkine's manuscript?

CM: I mean his memoirs. He has not completed them. We shall publish one chapter in *Images et Son*, "294 days on wheels." Did you know that Medvedkine's great patron was Lounatcharsky [Lunatcharsky], this extraordinary character who embodied the grandeur of Bolsheviks of the heroic times, protected Mayakovsky, Vertov, Meyerhold, and was translating Marcel Proust during his leisure time?

Interview with Chris Marker (1996)

DOLORES WALFISCH, *The Berkeley Lantern,* November 1996.

DOLORES WALFISCH: This may not be an Oscar-winning question, but can I start by asking, why Okinawa?

CHRIS MARKER: There's been a great deal of talk, recently, about a CD-ROM on World War II. Look up Okinawa. It says, "There were about 100,000 casualties, *including* numerous civilians . . .," which is doubly wrong. Japanese *military* casualties certainly totaled about 100,000. But the civilians were Okinawans, a separate community, with its own history, and its own culture, annexed first by China and then by Japan. . . . The number of Okinawan dead is estimated at 150,000, one-third of the population of the island—a snip. Take *The Grolier Multimedia Encyclopedia,* it says, "The Americans lost twelve thousand men, the Japanese a hundred thousand." No mention of the civilian dead. And many of those were mass suicides, even after the battle was over, because people had been brainwashed into not surrendering. The case is unique, one of the maddest and deadliest episodes in the Second World War, bypassed by history, erased from our collective consciousness, and that is why I wanted to bring it to light.

DW: That sounds like some kind of historical documentary. Which is not what it seems like at all. . . .

CM: Television has made a big difference. The entire Okinawa chapter in *Level Five* is based on an eyewitness account. Picture that in some kind of documentary, as you say (I've always hated the word, but the fact is no one has come up with anything better, though the Germans are a little more elegant with their *Kulturfilm* . . .). Slotted into the average viewing day, between some personal tragedy in Bosnia and a Holocaust survivor's story. How many successive tales of suffering can the average television viewer take in without losing a sense of uniqueness of each? There had to be another way.

DW: Meaning a video game? Computer graphics and a lady?

CM: My favorite hallucinations, yes. I use what I've got. Contrary to what people often say, using the first person in films tends to be a sign of humility: "All I have to offer is myself."

DW: Laura is a kind of blade runner, a missing link between the audience and the absolute horror of war?

CM: She is honest enough not to be self-conscious about placing her own personal tragedy within the abysmal tragedy of warfare, because every tragedy is unique. A woman imbued with petty bourgeois guilt would not have been able to do that, and not because she thought her tragedy was the less important (if anything she'd think it was *more* important). Laura knows that suffering confers no kinds of status. She places her own suffering beside the suffering of the Okinawa victims, like one of those bunches of flowers which the parents of the drowned children throw into the waves. For my part, I expect it is easier for the audience to identify with Laura's suffering than with the feelings of a man who massacred his entire family. I am willing to bet on that. And so I help the audience attain a level of compassion akin to hers as she plunges into the tragedy of Okinawa. But it is a bet.

DW: Is that level you refer to, *Level Five*?

CM: There are various levels in the game used as a metaphor to classify people and things. And then there is the way in which she enters into the game. What exactly she means at the end, I have no idea. The audience will have to decide for itself.

DW: Is that a form of respect for the audience or a way of ignoring it?

CM: I never have a potential audience in mind. I've been told this is contemptuous. Well, that's debatable. Complying with an imaginary audience means one has so high an opinion of oneself that one believes oneself capable of delving into that audience's mind and adapting oneself to suit it; or simply thinking that one is not so exceptional that what moves and amuses one couldn't amuse and move others in the same way. Which shows the greater contempt?

DW: Why Catherine Belkhodja?

CM: Obviously the obvious choice.

DW: Laura's work space where—almost always—she appears, seems to embody the place where the film itself is manufactured.

CM: Correct. One of the niceties of the setup was that the location was itself a tool in the formal process. The special effects were achieved on the computer which appears on screen—a good old Power Mac. The control panel visible in the foreground is part of my editing kit. Except for the Japanese footage, the film is a duet, manufactured by two people housed in a room six foot by ten, with no crew, no technical assistance. Recently, Lelouch was quoted as saying he longed to make a film without technicians. I can't think what is stopping him. If all he needs is a bankrupt producer, I can recommend one.

DW: So is this a manifesto for *cinéma pauvre* so unfashionable in film schools nowadays?

CM: A manifesto for one kind of cinema, one of several possible kinds of cinema, that's all. To call it anything else would be foolish. You could never make *Lawrence of Arabia* like this. Nor *Andrei Rublev.* Nor *Vertigo.* But we possess the wherewithal—and this is something new—for intimate, solitary, filmmaking. The process of making films in communion with oneself, the way a painter works or a writer, need not now be solely experimental. My comrade Astruc's notion of the camera as a pen was only a metaphor. In his day, the humblest cinematographic product required a lab, a cutting room and plenty of money. . . . Nowadays, a young filmmaker needs only an idea and a small amount of equipment to prove himself. He needn't kowtow to producers, TV stations, or committees.

DW: You never give interviews. What got into you?

CM: Berkeley is my second home. Or third, the other being a bar in Tokyo called *La Jetée*. . . . And I wanted to use this opportunity of clearing up a few points which might be open to question. But generally, if a film does not provide its own answers to any of the questions people may want to raise with the filmmaker, then the film wasn't worth making.

Interview with Chris Marker (1997)

JEAN-MICHEL FRODON, "I never wonder about if, why, how . . . ," *Le Monde*, 20 February 1997. (Translated from the French.)

For more than 30 years Chris Marker, who indulges in his taste for secrecy and has long known the media's informational drifts, has been refusing to give interviews to the press. However, he accepted to answer our questions submitted by fax.

JEAN-MICHEL FRODON: *Level Five* combines classical film features (scenario, actress, commentary) with "new technologies." How did you conceive this combination?

CHRIS MARKER: Scenario, actress, use of a text. . . . All that is really meaningless as I am concerned. Film is a totality; I let my intuition guide me into it; features combine like parts of my imaginary Mecano [construction toy]; I never wonder about if, why, how.

J-MF: The images in the film are generated by heterogeneous sources. How did you assembly them?

CM: The great majority of the images was generated by two cameras: a small video camera and a digital camera when I was working in the studio. In theory, the digital image is better and is better transferred on a 35 mm film; but in reality the scenes filmed with my little Handycam do fit quite well with those that Catherine Belkhodja filmed with the Sony 3CCD. The first Okinawa images had been filmed with a 16 mm camera together with the cameraman Gerard de Battista in 1985, already with an eye toward *Level Five*. I took several other trips to that island after *Sunless*—a matter of personal fascination, and several times I went back to it alone with my video camera, always thinking about *Level Five*. There are also a few exterior sequences filmed by the cameraman in chief Yves Angelo. These images originated in a totally different universe: I hired Yves Angelo to film a video clip with an English team. I used the scenes that were left unused when it appeared to me that I needed at least one time to show Laura in a context outside the studio, and also that I did not want any identifiable clue about the place and time.

J-MF: Did you write up, or had to write up, a specific computer editing program for filming *Level Five*?

CM: I did not write up, strictly speaking, a specific program: I combined several, ranging from the classic image processing (Photoshop, Painter) to Roger Wagner's brilliant Hyper Studio, the most extraordinary tool of creation that I experienced since I had learned to write. It is a multimedia program (an overused term but it fits well its meaning) that makes it possible to combine text, images, animation. It enabled me to create most of the game's "figures," including the sequence with masks.

J-MF: How does that software work?

CM: Hyper Studio works (like HyperCard but with much greater speed and intuition) on the basis of stacks [piles] that contain a certain number of screens, connected by "buttons" that can in turn call in reels of texts, music, animation, fragments of QuickTime films. Surfing from screen to screen, then from stack to stack, one gets the arborescence [flowering] of a game [in the film] or a CD-ROM like the one I am making right now on the topic of memory: *Immemory*. This program makes it possible to be totally free to surf and to follow a nonlinear narrative, particularly well suited for the CD-ROM because it is the only technique that enables us to simulate the aleatory and capricious character of memory—which by definition a film cannot do.

J-MF: In what way is the montage [editing] of *Level Five* different from that of a "classic" film?

CM: The only, but decisive, difference stems from the choice I made when I started working with a video to apply a montage that I am calling "zen," or online, i.e., which is linear, from the beginning to the end of the film, without any right to regret, to remorse, to retrace one's steps, to anything that begins with *re*. This method has something in common with Russian roulette, and it is stimulating: In contrast to the virtual montage, which enables us to do slapdash work because, in our mind, we can always return to it, there is no second chance in this case. Needless to say, this idea would horrify all self-respecting directors and would cause all the professors of the FEMIS (French national film school) to faint. In addition, there is a gain of time and budget in it. An edited minute is a total minute: image, words, music, and special effects (far removed from the atrocious cinema tradition whereby music is added "at the end," whereas, so often, it is music that is responsible for the mood of a scene. . . .

J-MF: In addition to the filmmaker Nagisa Oshima and Rev. Shigeaki Kinjo, a former protagonist [participant] in the Okinawa massacre, who are the other two Japanese witnesses who appear in the film?

CM: Kenji Tokitsu is a karate grand master who has his dojo [studio] in Saint-Germain-des-Pres and has written a remarkable book: *La Voie du karate* (The Way of Karate; Editions du Seuil). I required his presence because there are things about Japan (the war, seppuku) that can only be said by a Japanese who meditated for a long time about them. Ju'nishi Ushiyama is the founder of the documentary film institute in Tokyo. He was the one who first sent me to Okinawa, and I owe my discovery of the documentary work of Oshima to him. Hence my acknowledgment of my gratitude.

Chris Marker on *Immemory*, taken from Tapies catalog, 1998

In this age of delusions of grandeur, we would all like to leave our names in the history books. We have won battles or lost them, we have discovered kingdoms and lost them. Or, at least, we see ourselves as the leading characters of a novel like Napoleon, who once exclaimed: "What a novel my life has been!" A more modest, but also more useful, enterprise would be to represent each memory with the tools of geography. In each life there are continents, islands, deserts, dams, overpopulated countries and unexplored territories. In memory we can represent maps and landscapes more easily (and more precisely) than songs or stories.

For a photographer or a film director to become an object of memory does not mean that he or she is more interesting than anyone else, simply that there are lines one can work with, forms from which maps can be drawn, and figures that can be inserted into those images.

Around me are thousands of photographs I have never used. Bill Klein once said that if the works of a famous photographer were projected at a rate of fifty images per second, the whole production would last three minutes. . . . I have many fragments of images I have never used and which, as one might say, stream off my films like the tail of a comet. From every country I visit I return with postcards, newspaper cuttings and posters which I tear off walls. The idea behind all that is to immerse myself in that whirlpool of images and construct their geography.

I think that any reasonably long memory (like every collection) is more structured than it seems at first sight. For example, in some images apparently taken at random, on postcards bought without thinking, we can recognize the first steps of a road on which we can draw a map of that particular imaginary landscape. I am sure that if I study my documents systematically, I shall find, hidden in that disorder, a secret map, like the map of the treasure in a tale of pirates. That has been no more than a scrap of rhetoric; in fact it is some time since I began that small study of classification of my archive of images, mine and other people's.

The objective of this project is to provide a guide for some person's particular archive, creating a geography book of my own with the help of a computer, either through free choice or through a random tour of the programmes.

Feature Films

Olympia 52 (1952; feature)
Finland
Production: Peuple et Culture with support from the Ministère de
l'Education Nationale.
Direction: Chris Marker
Photography: Chris Marker, Robert Cartier, Charles Sabatier, Joffre
Dumazedier
Screenplay: Chris Marker
Narration: Joffre Dumazedier
Editing: Suzy Benguigui
Sound: Robert Barthès
Special Effects: Etienne Lalou, Georges Magnage
Black and white
16 mm
82 minutes
Unofficial documentary about the 1952 Olympics in Helsinki. The film was
controversial because of its suggestion that Olympic champions often drift
into obscurity and even poverty once they are no longer able to compete.

Lettre de Sibérie (Letter from Siberia; 1958; feature)
Production: Anatole Dauman (Argos Films)
Direction: Chris Marker
Photography: Sacha Vierny
Narration: George Rouquier
Sound: Studios Marignan
Music: Pierre Barbaud
Special Effects/Animation: Equipe Arcady
Color
16 mm
62 minutes

Award: Prix Lumière, 1958
An essay travel film sponsored by the periodical *France-URSS* and the
  Foreign Ministry of the Soviet Union. Marker, Sacha Vierny, Armand Gatti,
  and Pierrard traveled to Siberia in 1957. The resulting travelogue consists
  of sequences on nature, modernization, ritual performances, as well as
  animation clips. An overarching voice-over commentary structures the
  narrative.

Description d'un combat (Description of a Struggle; 1960; feature)
Israel
Production: Yitzhak Zohar (Wim van Leer, Israel; SOFAC, Paris)
Direction: Chris Marker
Photography: Ghislain Cloquet, Meyer Levin, Bertrand Hesse
Screenplay: Chris Marker
Narration: Jean Vilar, Howard Vernon, Alan Adair
Editing: Eva Zorz
Sound: Pierre Fatosme, SIMO
Color
35 mm
60 minutes
Awards: Golden Bear Berlin, 1961; Jugendfilmpreis des Senats von Berlin,
  1961
Documentary shot in Israel focuses on the challenges and opportunities
  facing the new nation, including the trauma of the Holocaust, the
  democratic socialist idealism of the kibbutzniks, the poverty of the Israeli-
  Arab sector, and the ongoing border wars. After 1967, Marker sought to
  withdraw the film from public screenings.

Cuba Si! (Cuba, Yes!; 1961; feature)
Cuba
Production: Juan Vilar, Roger Fleytoux (Films de la Pléiade/Pierre
  Braunberger)
Direction: Chris Marker
Assistant Directors: Dervis P. Espinosa, Saul Yelin, Eduardo Manet, Selma
  Diaz
Photography: Chris Marker
Screenplay: Chris Marker
Narration: Nicolas Yumatov
Interviewers: Etienne Lalou, Igor Barrere
Editing: Eva Zora
Sound: Jean Nêny
Music: E. G. Mantici, J. Calzada, Carlos Puebla
Special Effects: Paul Grimault, William Guêry

Black and white
16 mm
52 minutes
Award: Prix Terrenoire, 1962
Marker's first film about postrevolutionary Cuba, in which he tries to
counter the international media's effort to ignore the successes of Castro's
government. The film was censored from 1961 to 1963.

Le joli mai (The Merry Month of May; 1962; feature)
France
Production: Cathérine Winter, Gisèle Rebillon (Sofracima)
Production Manager: André Heinrich
Direction: Chris Marker, Pierre Lhomme
Assistant Director: Pierre Grunstein
Photography: Pierre Lhomme, Etienne Becker, Denys Clerval, Pierre
Villemain
Screenplay: Chris Marker, Catherine Varlin
Narration: Simone Signoret (English), Yves Montand (French)
Interviewers: Henri Belly, Henri Crespi
Editing: Eva Zora, Annie Meunier, Madeleine Lecompère
Sound: Antoine Bonfanti, René Levert
Music: Michel Legrand, Boris Mokroussow
Black and white
16 mm
123–minute and 165–minute versions
Awards: Fipresci Award Cannes, 1963; Golden Dove Leipzig, 1963
Shot in Paris, this film consists of two parts: "Prière sur la Tour Eiffel" and
"Le retour de Fantômas." Shot shortly after the referendum on Algerian
independence, Marker examines and exposes, through interviews, the
hypocrisy of bourgeois French attitudes about happiness and freedom,
while demonstrators are being beaten by police and prisoners languish in
jail cells. This film represents Marker's first systematic use of synchronized
sound.

Le mystère Koumiko (The Koumiko Mystery; 1965; feature)
Japan
Production: Apec Joudioux, Sofracima, Service de la Recherche de l'ORTF
Direction: Chris Marker
Photography: Chris Marker
Screenplay: Chris Marker
Narration: Chris Marker
Editing: Chris Marker
Sound: SIMO

Music: Toru Takemitsu
Cast: Kumiko Muraoka
Color
16 mm
54 minutes
Award: Oberhausen Grand Prize, 1966
Marker travels to Tokyo, Japan, to film the 1964 Olympics, where he meets
a young Japanese woman named Kumiko Muraoka. The film is a personal
investigation of the society of postwar Japan.

Si j'avais quatre dromadaires (If I Had Four Camels; 1966; feature)
Production: Henri Régnier, Claude Joudioux (ISKRA, APEC)
Direction: Chris Marker
Photography: Chris Marker
Screenplay: Chris Marker
Narration: Pierre Vaneck, Nicolas Yumatov, Catherine Le Couey
Assistance From: J. F. Larivière-Brochard, Christine Lecouvette, Wolfgang
Teile
Sound: Antoine Bonfanti
Music: Lalan et Trio, Barney Wilen
Black and white
35 mm
49 minutes
This "photo-film" consists of 800 still images taken from 26 countries around
the world. The commentary is in the form of three friends who discuss the
nature of photography and comment on the screened images.

La bataille des dix millions (The Battle of the Ten Million; 1970; feature)
Cuba
Production: K. G. Production, SLON, RTB, ICAIC
Direction: Chris Marker and Valérie Mayoux
Photography: Santiago Alvarez
Screenplay: Chris Marker
Narration: Georges Kiejman, Edouard Luntz
Editing: Jacqueline Meppiel
Black and white
16 mm
58 minutes
Documentary about economic development in Cuba, particularly the effort
to boost output of sugar cane. This film is made from a compilation of
newsreel footage from the Cuban Film Institute ICAIC and from Santiago
Alvarez's film *Despegue a las 18.00* (Departure: 18:00).

Puisqu'on vous dit que c'est possible (Because You Said It Was Possible; 1973; feature)
Production: Crepac-Scopcolor (Roger Louis)
Direction: Chris Marker
Editing: Chris Marker
Color (German text says black and white)
16 mm
60 minutes
This film depicts the strike at the Ebaucha S.A. clock factory in Lip (France). Marker was responsible for assembling clips from various photographers into one cohesive film.

La solitude du chanteur de fond (The Loneliness of the Long-Distance Singer; 1974; feature)
Production: Seuil Audio-Visuel (Jean-Marie Bertrand, François Lesterlin)
Direction: Chris Marker
Photography: Pierre Lhomme, Yannle Masson, Jacques Renard
Camera Assistants: Guy Testa-Rosa, Michel Cemet, Richard Kopans
Editing: Monique Christel-Adamov with assistance from Laurence Cuvillier
Sound: Antoine Bonfanti, Michel Destrois, with assistance from Jean-François Chevalier, Auguste Galli
Cast: Yves Montand
Color
16 mm
60 minutes
Portrait of singer Yves Montand on the occasion of a concert given for the benefit of refugees of the coup d'état in Chile.

Le fond de l'air est rouge (A Grin without a Cat; 1977; feature)
Production: Grupo Iskra, Institut National de l'Audiovisuel, Dovidis
Direction: Chris Marker
Assistants: Valerie Mayroux, Luce Marsant, Pierre Camus, Annie-Claire Mittelburger
Christine Aye, Patrick Sauvion, Jean-Roger Sahunet
Editing: Chris Marker
Sound: Chris Marker
Music: Luciano Berio
Cast: Simone Signoret, Jorge Semprun, Davos Hanich, Sandra Scarnati, François Maspere, Laurence Cuvillier
Color
16 mm
240 minutes

Originally divided into four parts for television broadcast, Marker, through the use of film archives, Super 8 films, photographs, posters, audio tapes, and newsreels, examines the fate and gradual dissolution of the Left of the 1960s. The film covers the anti–Vietnam War movement, revolutionaries in Latin America, the Prague Spring, and the May 1st demonstrations in France. Marker released a reedited and updated version of the film in 1993 under the title *A Grin without a Cat.*

Sans soleil (Sunless; 1982; feature)
Production: Argos Films
Direction: Chris Marker
Assistant Director: Pierre Camus
Assistance From: Kazuko Kawakita, Hayao Shibata Ichiro, Hagiwara, Kazue Kobata, Keiko Murata, Yuko Fukusaki, Tom Luddy, Anthony Reveaux, Manuela Adelman, Pierre Lhomme, Jimmy Glasberg, Ghislain Cloquet, Eric Dumage, Dominique Gentil, Arthur Cloquet
Photography: Sandor Krasna
Still Photography: Martin Boschet, Roger Grange
Film Extracts: Sana na N'hada (Carnival in Bissau), Jean-Michel Humeau (Ranks ceremony), Mario Marret and Eugenio Bentivoglio (Guerilla in Bissau), Danièle Tessier (Death of a giraffe), Haroun Tazieff (Iceland 1970).
Narration: Alexandra Stewart (English), Florence Delay (French)
Editing Assistants: Anne-Marie L'Hôte, Catherine Adda
Sound Mix: Antoine Bonfanti, Paul Bertault
Music: Modest Mussorgski, Jean Sibelius (treated by Isao Tomita)
Song: Arielle Dombasle
Electronic Sound: Michel Krasna, Isao Tomita
Image Synthesiser: EMS Spectre
Sound Synthesiser: EMS/VCS3, Moog Source
Special Effects: Hayao Yamaneko
Color
16 mm blowup to 35 mm
110 minutes
Awards: International Critics Prize, London, 1983; Grand Prize Festival of the People, Florence, 1983; BFI Award, London, 1983
Considered by critics to be the classic essay film, *Sans soleil* consists of "letters," read by an unknown woman, from a freelance cameraman, Sandor Krasna. The comments and the accompanying footage concern everyday life in the farthest reaches of the world: from the Cape Verde Islands to Guinea-Bissau to Iceland and Japan and back again.

A. K. (*Portrait of Akira Kurosawa;* 1985; feature)
Production: Serge Silberman/Greenwich Film Productions, Herald Ace,
    Herald Nippon
Direction: Chris Marker
Photography: Frans-Yves Marescot
Assistant Camera: Tsutomu Ishizuka, Hiroshi Ishida
Narration: François Maspero (French), Hanns Zischler (German)
Editing: Chris Marker
Sound: Jun'ichi Shima
Sound Editor: Catherine Adda
Music: Toru Takemitsu
Special Effects: Patrick Duroux
Cast: Akira Kurosawa
Color
35 mm
71 minutes
A personal portrait of Akira Kurosawa while on the set of *Ran.* Marker
    exposes Kurosawa's precise directing and filming techniques.

Mémoire de Simone (Simone's Memory; 1986; feature)
Production: Festival International du Film de Cannes
Direction: Chris Marker
Script: Chris Marker
Narration: François Périer
Editing: Chris Marker
Color
35 mm
61 minutes
A tribute to the work of Simone Signoret, who had died the previous year.
    Assembled by Marker, the film consists of clips from different time periods
    in the actress's life. The film has been rarely screened publicly, the most
    important being the Cannes Film Festival in 1986.

Le tombeau d'Alexandre (The Last Bolshevik; 1993; feature)
Production: Les Films de l'Astrophore (Paris), Michael Kustow Productions
    (Great Britain), La Sept/Arte (France), Epidem Oy (Finland), Channel 4
    (London)
Production coordinator: Francoise Widhoff and the ghost of A. I.
    Medvedkine
Direction: Chris Marker, in association with Andrei Paschkevich (Moscow)
Memory Manager: Julia Bodin
Assistants: Sergei Nekipelov, Tony Boulihet

Script: Chris Marker
Narration: Michael Pennington
Editing: Chris Marker
English Version: Orna and Michael Kustow
Music: Alfred Schnittke (In Memorian, Quintet, Trio, Violin Concerto)
Additional Music: Michael Krasna
Color, black and white
Super 8 Video
118 minutes
Marker's second portrait of Russian filmmaker Alexander Medvedkine, shot
this time in the shadow of the downfall of the Soviet Union. *The Last
Bolshevik,* filmed after Medvedkine's death, constitutes a farewell both to
the filmmaker and to the Soviet Union. Although critical of the excesses
of the totalitarian regime, Marker is quick to remind the viewer of the
social injustices and dire circumstances prior to the revolution. The film is
dedicated to the memory of Marker's friend Jacques Ledoux.

Level Five (1996; feature)
Production: Argos Films, Les films de l'Astrophore
Direction: Chris Marker
Assistance: Kenji Tokitsu
Cast: Catherine Belkhodja
Color
35 mm
106 minutes
Laura has inherited the task of completing the programming of a computer
game about the battle of Okinawa that her deceased beloved has left
undone. Unable to change the course of the game, she engages the help
of Chris, a filmmaker who has experience in Japan and acts as off-camera
advisor. As she becomes increasingly involved with the details of the war,
she comes ever closer to reaching "Level Five," a status she and her lover
had invented.

One Day in the Life of Andrei Arsenevich (1999; feature)
Direction: Chris Marker
Color
55 minutes
A portrait of Russian director Andrei Tarkovsky and an analysis of his films.

Avril inquiet (Worried April; 2001; feature)
Direction: Chris Marker
52 minutes
An unfinished series of portraits from Kosovo.

Short Films

Dimanche à Pekin (Sunday in Peking; 1956; short)
Production: Madeleine Casanova-Rodriguez (Pavox Films, Argos Films),
    People's Republic of China
Direction: Chris Marker
Photography: Chris Marker
Screenplay: Chris Marker
Narration: Gilles Quéant
Editing: Francine Grubert
Music: Pierre Barbaud
Special Effects: Arcady
Color
16 mm
22 minutes
Awards: Grand Prix de Court-Métrage, Tours, 1956; Médaille dárgent,
    Moscow, 1957
A short travel film giving a rare and official glimpse of the People's Republic
    of China in the 1950s.

La jetée (1962; short)
France
Production: Anatole Dauman (Argos Films)
Production Design: Jean-Pierre Sudre
Direction: Chris Marker
Photography: Chris Marker
Still Photography: Jean Chibaud
Screenplay: Chris Marker
Narration: Jean Négroni
Editing: Jean Ravel
Sound: SIMO, Antoine Bonfanti
Music: Trevor Duncan, Music from Russian Liturgy of Good Saturday
Special Effects: DSA
Cast: Hélène Chatelain, Davos Hanich, Jacques Ledoux, André Heinrich,
    Jacques Branchu, Pierre Joffroy, Etienne Becker, Philbert von Lifchitz,
    Ligia Borowczyk, Janine Klein, William Klein
Black and white
35 mm
28 minutes
Awards: Astronef d'or, Trieste, 1963; Prix Jean Vigo, 1963; Goldener Dukat,
    Mannheim, 1963; Prix Giff-Wiff, 1963
Composed almost entirely of still photos, this is a futuristic story about a
    prisoner of war who, by virtue of his advanced memory abilities, learns to

travel back in time, where he meets and falls in love with a woman he once saw as a child during a traumatic event at the Orly airport terminal. When his captors finally "catch up" with him in the past and kill him—again at the Orly terminal—his "child self" paradoxically witnesses his own future death, thus explaining the trauma of his childhood experience. Served as the basis for Terry Gilliam's *12 Monkeys*.

Jour de tournage (Filming Day; 1969; short)
Production: SLON
Direction: Chris Marker
Assistant: Pierre Duponey
Black and white
16 mm
11 minutes

On vous parle de Brésil: Torture (Report on Brazil: Torture; 1969; short)
Brazil
Production: SLON
Direction: Chris Marker
Screenplay: Chris Marker
Photography: Pierre Duponey
Narration: Chris Marker and others
Editing: Chris Marker
Black and white
16 mm
20 minutes
Third in SLON's *On vous parle . . .* series. Four men and women arrested in connection with the 1969 kidnapping of the U.S. ambassador in Brazil report on the methods of torture utilized by the military government.

On vous parle de Prague: Le deuxième procès d'Artur London (Report on Prague: The Second Trial of Artur London; 1969; short)
France
Production: SLON
Direction: Chris Marker
Black and white
16 mm
28 minutes
Documentary of the making of Costa-Gavras's film *L'Aveu* about the Stalinist show trials of Eastern Europe.

On vous parle de Brésil: Carlos Marighela (Report on Brazil: Carlos Marighela; 1970; short)

Production: SLON
Direction: Chirs Marker
Black and white
16 mm
17 minutes
About the execution of Carlos Marighela, one of four terrorists convicted of
kidnapping the American ambassador to Brazil.

On vous parle de Paris: Les mots ont un sens (Report on Paris: Words Have a
Meaning; 1970; short)
Production: SLON
Direction: Chris Marker
Narration: Chris Marker
Black and white
16 mm
20 minutes
A portrait of the left-leaning publisher and bookstore owner François
Maspéro, who provided counterinformation; the most intellectual and
optimistic of the *On vous parle . . .* series.

Le train en marche (The Train Rolls On; 1971; short)
Production: SLON
Direction: Chris Marker
Photography: Jacques Loiseleux
Script: Chris Marker
Narration: François Périer
Black and white
16 mm
32 minutes
Awards: Silver Dove, Leipzig, 1971; Fipresci Award, Leipzig, 1971
A portrait of Soviet filmmaker Alexander Medvedkine and his remarkable
ciné-train. The film was made as an introductory short for SLON's
rerelease of Medvedkine's *Happiness* (1934). Includes an interview with
Medvedkine filmed at the Noisy-le-Sec train depot near Paris in 1971.

L'Ambassade (The Embassy; 1973; short)
France
Production: E. K.
Direction: Chris Marker
Narration: Chris Marker
Color
Super 8
20 minutes

Intertitles tell the viewer that this film was found in an embassy. The footage appears to have been originally taken without sound, but the filmmaker's voice-over commentary tells us that what we are seeing is the processing of political refugees who have sought asylum in the embassy. As the film draws to a close, the camera pans down from the embassy window, tracking the departure of the refugees, and as it pans back up, we see the Parisian skyline and realize we are not in Latin America but in France. This is Marker's first use of Super 8 technology.

Junkopia (San Francisco) (1981; short)
Production: Argos Films
Direction: Chris Marker
Photography: Chris Marker, Frank Simeone, John Chapman
Singing Voice: Arielle Dombasle
Sound: Antegor
Music: Michel Krasna
Special Effects: Manuela Adelman, Tom Luddy, Sara Ström
Color
16 mm
6 minutes
Short observation of an uninhabited Pacific inlet near San Francisco, where unknown artists have fashioned objects (an old German plane, a huge fish, a bird, etc.) out of wood planks.

Berliner Ballade (1990; short)
Production: Antenne 2
Direction: Chris Marker
Interviews with Jürgen Böttcher and Stephan Hermlin
Color
Super 8, video
29 minutes
On the occasion of the first elections in East Germany following the fall of the Berlin Wall, Marker documents the events for French television *(Envoye Spécial)*, parts of which were also used in the Zapping Zone exhibit *(Berlin '90)*.

Getting Away with It (1990; music video)
Production: Michael Shamberg, Cascando Studios
Direction: Chris Marker
Color
Video
4 minutes

Music video for London group Electronic. The music was then used for the sound track in Zapping Zone

Les 20 heures dans les camps (Prime Time in the Camps; 1993; short)
Production: Les Films de l'Astrophore
Direction: Chris Marker and the video team of the Roska camp
Photography: Chris Marker
Script: Chris Marker
Editor: Chris Marker
Music: Leonard Cohen ("Everybody Knows")
Color
Super 8 Video
27 minutes
In this video Marker reports from a camp for Bosnian refugees in the Croatian town of Roska, near Ljubljana, where six refugees—including two Serbian deserters—are producing a nightly live news program with a Super 8 video camera and captured signals from CNN, Radio Sarajevo, and Sky News.

3 Video Haikus (1994)
"Petite Ceinture," 1 minute
"Chaika," 1 minute 29 seconds
"Owl Gets in Your Eyes," 1 minute 10 seconds

Casque bleu (Blue Helmet; 1992)
Production: Les Films de l'Astrophore
Direction: Chris Marker
Color
Video
27 minutes
In this interview, conducted by Marker, François Crémieux talks about his experience as a Blue Helmet (an enlisted man in the French army deployed to protect the Bosnian enclave of Bihac from Serbian aggression) and the disillusionment he experienced in relation to the commanding officers, who openly sided with the Serbs.

Un maire au Kosovo (A Mayor in Kosovo; 2000; short)
Direction: Chris Marker
27 minutes
Unfinished portrait of Dr. Bajram Rexhepi, mayor of Mitrovica.

Television

L'Héritage de la chouette (The Legacy of the Owl; 1989; 13–part television
  series)
Production: La Sept, Attica Art Production (Goupe Fondation Onassis), FIT
  Productions
Direction: Chris Marker
Photography: Peter Chapell, Emiko Omori, Andreas Sinanos, Pierre
  Dupouey, Jimmy Glasberg, Arnaud de Boisberranger, Peter Arnold, Levan
  Paatachvili, Sandor Krasna
Script: Chris Marker
Narration: André Dussollier
Editing: Khadicha Bariha, Nedjma Scialom
Sound: Harald Maury, Harrick Maury, Jean-Charles Martel, Ann Evans, Eoin
  McCann, Mervyn Gerrard, Guarri Kountsev, Dinos Kittou, Arst Axel
Music: Eleni Karaindrou, Krzystof Penderecki, Herbert Windt, Iannis
  Xenakis, François-Bernard Mâche, Christelle Kose, Pierre Bernard,
  Florence Malraux, Valérie de Ricquebourg, Carline Bouilhet, Diana
  García, Laurence Braunberger, François Widhoff
Cast: Theo Angelopoulos, Cornelius Castoriadis, Elia Kazan, George Steiner,
  Iannis Xenakis
Color
16 mm
26 minutes
The television series consists of the following thirteen parts: "Symposium ou
  les idées reçu," "Olympisme ou la Grèce imaginaire," "Démocratie ou la
  cité des songes," "Nostalgie ou le retour impossible," "Amnésie ou le sens
  de l'histoire," "Mathématique ou l'empire des signes," "Logomachie ou
  les mots de la tribu," "Musique ou l'espace du dedans," "Mythologie ou la
  vérité du mensonge," "Cosmogonie ou l'usage du monde," "Misogynie ou
  les pièges du desir," "Tragedie ou l'illusion de la mort," "Philosophie ou le
  triomphe de la chouette."

Mutimedia/Installation

Quand le siècle a pris formes (When the Century Assumed Form; 1978;
  multimedia video)
Production: CNAC GP (Centre Georges Pompidou)
Direction: Chris Marker
Assistant Director: Pierre Camus
Music: Hanns Eisler
Color
16 mm converted to video and edited

15 minutes 30 seconds
Video installation for two monitors produced for the Centre Georges
Pompidou exhibition Paris-Berlin 1900–1930 (July 12–November 6,
1978). This installation depicts scenes from World War I and the Russian
Revolution, which Marker sees as the defining moments of the twentieth
century, as well as the failed revolutions of Western Europe. Reedited and
rereleased in 1993.

Zapping Zone: Proposals for an Imaginary Television (multimedia installation
for the Centre Georges Pompidou; 1991)
Production: Musée National d'Art Moderne (MNAM)
Direction: Chris Marker
Equipment: 14 video monitors, 13 laser disc players, 13 loudspeakers, 13
video recorders
Christo also from Chris to Christo, 24 minutes (1985)
Matta, 14 minutes 18 seconds (1985)
Tarkovski, 26 minutes (1986)
Eclats, 20 minutes
Bestiare, in three parts:
Chat écoutant la musique (Cat Listening to Music), 2 minutes 47 seconds
An Owl Is an Owl Is an Owl, 3 minutes 18 seconds
Zoo Piece, 2 minutes 45 seconds
Spectre, 27 minutes
Tokyo Days, 24 minutes
Berlin '90, 20 minutes 35 seconds
Photo Browse, 301 photographs, 17 minutes 20 seconds
Détour Ceaucescu, 8 minutes 2 seconds
Théorie des ensembles, 11 minutes.
Later additions include:
Azulmoon (1992), loop
Coin fenêtre (1992), 9 minutes 35 seconds
Slon Tango (1993), 4 minutes 15 seconds
Bullfight/Okinawa (1994), 4 minutes 12 seconds
A multimedia installation (video, photographs, computer) for the Centre
Georges Pompidou "Passage de l'Image, September 18, 1990–January 13,
1991." Divided into "Zones."

Silent Movie (1995; installation for the Wexner Center for the Arts,
Columbus, Ohio)
Production: Wexner Center for the Arts
Direction: Chris Marker
Cast: Catherine Belkhodja

Equipment: five Sony 25" video monitors, five Pioneer laser disc players, five laser discs (20 minutes each).

Top monitor: "The Journey"
Second monitor: "The Face"
Middle monitor: "Captions"
Fourth monitor: "The Gesture"
Bottom monitor: "The Waltz"
Sound track: Scott Joplin, "Bethena"; Artur Lourié, "Dodo"; Alexander Scriabin, Mazurka op. 3, no. 2; Domenico Scarlatti, Sonata in B minor Kk 87; Billy Strayhorn, "Lotus Blossom"; Nino Rota, "Cantilena"; Alexander Scriabin, Mazurka op. 3, no. 7; Federico Mompou, "Cançó VI"; Duke Ellington, "Reflections in D"; Artur Lourié, "Valse"; Frederico Mompou, "Cançó VIII"; Leonard Bernstein, "Lucky to Be Me"; Alexander Scriabin, Prelude op. 11, no. 10; Alexander Scriabin, Etude op. 2, no. 1; Peter Illich Tchaikovsky, "June"; Cesar Cui, Prelude op. 64, no. 2; Alexander Borodin, "Nocturne"; Frederico Mompou, "Pajaro triste."
An installation for the Wexner Center for the Arts in Columbus, Ohio (January 26–April 9, 1995). The installation consists of five monitor towers with each monitor screening material from a laser disk. The monitors are controlled by a computer so that they maintain a random sequence.

Immemory One (1997; multimedia installation at the Centre Georges Pompidou, Paris)
Production: Musée National d'Art Moderne, Centre Georges Pompidou/Les Films de l'Astrophore
Creator: Chris Marker
Multimedia installation: June 4–September 29, 1997, Paris (Centre Georges Pompidou).

Immemory (1998; CD-ROM)
Released at the Centre Georges Pompidou, Paris, 1998.

Roseware (1999; multimedia installation at the Tapies Foundation, Barcelona, January 11–24, 1999)
Production: Constant, Brussels (in association with the Atelier des Jeunes Cinéastes)
Creators: Chris Marker and Laurence Rassel
Equipment: 1 Omega Jaz Disk, 2 PC Apple G3 AV Power Mac, 1 PC Apple 200 MHz Power Mac, 2 AV monitors, 1 scanner, 1 video camera, 1 Jaz player, 1 slide projector and screen, tables, chairs, drawing material

Owls at Noon Prelude: The Hollow Men (2005; multimedia installation at the
   Museum of Modern Art)
Production: The Museum of Modern Art
Direction: Chris Marker
19 minutes
Equipment: 2 video feeds, 8 monitors

Codirected, Collective, and Collaborations on Films

Les statues meurent aussi (Statues Also Die; 1952; collaboration)
France
Production: Présence Africaine, Tadié-Cinéma
Direction: Alain Resnais, Chris Marker
Photography: Ghislain Cloquet
Screenplay: Chris Marker
Narration: Jean Negroni
Editing: Henry Colpi
Sound: René Louge, Studios Marignan
Music: Guy Bernard
Black and white
35 mm
30 minutes
Award: Prix Jean Vigo, 1954
Documentary about the disintegration and desecration of black African art
   by white Europeans, who have removed it from its sacred animist context
   to be viewed in sterile museums. The strong anticolonialist message
   precipitated a ten-year ban after its premier at the Cannes Film Festival in
   1953.

Nuit et brouillard (Night and Fog; 1955; collaboration)
Production: Argos Films, Como, Cocinor
Direction: Alain Resnais
Assistant Director: André Heinrich
Photography: Ghislain Cloquet, Sacha Vierny
Screenplay: Jean Cayrol
Narration: Michel Bouquet
Editing: Henri Colpi, Jasmine Chasney
Music: Hanns Eisler
32 minutes
Chris Marker has an uncredited collaboration as both cameraman and script
   editor on this documentary exposing the horrors of the concentration
   camps.

Les hommes de la baleine (The Men of the Whale; 1956; collaboration)
Production: Argos Films, Les Films Armorial
Direction: Mario Ruspoli
26 minutes
Vive la baleine is the title for the film when it was reissued by SLON in 1970 (which some sources list as 1972). Chris Marker did the commentary for this film under the pseudonym Jacopo Berenizi. Short film about whale hunters in the Azores.

Toute la mémoire du monde (All the Memory of the World; 1956; collaboration)
Production: Pierre Braunberger, Les Films de la Pléiade. With the collaboration of Gérard Willemetz, Pierre Goupil, Anne Sarraute, Roger Fleytoux, Claude Joudioux, Jean Cayrol, André Goefers, Jean-Claude Lauthe, Chris and Magic Marker, Phil Davis, Robert Rendigal, Giuletta Caput, Claudine Merlin, Dominique Raoul Duval, Chester Gould, Denise York, Benigno Caceres, Agnès Varda, Monique le Porrier, Paulette Borker, André Heinrich, Mme. Searle, Marie-Claire Pasquier, François-Régis Bastide, Joseph Rovan
Direction: Alain Resnais
Photography: Ghislain Cloquet
Screenplay: Rémo Forlani
Narration: Jacques Dumesnil
Editing: Alain Resnais
Music: Maurice Jarre
22 minutes
A short documentary about France's national library, the Bibliothèque Nationale.

Broadway by Light (1957; collaboration)
Production: Argos Films
Direction: William Klein
Color
16 mm
10 minutes
Defense and illustration of the Times Square movie marquee. Marker is credited with writing the opening text.

Le mystère de l'atelier 15 (The Mystery of Studio 15; 1957; collaboration)
Production: Les films Jacqueline Jacoupy, with the collaboration of Chris Marker, Yves Peneau, Jean Brugot, Fernand Marzelle, Claude Joudioux, André Schlotter, Fearless Fosdick, Elisabeth Seibel
Direction: Alain Resnais, André Heinrich

Photography: Ghislain Cloquet, Sacha Vierney
Screenplay: Chris Marker
Narration: Jean-Pierre Grenier
Editing: Anne Sarraute
Music: Pierre Barbaud
18 minutes
About a doctor trying to discover the cause of a factory worker's sudden
illness.

Des hommes dans le ciel (Men in the Sky; 1958; collaboration)
Direction: Jean-Jacques Languepin
Commentary: Chris Marker

La Mer et les jours (The Sea and the Days; 1958; collaboration)
Production: Son et Lumière, Pierre Long
Direction: Raymond Vogel, Alain Kaminker
Scenario: Chris Marker
Screenplay: Chris Marker
22 minutes
Everday life of fishermen on Brittany's Ile de Sein.

Le siècle a soif (The Century Is Thirsty; 1958; collaboration)
Direction: Raymond Vogel
Screenplay: Chris Marker
A short about the qualities of fruit juice framed by a commentary written in
Alexandrine verse.

L'Amérique insolite (Strange America; 1958; collaboration)
Direction: François Reichenbach
Incorporating generous portions of Marker's commentary from *L'Amérique
rêve,* this film is a scathing critique of the American dream in the 1950s.

Les astronautes (The Astronauts; 1959; collaboration)
Production: Anatole Dauman (Argos Films, Films Armorial)
Direction: Walerian Borowczyk, Chris Marker
Photography: Antonio Harispe
Screenplay: Walerian Borowczyk
Editing: Jasmine Chasney
Music: Jan Markowsky
14 minutes
About an amateur space traveler and his pet owl, Anabase.

Django Reinhardt (1959; collaboration)
Production: Pavox films
Direction: Paul Paviot
Narration: Chris Marker
22 minutes
A short sketch of Reinhardt's career.

Jouer à Paris (Playing in Paris; 1962; collaboration)
France
Production: Sofracima
Direction: Catherine Varlin
Editing: Chris Marker
27 minutes
This film is a twenty-seven-minute postscript to *Le joli mai* assembled from leftover footage and organized around a new commentary.

A Valparaiso (1963; collaboration)
Chile
Production: Anatole Dauman (Argos Films), Cine Experimental de al Universidad de Chile
Direction: Joris Ivens
Assistants: Sergio Bravo, Augustin Altez, Rebecca Yanez, Joaquin Olalla, Carlos Böker
Photography: Georges Strouvé
Camera Assistants: Patricio Guzmán, Leonardo Martinez
Screenplay: Joris Ivens
Commentary: Chris Marker
Narration: Roger Pigaut
Editing: Jean Ravel
Music: Gustavo Becerra, Orchestra conducted by Georges Delerue, song "Nous irons à Valparaiso" sung by Germaine Montero
Black and white, color
29 minutes
Ivens and Marker draft a poetic map of Valparaiso, once the most important port in all of South America.

Les chemins de la fortune (The Ways of Fortune; 1964; collaboration)
Venezuela
Direction: Pierre Kassovitz
42 minutes
Marker helped Kassovitz finish this travelogue about Venezuela.

La douceur du village (The Softness of the Village; 1964; collaboration)
France
Production: Films de la Pléiade
Direction: François Reichenbach
Editing: Chris Marker
47 minutes
About life in the small rural town of Loué, France.

La brulure de mille soleils (The Burn of a Thousand Suns; 1964; collaboration)
Production: Argos Films, Clara d'Ovar, Service de la Recherche de l'ORTF
Direction: Pierre Kast
Screenplay: Chris Marker
Editing: Chris Marker
Animated science fiction short about a depressive millionaire-poet who travels through time—with his cat Marcel and a robot semanticist in tow—to fall in love with a woman from another planet.

Le volcan interdit (The Forbidden Volcano; 1965; collaboration)
Production: Ciné Document Tazieff
Direction: Haroun Tazieff
Commentary: Chris Marker
55 or 79 minutes
Tazieff was one of the world's foremost volcanologists. The film depicts a series of active volcanoes and documents an expedition to the bottom of Mount Nyiragongo in the former Congo.

Europort-Rotterdam (1966; collaboration)
Production: Nederlandse Filmproduktie Mij, Argos Films
Direction: Joris Ivens
Assistant Directors: Mirek Sebestik, Marceline Loridan
Photography: Eduard Van der Enden, Etienne Becker
Screenplay: Gerrit Kouwenaar; adaption to French: Chris Marker
Narration: Yves Montand (French)
Editing: Catherine Dourgnon, Geneviève Louveau, Andrée Choty
Music: Pierre Barbot, Konstantin Simonovitch
20 minutes
Marker is credited with adapting Dutch poet and novelist Gerrit Kouwenaar's original text, which reworks the legend of the Flying Dutchman. Condemned to eternal wandering, the Dutchman is permitted to visit Rotterdam once a century. When he returns this time, he sees the city with fresh eyes and in return inspires others to question their assumptions about urban space.

Loin du Vietnam (Far from Vietnam; 1967; collaboration)
Production: Chris Marker and SLON
Direction: William Klein, Joris Ivens, Claude Lelouch, Jean-Luc Godard,
   Chris Marker
Coordination: Chris Marker, Alain Resnais, Agnès Varda
Photography: Jean Boffety, Denys Clerval, Ghislain Cloquet
Screenplay: Jacques Sternberg
Narration: Maurice Garrel
Editing: Colette Semprun, Ragnar van Leyden, Jean Ravel, Colette Leloup,
   Eric Pluet, Albert Jurgenson
Sound: Antoine Bonfanti, Harald Maury, Harrick Maury, René Levert
Music: Michel Fano, Michel Chapdenat, Georges Aperghis
Cast: Bernard Fresson, Karen Blanguernon, Anne Bellec, Maurice Garrel,
   Valerie Mayoux
Color
35 mm and 16 mm
115 minutes
Award: Silver Dove, Leipzig, 1968
This film is a collective work in eleven episodes conceived as a artistic
   response to the horrors of the war in Vietnam. Marker was responsible for
   giving the the montage its final cohesive form, in which most, but not all, of
   the participating filmmakers' episodes come together.

A bientôt j'espère (Be Seeing You; 1968; short)
Production: SLON, ORTF
Direction: Chris Marker, Mario Marret
Photography: Pierre Lhomme, Michel Bourder
Narration: Chris Marker
Editing: Carlos de los Llanos
Sound: Michel Desrois
Black and white
16 mm
43 minutes
Short documentary about a factory strike in Besançon, France, which was
   intended to provide moral support to striking workers at the Rhodiacéta
   factory. When the film was criticized for its "outsider" perspective, Marker
   encouraged the factory workers to start their own film cooperative, which
   came into being under the name Groupe Medvedkine and the leadership
   of Pol Cèbe.

La sixième face du Pentagon (The Sixth Face of the Pentagon; 1968; short)
Production: Pierre Braunberger (Films de la Pléiade)

Direction: Chris Marker, François Reichenbach
Photography: François Reichenbach, Chris Marker, Christian Odasso, Tony Daval
Sound: Antoine Bonfanti, Harald Maury
Music: Carlos de los Llanos
Color
16 mm
28 minutes
Award: Oberhausen Grand Prize, 1968
Short documentary about an antiwar demonstration at the Pentagon in October 1968 in which unarmed demonstrators break through an MP cordon and are beaten down at the doors of the building.

Ciné-tracts (1968; short)
Direction: Chris Marker, Alain Resnais, Jean-Luc Godard
Black and white
16 mm
24 minutes
In an effort to support the student revolt and labor strikes in May 1968, Marker contacted several moviemakers with the goal of making two to three films to encourage political resistance, the result of which was the *Ciné-tracts,* which were to be shown during meetings and demonstrations. Though the films are anonymous, it is believed that Marker made several of them, notably the fifth in the series, *Mouvement étudiant débouchant sur mouvement ouvrier (ou C'était la nuit . . .).*

Classe de lutte (1969; collaboration)
Production: SLON
Direction: Groupe Medvedkine de Besançon
16 mm
37 minutes
Directed by the labor union film cooperative whose formation Marker encouraged (see *A bientôt j'espère*), this film about a young factory worker and militant activist in the leftist CGT trade union is one of the most important examples of politically engaged documentary film of the late 1960s. Marker may have assisted in this project, but sources differ as to his role.

On vous parle de Flins (Report of Flins; 1969; short)
France
Production: SLON
Direction: Guy Devart
Black and white

16 mm

30 minutes

Number seven in SLON's *On vous parle . . .* series. Marker helped film and edit this short, which deals with how the exploitation of immigrant workers at a Renault factory in Flins was abetted by the mayor's office in nearby Meulan.

L'Afrique express (1970; collaboration)

Production: Argos

Direction: Danièle Tessier, Jacques Lang

Assistant Director: Sophie Veneck

18 minutes

Marker wrote the introductory text for this film under the name Boris Villeneuve.

L'aveu (The Confession; 1970; collaboration)

Production: Robert Dorfman, Bertrand Javal

Direction: Costa-Gavras

Screenplay: Jorge Semprun

Story: Artur London

Photography: Raoul Coutard

Still Photography: Chris Marker

Cast: Yves Montand, Simone Signoret, Gabriele Ferzetti, Michel Vitold, Jean Bouise

138 minutes

This political film is a dramatization of Artur London's experiences during the Communist purges in Czechoslovakia (see *On vous parle de Prague*). Marker was responsible for the still photography.

Die Kamera in Der Fabrik (The Camera in the Factory; 1970; feature)

Production: Norddeutsche Rundfunk (Hans Brecht)

Direction: Chris Marker/SLON, Groupe Medvedkine

Black and white

16 mm

88 minutes

Apparently, this rare film is a continuous edit of *A bientôt j'espère* and *Classe de Lutte,* made for the German television station NDR III.

L'Animal en question (Jacques Prévert et . . . un raton laveur; 1970; collaboration)

Production: SLON

Direction: André Pozner, Pierre Lhomme, Robert Doisneau, Michèle Wolf,

Sebastian Maroto, Michel Desrois, Antoine Bonfanti, Sacha Vierny, Jose They, Lionel Legros, J. F. Chevalier, Catherine Bachollet
Color
16 mm
38 minutes
Marker filmed the raccoon mentioned in the title for this documentary about poet Jacques Prévert's life and work.

El primer año (The First Year; 1971; collaboration)
Production: ISKRA (France)
Direction: Patricio Guzman
90 minutes
A documentary of the first year of the Allende government in Chile. Marker helped with the French version of the film.

Vive la baleine (Long Live the Whale; 1972; collaboration)
Production: Argos Films (German filmography lists Prodix)
Direction: Chris Marker, Mario Ruspoli
Photography: Mario Ruspoli
Script: Chris Marker
Narration: Chris Marker
Editing: Chris Marker
Sound: Chris Marker
Color
35 mm
17 minutes
Using footage from Ruspolis's 1956 *Les Hommes de la baleine,* drawings, oil paintings, and engravings, Marker's film about the barbarity of the whale hunt coincides with the beginning of a ten-year international moratorium on whaling, which is ignored by the major whaling nations, Japan and the Soviet Union.

On vous parle de Chili: Ce que disait Allende (Report on Chile: What Allende Said; 1973; collaboration)
Chile
Production: SLON-ISKRA
Direction: Miguel Littin
Editor: Chris Marker
Interviewer: Régis Debray
Black and white
16 mm
16 minutes

Tenth in SLON's *On vous parle . . .* series, this film uses footage from Littin's film *Compañero Presidente,* which depicts conversations between newly elected Chilean president Salvador Allende and Régis Debray, who spent three years in a Bolivian jail for his guerilla activities with Che Guevara. The film was released as a reaction to Allende's murder during the 1973 right-wing military putsch in Chile led by Augusto Pinochet.

Les deux mémoires (Two Memories; 1973; collaboration)
Direction: Jorge Semprun
141 minutes
Marker handled sound and helped with the editing on Semprun's documentary about the Spanish civil war.

Kashima Paradise (1974; collaboration)
Japan
Production: Co-ferc
Direction: Yann Le Masson, Bénie Deswarte
Screenplay: Chris Marker
Narration: Chris Marker
Black and white
35 mm
70 minutes
About the manipulation, exploitation, and destruction of farming communities in Narita and Kashima by Japanese corporations, including harrowing scenes from the resulting Narita airport protests.

La spirale (The Spiral; 1975; collaboration)
Chile
Production: Les Films Molière, Reggane Films, Seuil Audio-Visuel
Production Design: Jean-Michel Folon
Direction: Armand Mattelart, Jacqueline Meppiel, Valerie Mayoux
Assistance: Chris Marker, Silvio Tendler, Pierre Flament
Screenplay: Chris Marker
Narration: François Catonné, Med Hondo
Music: Jean-Claude Eloy, Luc Bérini, Antoine Bonfanti, J. F. Chevalier
Color
35 mm
155 minutes
A collective work about the downfall of the Allende government in Chile. The film is divided into seven acts (like the U.S. counterrevolutionary simulation game "Politica"), during which the political will of landowners, industry, the petit bourgeois, not to mention the CIA, is finally reimposed upon the Chilean masses.

La Batalla de Chile: La Lucha de un Pueblo Sin Armas (The Battle of Chile: The Struggle of a Powerless Town; 1975; feature)
Chile
Production: Equipo Tercer Ano with Chris Marker and ICAIC
Direction: Patricio Guzman
90 minutes
Marker helped produce Guzman's epic documentary about the extreme right's violent overthrow of the Allende government in Chile. He also contributed to the screenplay.

Viva el Presidente! (*Le recours de la méthode;* 1978; collaboration)
Direction: Miguel Littin
Color
35 mm
164 minutes
Marker prepared the subtitles for the French version of this satirical magical realist film, an adaptation of Alejo Carpentier's novel *Recourse to Method* by Chilean director Littin.

2084: Video clip pour une réflexion syndicale et pour le plaisir (Video Clip for the Trade Unions' Reflection and Pleasure; 1984; short)
Production: La Lanterne, Groupe Confédéral Audiovisuel CFDT
Direction: Chris Marker, Groupe Confédéral Audiovisuel CFDT
Assistant Director: Pierre Camus
Photography: Robert Millie, Christian Bordes, Pascal Le Moal
Script: Chris Marker
Narration: François Périer
Editing: Chris Marker
Special Effects: Hayao Yamaneko
Cast: Sophie Garnier, Bibiane Kirby, Atika Tahiri
Color
Video
10 minutes
Awards: Special prize of the Jury Festival of Nyon, 1984; Prize "la puce subversive" of the Octet Association, 1984
Filmed on the occasion of the 100th anniversary of the labor union laws in France, the quasi-science fiction film is set in the year 2084, and a robot moderator helps us look "back" at today's labor situation and shows different directions that the movement can take.

Les pyramides bleues (The Novice; 1988; collaboration)
Production: Catherine Winter, Sofracima, Fr3, Mexico Inc.
Direction: Arielle Dombasle

Cast: Arielle Dombasle, Omar Sharif, Hippolyte Girardot, Pierre Vaneck, Carole Davis, Pascal Greggory
Color
97 minutes
Marker and Eric Rohmer served as artistic consultants on this film, which stars Omar Sharif and Arielle Dombasle. A few stills and a short video clip are posted on the director's Web site.

Souvenir (1997; feature)
Production: Cascando Studios
Direction: Michael Shamberg
78 minutes
Marker created computer graphics for Shamberg's first film.

Remembrance of Things to Come (2001; short)
Direction: Chris Marker, Yannick Bellon
Black and white
42 minutes
Consisting entirely of still photos, the film focuses on the work of photographer Denise Bellon during the two decades between 1935 and 1955. Codirected by the photographer's daughter, Yannick.

Bibliography of Chris Marker's Writings |

Literary Works and Photo Books

"Till the end of time," *Esprit* 129 (1947): 145–51.

Le coeur net [The Sure Heart]. Collection "Esprit." Paris: Editions de Seuil, 1949; Collection "Roman." Paris: Le club français du livre, 1951; Collection "Le Petite Ourse." Lausanne: La Guilde du Livre, 1960.

L'homme et sa liberté. Collection "Veillées" no. 4. Paris: Editions de Seuil, 1949.

Giraudoux par lui-même. Collection "Les Ecrivains de toujours" no. 8. Paris: Editions de Seuil, 1952.

Regards sur le Mouvement Ouvrier. Cacérès, Benigno, and Chris Marker. Collection "Peuple et Culture" no. 5. Paris: Editions de Seuil, 1952.

Regards neufs sur la chanson. Barlatier, Pierre, and Chris Marker. Collection "Peuple et Culture" no. 9. Paris: Editions de Seuil, 1954.

La Strada: Un film de Federico Fellini. Bastide, Francis-Régis, Juliette Caputo, and Chris Marker. Paris: Edions du Seuil, 1955. With contributions by André Bazin, Alain Resnais, and Guido Cincotti.

Coréennes. Collection "Court-Métrage" no. 1. Paris: Editions de Seuil, 1959.

Commentaires. Paris: Editions du Seuil, 1961. Contains the text of *Les statues meurent aussi, Dimanche à Pékin, Lettre de Sibérie, L'Amérique rêve, Description d'un combat,* and *Cuba Si!*

Commentaires II. Paris: Editions du Seuil, 1967. Contains the text of *Le Mystère Koumiko, Soy Mexico* (an imaginary film), and *Si jávais quatre dromedaires.*

Le fond de l'air est rouge. Scènes de la troisiéme guerre mondiale 1967–1977. Paris: Editions François Maspero, 1978.

Le dépays. Paris: Editions Herrscher, 1982.

La renfermée: La Corse. Text by Marie Susini and photos by Chris Marker. Paris: Editions de Seuil, 1981.

La jetée. New York: Zone Books, 1992.

La petite illustration cinématographique: Chris Marker, Silent Movie. Columbus: Wexner Center for the Arts, Ohio State University, 1995.

Poetry

"Chant de l'endormition." *Le Mercure de France* 1067 (1947): 428–34.
"Romancero de la montagne." *Esprit* 135 (July 1947): 90–98.
"La dame à la licorne." *Le Mercure de France* 1024 (December 1948): 646–48.
"Les séparés." *Esprit* 162 (December 1949): 921–22.

Comic Strip Drawings

"La pathétique et réelle aventure du manuscrit génial . . ." *27, rue Jacob,* no. 1 (Spring 1952), no. 2 (Summer 1952), no. 3 (Fall 1952).
"Carte véritable des temps que nous voyvons" *27, rue Jacob,* no. 4 (Winter 1952/1953).

Translations

Hine, Al, Sergeant. "Christmas 1945." *DOC* 47, no. 2/3 (1947): 39.
Chapman, Frederick Spencer. *La jungle est neutre.* Paris: Editions de Seuil, 1951.
Thurber, James, and Elwyn Brooks-White: *La quadrature du sexe.* Paris: Editions de Seuil, 1952.
Powers, James Farl. *Le prince de ténèbres.* Translated by Charles Antonetti and Chris Marker. Paris: Editions de Seuil, 1952.
Stuart, Francis. *La fille du vendredi-saint.* Paris: Editions de Seuil, 1953.
Cuppy, Will. *Grandeur et décadence d'un peu tout le monde.* Paris: Editions de Seuil, 1953. Translated under the pseudonym Fritz Markassin.
Haldeman, Charles. *Le Gardien du soleil.* Paris: Editions de Seuil, 1965. Translated under the pseudonym T. T. Toukanov.
Lorenz, Konrad. *Tous les chiens, tous les chats.* Paris: Flammarion, 1970. Translated under the pseudonym Boris Villeneuve.

Commentaries about Others' Films

"Les hommes de la baleine." [Mario Ruspoli, 1956]. *Avant-Scène Cinéma* 24 (15 March 1963).
"Le mystère de l'atelier quinze." [Alain Resnais, André Heinrich, 1957]. *Avant-Scène Cinéma* 61/62 (July/September 1966): 73.
"Broadway by Light." [William Klein, 1957]. In *Anatole Dauman, Argos Films: Souvenir-Ecran,* edited by Jacques Gerber, 269. Paris: Editions du Centre Pompidou, 1989.

"La mer et les jours." [Raymond Vogel, 1958]. *Avant-Scène Cinéma* 68 (March 1967): 61–66.

"A Valparaiso." [Joris Ivens, 1963]. *Image et Son* 183 (April 1965): 73.

"Europort: Rotterdam." [Joris Ivens, 1966]. *Avant-Scène Cinéma* 99 (January 1970): 40.

Articles, Critiques, and Short Notes

"L'art noir." *Afrique Noire*, Collection "ODE." N.d., Paris.

"A propos de paradis terrestre." *Esprit* 129 (January 1947): 158.

"Une conférence de Louis Aragon." *Esprit* 129 (January 1947): 170–72.

"En attendant la société sans classés?" *Esprit* 130 (February 1947): 312.

"Mais revenons au sérieux." *Esprit* 130 (February 1947): 312.

"Les vaches maigres; Les vaches grasses; Les vaches moyennes." *Esprit* 130 (February 1947): 320–21.

"Importé d'Amérique." *Esprit* 130 (February 1947): 326.

"Nous avons un président." *Esprit* 130 (February 1947): 329–30.

"Les trios petits cochons." *Esprit* 131 (March 1947): 470.

"Le musicien errant." *Esprit* 131 (March 1947): 475.

"Vox populi." *Esprit* 131 (March 1947): 482–83.

"Deux petits nègres." *Esprit* 131 (March 1947): 488.

"La mort de Scarface, ou les infortunes de la vertu." *Esprit* 131 (March 1947): 488–91.

"Yves Salgues: Le Jeune homme endormi." *Esprit* 131 (March 1947): 524.

"Maurice Collis: La cité interdite." *Esprit* 131 (March 1947): 525.

"Bernard Voyenne: Honneur des hommes." *Esprit* 131 (March 1947): 531.

"Actualités imaginaires." *Esprit* 132 (April 1947): 643–44.

"Actualités éternelles." *Esprit* 132 (April 1947): 644–45.

"On le voit . . ." *Esprit* 132 (April 1947): 663.

"Les dernières feux du roman: Par Lagerkvist: Le Nain; Henri Queffélec: La Culbute; Célia Bertin: La Parade des Impies." *Esprit* 132 (April 1947): 703–7.

"Franz Villier: La vie et la mort de Richard Winslow." *Esprit* 132 (April 1947): 709–10.

"Pierre Daninos: Eurique et Amerope." *Esprit* 132 (April 1947): 710.

"L'apolitique du mois." *Esprit* 133 (May 1947): 808–12.

"L'apolitique de mois II." *Esprit* 133 (May 1947): 818.

"Un prologue que est tout un programme." *Esprit* 133 (May 1947): 824–25.

"Newsreel." *Esprit* 133 (May 1947): 836–38.

"Le sommeil de l'injuste." *Esprit* 133 (May 1947): 844–47.

"Le yogi et le commissaire—Stefan Zweig: Castellion contre Calvin." *Esprit* 133 (May 1947): 874–77.

"André Berry: Les expériences amoureuses." *Esprit* 133 (May 1947): 882–83.

"Le pain et le chien." *Esprit* 134 (June 1947): 1089.

"Pôles." *Esprit* 134 (June 1947): 1092.

"Actualités imaginaires." *Esprit* 135 (July 1947): 134–37.

"Information." *Esprit* 136 (August 1947): 285.

"Das tägliche Leben ohne Queffélec." *Esprit* 137 (September 1947): 400–405.

"Introduction à la représentation du *Mariage de Figaro.*" *Doc 47* I (September 1947).

"Grognement indistincts." *Esprit* 138 (October 1947): 562–65.

"Sartre noster." *Esprit* 139 (November 1947): 750–54.

"Le cheval blanc d'Henry Cinq." *Esprit* 141 (January 1948): 120–27.

"Meteo Maximoff: *Les Ursitory;* Fernand Gregh: *L'Age d'Or;* Bernard Pingaud: *Mon beau navire;* Allan Seager: *Equinoxe;* Langston Hughes: *Histoires de blancs;* Stefan Vincent Benet: *Le Roi des Chats;* James Gould Gozzens: *Hommes et frères;* Diana Frederica: *Diana;* Robert S. Close: *Prend-mois matelot.*" *Esprit* 141 (January 1948): 158–59.

"La science et la vie." *Esprit* 143 (March 1948): 472.

"Sauvages blancs seulement confondre." *Esprit* 146 (July 1948): 1–9.

"Newsreel." *Esprit* 146 (July 1948): 93–94.

"Du Jazz considéré comme une prophétie." *Esprit* 146 (July 1948): 133–38.

"L'affaire Tito vue de Yougoslavie; Lumière pour tous; Le Tito entre les dents." *Esprit* 147 (August 1948): 207–12.

"Le male comportement de l'américain sexuel." *Esprit* 147 (August 1948): 226–29.

"L'imparfait du subjectif." *Esprit* 148 (September 1948): 387–91.

"Fernand Deligny: *Les vagabonds efficaces.*" *Esprit* 148 (September 1948): 131–35.

"Jean Auger-Duvignaud: *Les dents ne poussent pas sur des chicots.*" *Esprit* 149 (October 1948): 595.

"Loys Masson: *L'illustre Thomas Wilson.*" *Esprit* 150 (November 1948): 753–54.

"C. S. Lewis: *Le Grand Divorce.*" *Esprit* 150 (November 1948): 754–55.

"'K' revue de la poésie. Nos. 1 et 2 consacré à Antonin Artaud." *Esprit* 150 (November 1948): 755–56.

"L'aube noire." *DOC* 49 (1949): n.p.

"Corneille au cinéma." *Esprit* 153 (February 1949): 282–85.

"Fêtes de la victoire." *Esprit* 156 (June 1949): 862–63.

"Les cent chef-d'oeuvre du cinéma." *Esprit* 156 (June 1949): 878–80.

"Le passager clandestin." *Esprit* 157 (July 1949): 1097–99.

"Le rosier de Madame Isou." *Esprit* 158 (August 1949): 297–99.

"Cachez donc les poètes." *Esprit* 162 (December 1949): 967–68.

"Le théâtre du peuple en Angleterre." *Parallèles* 50 (3 January 1950): n.p.

"Aus dem Bereich des Amateurfilms." In *DOK 50*, Sondernummer "Film und Kultur," 64. Stuttgart, West Germany: Joseph Rovan, 1950.

"Der Trickfilm." In *DOK 50* Sondernummer "Film und Kultur," 75–76. Stuttgart, West Germany: Joseph Rovan, 1950.

"Orphée." *Esprit* 173 (November 1950): 694–701.

"Croix de bois et chemin de fer." *Esprit* 175 (January 1951): 88–90.

"Bernard Pingaud: *L'amour triste.*" *Esprit* 176 (February 1951): 314–15.

"Réunions contradictoires." *Esprit* 178 (April 1951): 599–600.

"Petite suite sur thème de chansons." *Esprit* 179 (May 1951): 765–69.

"Siegfried et les Argousins ou le cinéma allemand dans les chaînes." *Cahiers du Cinéma* 4 (July/August 1951): 4–11.

"L'esthétique du dessin animé." *Esprit* 182 (September 1951): 368–69.

"Gérald Mc Boing-Boing." *Esprit* 185 (December 1951): 826–27.

"Le chat aussi est une personne." *Esprit* 186 (January 1952): 78–79.

"Das Blut eines Dichters." *Filmforum* 4 (January 1952): 3.

"Une forme d'ornement." *Cahiers du Cinéma* 168 (January 1952): 66–68. Also in *Images documentaires* 15 (1993).

"La passion de Jeanne d'Arc." *Esprit* 190 (May 1952): 840–43.

"Lettre de Mexico." *Cahiers du Cinéma* 22 (April 1953): 33–35.

"Lettre de Hollywood." *Cahiers du Cinéma* 25 (July 1953): 26–34.

"Le cinérama." *Cahiers du Cinéma* 27 (October 1953): 34–37.

"L'avant-garde français: Entr'acte; Un chien andalou; Le sang d'un poète." In *Regards neufs sur le cinéma*, Collection "Peuple et Culture" no. 8, edited by Jacques Chevalier, 249–55. Paris: Editions du Seuil, 1953.

"Un film d'auteur: La passion de Jeanne d'Arc." In *Regards neufs sur le cinéma*, Collection "Peuple et Culture" no. 8, edited by Jacques Chevalier, 256–61. Paris: Editions du Seuil, 1953.

"Cinéma, art du XXIe siècle?" In *Regards neufs sur le cinéma*, Collection "Peuple et Culture" no. 8, edited by Jacques Chevalier, 499–502. Paris: Editions du Seuil, 1953.

"And Now This Is Cinerama." In André Bazin et al. *Cinéma 53 à travers le monde*. Paris: Éditions du Cerf, 1953.

"Hollywood: sur place." In André Bazin et al. *Cinéma 53 à travers le monde*. Paris: Éditions du Cerf, 1953.

"Cinéma d'animation: U.P.A." In André Bazin et al. *Cinéma 53 à travers le monde*. Paris: Éditions du Cerf, 1953.

"Une conversation sur la chanson entre un critique: Pierre Barlatier, un auteur: Francis Lemarque, un professeur: Solange Demolière, un folkloriste: Maurice Delarue, et un auditeur: Chris Marker." In *Regards neufs sur la chanson*. Collection "Peuple et Culture" no. 9, 16–24. Paris: Editions du Seuil, 1954.

"Demi-dieux et doubles croches." In *Regards neufs sur la chanson*. Collection "Peuple et Culture" no. 9, 79–89. Paris: Editions du Seuil, 1954.

"Petite Planète." *27, rue Jacob* 10 (Summer 1954): 1.

"Le monde animal ne connaît pas la vedette . . ." *27, rue Jacob* 10 (Fall 1954): 1, 6.

"Adieu au cinéma allemand?" *Positif* 12 (November/December 1954): 66–71. German version: "Deutscher Film adieu?" In *Der Film—Manifeste, Gespräche, Dokumente,* Band 2, edited by Theodor Kotulla, 132–38. Munich: Piper Verlag, 1964.

"Wolfgang Staudte." *Cinéma* 55 I (November 1954): 33–36.

"On the Waterfront." *Esprit* 224 (March 1955): 440–43.

"Clair de Chine. En guise de carte de voeux, un film de Chris Marker." *Esprit* 234 (Suppl., January 1956): n.p.

"Der Film von morgen." *Film* 56 2 (February 1956): 67–71.

"Un film blanc: Moranbong." [Jean Claude Bonnardot, Armand Gatti]. *Spectacles* I, Nouvelle Série, (1960): n.p..

"Zu einem Skandal." *Filmstudio* 43 (10 May 1964): 31.

"Beitrag auf dem freien Forum in Leipzig." *Filmwissenschaftliche Mitteilungen* I (Berlin, 1964): 199–201.

"L'objectivité passionnée." *Jeune Cinéma* 15 (May 1966): 12–13.

"Let Us Praise Dziga Vertov." In *Sowjetischer Dokumentarfilm,*edited by W. Klaue and M. Lichtenstein, 70–71. Berlin: Staatliches Filmarchiv der DDR, 1967.

"Les révoltés de la Rhodia." *Le Nouvel Observateur* 123 (March 1967): 26.

"L'Aurore d'un cinéma ouvrier: Transcription d'un débat entre Chris Marker, Bernard P, and CG et le public après une projection à Bançon de films du Groupe Medvedkine." A nonreferenced press article from the ISKRA archives.

"Cinéma cubain: Che Guevara à 24 images/seconde." *Cinémonde* 1832 (21 April 1970).

"Le ciné-ours." La *Revue du Cinéma\Image et Son* 255. Themenheft Medwedkin (December 1971): 4–5.

"Reci Tridniho Boje." *Film a doba* 18, no. 2 (1972): 86.

"Au Creusot un musée de question." *L'Estampille* 42 (May 1973): 37–40.

"Kashima Paradise." *Ecran* 74 30 (November 1974): 74–75. Also appeared as the forward in Deswarte, Bénie, ed. *Kashima Paradise: un film de Yann Le Masson et Bénie Deswarte.* Lyon: Deswarte/Garnier, 1975.

"William Klein: peintre, photographe, cinéaste." *Graphis* 33 (May/June 1978): 495.

"Les gribouilles d'Antenne 2." *Libération,* 22 December 1983, n.p.

"Terminal Vertigo." *Monthly Film Bulletin* 51, no. 606 (July 1984): 196–97. A conversation between Chris Marker and his computer.

"Photos of Kurosawa's *Ran* and of Japan." *Traverses* 38/39 (November 1986): 13, 80, 137. "L'Héritage de la chouette." *XXV Mostra Internationale Del Nuovo Cinema.* Pesaro, Italy: Pesaro Film Festival XXV Catalog, 1989.

"De l'ordre du miracle." [Alain Cuny]. *Libération,* 18 May 1994, 40.

"A Free Replay: Notes sur 'Vertigo.'" *Positif* 400 (June 1994): 40.

"Le tombeau d'Alexandre." *Le Nouveau Commerce,* 88/89 (Fall/Winter, 1993), 17–48.

"Le tombeau d'Alexandre." In *Presseheft* Locarno, 1994.

"Effets et gestes." *Vogue,* December/January 1994/95, 208–11, 263. Text from Jean-Claude Carrière, photos by Chris Marker.

"The Rest Is Silent." *Chris Marker: Silent Movie.* Columbus: Wexner Center for the Arts, Ohio State University, 1995.

"Marker's Slide Show." Macintosh Director File of Xplugs. Un Regard Moderne. http://www.unregardmoderne.com/spip.

Interviews

Dubreuilh, Simone. *Lettres Françaises,* 28 March 1957.

Gendron, Francis. "Le socialisme dans la rue." *Miroir du Cinéma* 2 (May 1962): 12.

h. h. (possibly Hermann Herlinghaus). "Chris Marker: Ich werde bestimmt wiederkommen." *Deutsche Filmkunst* I (1962): 26–27.

Pay, Jean-Louis. *Miroir du Cinéma* 2 (May 1962): 4–7. Also in Jacques Gerber, ed. *Anatole Dauman: Souvenir-Ecran.* Paris: Editions du Centre Pompidou, 1989.

Anonymous. "Chronisten unserer Zeit: Chris Marker ["Gespannt auf 1964"]." *Filmspiegel* 23 (1963): 3.

Gersch, Wolfgang. "Der schöne Mai." *Filmwissenschaftliche Mitteilungen* I (1964): 194–98. Also in Hermann Herlinghaus, ed. *Dokumentaristen der Welt in den Kämpfen unserer Zeit.* Berlin: Henschel, 1982.

Ritterbusch, R. "Entretien avec Chris Marker." *Image et Son* 213 (February 1968): 66–68.

Philipe, Anne. "Medvedkine, tu connais? Interview avec Slon et Chris Marker." *Le Monde,* 2 December 1971, 17.

Walfisch, Dolores (possibly Chris Marker). "Level Five." *The Berkeley Lantern* (November 1996). Cited in *Level Five.* Paris: Argos Presseheft, 1997.

Frodon, Jean-Michel. "Je ne me demande jamais si, pourquoi, comment . . ." *Le Monde,* 20 February 1997.

Douhaire, Samuel, and Annick Rivoire. "Marker Direct." *Filmcomment,* May/June 2003, 38–41. Originally published in *Libération,* 5 March 2003.

Bibliography

Adamowsky, Natascha. "*La Jetée*—oder warum die Lanze ins Herz geht." In "*Sie wollen eben sein, was sie sind, nämlich Bilder*": Anschlüsse an Chris Marker, edited by Natalie Binczek and Martin Rass, 75–84. Würzberg, Germany: Königshausen & Neumann, 1999.

Ahlheim, Klaus, and David Wittenberg. "Die Dinge, die das Herz schneller schlagen lassen. Chris Marker: *Sans Soleil.*" In *Autorenfilme: Elf Werkanalysen*, edited by Thomas Koebner, 9–21. Münster, Germany: Maks, 1990.

Allard-Chanial, Laurence. "Le spectacle de la mémoire vive. A propos des créations numérique de Chris Marker." In "Recherches sur Chris Marker," edited by Phillippe Dubois. Special issue, *Théorème* 6 (2002): 132–40.

Almereyda, Michael. "Deciphering the Future: *Remembrance of Things to Come* Examines the Period between the Wars through the Prophetic Camera-eye of Denise Bellon." *Film Comment* (May/June 2003): 36–37.

Amengual, Barthélemy. "Le présent du futur: Sur *La Jetée.*" Special issue, *Positif* 433 (1997): 96–98.

Amiel, Vincent. "Il faut aller jusqu'à Tokyo pour que l'image et le regard se croisent: Sur *Sans soleil* et *Tokyo-Ga.*" Special issue, *Positif* 433 (1997): 99–101.

Andrew, Dudley. *André Bazin*. New York: Columbia University Press, 1990.

Arthur, Paul. "The Legacy of Soviet Cinema as Refracted through Chris Marker's Always Critical Vision." *Film Comment* (July/August 2003): 32–34.

Astruc, Alexandre. "The Birth of a New Avant Garde: La Caméra Stylo." In *The New Wave: Critical Landmarks*, edited by Peter Graham. Garden City, N.Y.: Doubleday, 1968.

Audé, Françoise. "*Level Five:* La migraine du temps." Special issue, *Positif* 433 (1997): 76–78.

Baetens, Jan. "Trois métalepses." In *Faux Titre: Etudes de Langue et Littérature Françaises*, edited by Ribiére Mireille, 171–78. Amsterdam: Rodopi, 2001.

Baker, Bob. "Chris Marker." *Film Dope* 40, no. 1072 (1989): 8–10.

Barthes, Roland. *The Empire of Signs*. Translated by Richard Howard. New York: Hill and Wang, 1982.

Bazin, André. "Chris Marker, *Lettre de Sibérie*." In *Le Cinéma français de la Libération à la Nouvelle Vague*, 179–81. Paris: Cahiers du Cinéma, 1983.

———. "Sur les routes de l'URSS et *Dimanche à Pekin*," *France Observateur* 372 (1957): 19.

Béghin, Cyril. "Des images en sursis." In "Recherches sur Chris Marker," edited by Phillippe Dubois. Special issue, *Théorème* 6 (2002): 158–66.

Beilenhoff, Wolfgang. "Andere Orte: *Sans soleil* als mediale Errinerungsreise." In *Chris Marker: Filmessayist*, edited by Birgit Kämper and Thomas Tode, 109–28. Munich: Institut Français de Munich, 1977.

Bellour, Raymond. "The Book, Back and Forth." In *Qu'est-ce Qu'une Madeleine?: A propos du CD-ROM Immmemory de Chris Marker*, edited by Yves Gevaert, 109–54. Paris: Centre Georges Pompidou, 1997.

———. "The Double Helix." Translated by James Eddy. In *Passages de l'image*, 48–75. Barcelona: Fundació Caixa de Pensions, 1991.

———. "Eloge in b-moll—*Zapping Zone*." In *Chris Marker: Filmessayist*, edited by Birgit Kämper and Thomas Tode, 129–34. Munich: Institut Français de Munich, 1997.

———. *L'Entre Images: Photo, Cinéma, Vidéo*. Paris: La Difference, 1990.

———. "Eulogy in B Minor." Translated by Joan Olivar. In *Passages de l'image*, 190–94. Barcelona: Fundació Caixa de Pensions, 1991.

———. "The Film Stilled." *Camera Obscura* 24 (1990): 98–123.

———. "Von Neuen." In *"Sie wollen eben sein, was sie sind, nämlich Bilder": Anschlüsse an Chris Marker*, edited by Natalie Binczek and Martin Rass, 85–98. Würzberg, Germany: Königshausen & Neumann, 1999.

———. "Zwischen Sehen und Verstehen: Sechs Filme (en passant)." In *Schreiben Bilder Sprechen: Texte zum essayistischen Film*, edited by Christa Blümlinger and Constantin Wulff, 61–94. Vienna: Sonderzahl, 1992.

Belmans, Jacques. "Méditations sur un concept." In *Cinéma et violence*. Paris: La Renaissance du Livre, 1980.

Benjamin, Walter. "On Some Motifs in Baudelaire." In *Illuminations*, translated by Harry Zohn, 155–200. New York: Schocken Books, 1969.

Bensmaïa, Réda. "From the Photogram to the Pictogram: On Chris Marker's *La Jetée*." *Camera Obscura* 24 (1990): 140–61.

Binczek, Natalie. "Zwischen akustischen und visuellen Spuren: Kommunikative Rahmenbedingungen des Kinos von Chris Marker." In *"Sie wollen eben sein, was sie sind, nämlich Bilder": Anschlüsse an Chris Marker*, edited by Natalie Binczek and Martin Rass, 173–87. Würzberg, Germany: Königshausen & Neumann, 1999.

Binczek, Natalie, and Martin Rass, eds. *"Sie wollen eben sein, was sie sind, nämlich Bilder": Anschlüsse an Chris Marker*. Würzberg, Germany: Königshausen & Neumann, 1999.

Biro, Yvette. "In the Spiral of Time." *Journal of Film and Video* 14/15 (1984–85): 173–77.

Blangonnet, Catherine. "Chris. Marker: Introduction." *Images Documentaires* 15 (Fall 1993): 9–10.

Blümlinger, Christa. "*La Jetée:* Nachhall eines Symptoms-Films." In *Chris Marker: Filmessayist*, edited by Birgit Kämper and Thomas Tode, 65–72. Munich: Institut Français de Munich, 1997.

———. "The Imaginary in the Documentary Image: Chris Marker's *Level Five.*" *Iris* 29 (Spring 2000): 133–42.

Bongers, Wolfgang. "Inseln: Gespentische Effekte in Bildern und Texten." In *"Sie wollen eben sein, was sie sind, nämlich Bilder": Anschlüsse an Chris Marker*, edited by Natalie Binczek and Martin Rass, 99–112. Würzberg, Germany: Königshausen & Neumann, 1999.

Braun, Peter. "Begegnungen—Abschiede: Chris Marker als Fotograf." In *Chris Marker: Filmessayist*, edited by Birgit Kämper and Thomas Tode, 87–100. Munich: Institut Français de Munich, 1977.

Braunberger, Pierre. *Cinémamémoire.* Paris: Centre Georges Pompidou, Centre National de la Cinématographie, 1987.

Brenez, Nicole, and Christian Lebrat, eds. *Jeune, Dure, et Pure!: Une histoire du cinéma d'avant-garde et expérimental en France.* Paris: Cinémathèque Française/Mazzotta, 2001.

Burch, Noël. "Four Recent French Documentaries." *Film Quarterly* 13, no. 1 (1959): 56–61. Also published in Lewis Jacobs, ed. *The Documentary Tradition*, 318–26. New York: Norton, 1979.

Callenbach, Ernest. "*La Jetée.*" *Film Quarterly* 19, no. 2 (1965–66): 50–52.

Casebier, Allan. "A Deconstructive Documentary." *Journal of Film and Video* 40, no. 1 (1988): 34–39.

Cauwenberge, Geneviève Van. "Le point de vue documentaire dans *Le joli mai.*" In "Recherches sur Chris Marker," edited by Phillippe Dubois. Special issue, *Théorème* 6 (2002): 83–99.

Cèbe, Pol. "Recontre avec Medvedkine." *L'Avant-Scène* 120 (December 1971): 9.

Chaiken, Michael, and DiIorio, Sam. "The Author behind the Auteur: Pre-Marker Marker." *Film Comment* (July/August 2003): 42–43

Chateau, Dominique. *Cinémas de la modernité.* Paris: Editions Klincksieck, 1981.

Chevrier, Jean-François, and Catherine David. "The Present State of the Image." In *Passages de l'image*, translated by James Eddy, 26–47. Barcelona: Fundació Caixa de Pensions, 1991.

Coates, Paul. "Chris Marker and the Cinema as Time Machine." *Science-Fiction Studies* 14 (1987): 307–15.

Cohen, Alain J. J. "*12 Monkeys, Vertigo,* and *La jetée:* Postmodern Mythologies and Cult Films." *New Review of Film and Television Studies* 1 (2003): 149–64.

Collas, Gérald. "Le sourire du chat." *Images Documentaires* 15, (Fall 1993): 23–28.

Darke, Chris. "Eyesight." *Film Comment* (May/June 2003): 48–50.

Debray, Régis. "*Le fond de l'air est rouge*, l'apprentissage de notre génération." *Images Documentaires* 15, (Fall 1993): 39–40.

DiIorio, Sam. "The Truth about Paris: Reconsidering *Le Joli Mai's* Investigation of French Social Attitudes in the Early Sixties." *Film Comment* (May/June 2003): 46–47.

Dresp, Wolf. "Die romantische Pose des Revolutionärs." In *Chris Marker: Film-essayist*, edited by Birgit Kämper and Thomas Tode, 53–64. Munich: Institut Français de Munich, 1977.

Dubois, Philippe, ed. "*La Jetée*, de Chris Marker ou le cinématogramme de la conscience." In "Recherches sur Chris Marker," edited by Phillippe Dubois. Special issue, *Théorème* 6 (2002): 8–45.

———. "Recherches sur Chris Marker." Special issue, *Théorème* 6 (2002).

Durgnat, R. "Resnais and Co.: Back to the Avant-garde." *Monthly Film Bulletin* 54, no. 640 (1987).

Ebert, Jürgen. "Der Film von Morgen—Chris Marker und das Kino." In "*Sie wollen eben sein, was sie sind, nämlich Bilder*": *Anschlüsse an Chris Marker*, edited by Natalie Binczek and Martin Rass, 113–25. Würzberg, Germany: Königshausen & Neumann, 1999.

Eisen, Ken. Review of *Sans Soleil. Cinéaste* 14, no. 2 (1985): 44.

Eisenschitz, Bernard. "Chris. Marker. Quelquefois les images." *Trafic* 19 (1996): 46–57.

Ertener, Orkun. "Filmen, als ob sich filmen ließe: Über das Bildersammeln und Filmemachen in Chris Markers *Sans soleil*." *Augenblick* 10 (1991): 35–49.

Exposito, Marcelo. "Letter from Chris Marker (When you go on a journey, you can at least tell something)." In *Chris Marker*, 1–10. Barcelona: Fundacio Antoni Tapies, 1998.

Fargier, Jean-Paul, Thérèse Girard, Serge Le Péron, Jean Narboni, and Serge Daney. "Table ronde sur *Le fond de l'air est rouge* de Chris Marker." *Cahiers du Cinéma* 284 (1978): 46–51.

Feigelson, Kristian. "Regards croisés EST/Ouest: l'histoire revisitée au cinéma (Medvedkine/Marker)." In "Recherches sur Chris Marker," edited by Phillippe Dubois. Special issue, *Théorème* 6 (2002): 118–31.

Fieschi, Jean-André. "*L'Ambassade*." *Trafic* 19 (1996): 73–74.

Friedlander, Eli. "*La Jetée*: Regarding the Gaze." *Boundary 2: An International Journal of Literature and Culture* 28, no. 1 (2001): 75–90.

Frodon, Jean-Michel. *L'Age moderne du cinéma français: De la Nouvelle Vague à nos jours*. Paris: Flammarion, 1995.

Gaggi, S. "Marker and Resnais: Myth and Reality." *Literature Film Quarterly* 12, no. 1 (1979).

Gauthier, Guy. Review of *Si J'avais Quatre Dromadaires* and *La Solitude du Chanteur de Fond. Image et Son* 293 (February 1975): n.p.

———. *Le Documentaire, un autre cinéma*. Paris: Nathan, 1995.

————. "Die Jagd nach dem Snark." In *Chris Marker: Filmessayist*, edited by Birgit Kämper and Thomas Tode, 15–30. Munich: Institut Français de Munich, 1997.

————. *Chris Marker, écrivain multimédia ou Voyage à travers les médias*. Paris: l'Harmattan, 2001.

————. "Image-mémoire et image-anticipation: Documentaire et fiction chez Chris Marker." *Licorne*, 24 (1992): 27–37.

————. "Images d'enfance." In "Recherches sur Chris Marker," edited by Phillippe Dubois. Special issue, *Théorème* 6 (2002): 46–59.

Geldin, Sherri. "Foreword and Acknowledgments." In *La Petite Illustration Cinématographique: Chris Marker, Silent Movie*, 5–7. Columbus, Ohio: Wexner Center for the Arts, 1995.

Gerber, Jacques. *Anatole Dauman, Argos Films: Souvenir-Ecran*. Paris: Editions du Centre Pompidou, 1989.

————. *Anatole Dauman: Pictures of a Producer*. Translated by Paul Willemen. London: BFI Publishing, 1992.

Gibson, Ross. "What Do I Know?: Chris Marker and the Essayist Mode of Cinema." *Filmviews* (Summer 1988): 26–32.

————. "Letters from Far-off Lands: Two Studies of Writing in Exile." In *South of the West: Postcolonialism and the Narrative Construction of Australia*, 19–62. Bloomington: Indiana University Press, 1992.

Gillet, Catherine. "Visages de Marker." In "Recherches sur Chris Marker," edited by Phillippe Dubois. Special issue, *Théorème* 6 (2002): 74–82.

Graham, Peter. "'Cinéma-Vérité' in France." *Film Quarterly* 17, no. 4 (1964): 30–36.

Gregor, Ulrich. "Filmessayist und Foto-Romancier." *Hefte der deutschen kinemathek* 18 (1965).

Hampton, Howard. "Chris Marker's Anatomies of Melancholy." *Film Comment* (May/June 2003): 32–35.

Hesper, Stefan. "Die Stimme der Erinnerung—Bilder des Vergessens. Chris Markers *Sans soleil*." In *"Sie wollen eben sein, was sie sind, nämlich Bilder"*: *Anschlüsse an Chris Marker*, edited by Natalie Binczek and Martin Rass, 39–50. Würzberg, Germany: Königshausen & Neumann, 1999.

Hilliker, Lee. "The History of the future in Paris: Chris marker and Jean-Luc Godard in the 1960s." *Film Criticism* 24, no. 3 (2000): 1–22.

Hoberman, J. "Dis Orient, Dat Occident." *Village Voice* (1 November 1983): 56–57.

————. "Japant-Garde Japanorama." *Artforum* (October 1985): 97–101.

————. "Postcard from the Edge." *Film Comment* (July/August 2003): 48–49.

Holborn, Mark. "Standing in the Shadow." *Artforum* (May 1986): 94–99.

Horak, Jan-Christophe. "Die Jagd nach den Bildern: Fotofilme von Chris Marker." In *Chris Marker: Filmessayist*, edited by Birgit Kämper and Thomas Tode, 73–86. Munich: Institut Français de Munich, 1997.

Horrigan, William. "Another Likeness." In *La Petite Illustration Ciné-matographique: Chris Marker, Silent Movie,* 9–13. Columbus, Ohio: Wexner Center for the Arts, 1995.

Howe, Susan. "Sorting Facts: Or Nineteen Ways of Looking at Marker." In *Beyond Document: Essays on Nonfiction Film,* edited by Charles Warren, 295–343. Hanover, N.H.: Wesleyan University Press, 1996.

Hüser, Rembert. "Herzliche Grüße, die Kultur ist das, was übrig bleibt, wenn alles weg ist, herzliche Grüße, aber man kann nicht alles haben, das ist richtig." In *"Sie wollen eben sein, was sie sind, nämlich Bilder": Anschlüsse an Chris Marker,* edited by Natalie Binczek and Martin Rass, 143–58. Würzberg, Germany: Königshausen & Neumann, 1999.

Ivens, Joris. "Rendez-vous des amis." In *Chris Marker: Filmessayist,* edited by Birgit Kämper and Thomas Tode, 197–98. Munich: Institut Français de Munich, 1997.

Jacobs. Gilles. "Chris Marker and the Mutants." *Sight and Sound* 35, no. 4 (1966): 164–68.

Jeancolas, Jean-Pierre. "La centrale Marker, 1967–1976." Special issue, *Positif* 433 (1997): 86–89.

Jenkins, S. "*Sunless.*" *Monthly Film Bulletin* 51 (1984).

"La Jetée." *L'Avant-Scène Cinéma* 38 (1964): 26.

Jones, Kent. "Chris Marker's Maiden Voyage into the Uncharted Waters of CD-ROM." *Film Comment* (July/August 2003): 46–47.

Jousse, Thierry. "Mr. and Mrs. Memory: *Level Five* de Chris Marker." *Cahiers de Cinéma* 510 (1997): 60–62.

Kämper, Birgit. "*Sans Soleil*—'ein Film erinnert sich selbst.'" In *Schreiben Bilder Sprechen: Texte zum essayistischen Film,* edited by Christa Blümlinger and Constantin Wulff, 33–60. Vienna: Sonderzahl, 1992.

———. "Das Bild als Madeleine—*Sans Soleil* und *Immemory.*" In *Chris Marker: Filmessayist,* edited by Birgit Kämper and Thomas Tode, 143–59. Munich: Institut Français de Munich, 1997.

Kämper, Birgit, and Thomas Tode, eds. *Chris Marker: Filmessayist.* Munich: Institut Français de Munich, 1997.

Kappest, Klaus-Peter, and Stefan Schallenberger. "Die Suche nach Zeit-Isotopien Film: Von der Möglichkeit und Unmöglichkeit, Zeitstrukturen in Chris Markers *La Jetée* zu durchschauen." In *"Sie wollen eben sein, was sie sind, nämlich Bilder": Anschlüsse an Chris Marker,* edited by Natalie Binczek and Martin Rass, 51–62. Würzberg, Germany: Königshausen & Neumann, 1999.

Kawin, Bruce. "Time and Stasis in *La Jetée.*" *Film Quarterly* 36, no. 7 (1982): 15–20.

Khalili, Bouchra. "*Level 5* ou le Reposoir." In "Recherches sur Chris Marker," edited by Phillippe Dubois. Special issue, *Théorème* 6 (2002): 141–57.

Kohn, Olivier. "Si loin, si proche." Special issue, *Positif* 433 (1997): 79–82.

König, Amy H. "Where Do Statues Go When They Die?" *h2so4* 14 (Winter/ Spring 2004). http://h2so4.net/artlove/statues.html.

Kustow, Michael. Review of *Le Joli Mai. Sight and Sound* 33, no. 2 (1964): 93–94.

Labarthe, André S. *Essai sur le jeune cinéma français.* Paris: Editions Le Terrain Vague, 1960.

Langmann, Ursula. *Chris Marker.* Munich: Revue CICIM, 1984.

Lanzoni, Rémi Fournier. *French Cinema: From Its Beginnings to the Present.* New York: Continuum, 2002.

Lardeau, Yann. "L'empire des mots." *Cahiers du Cinéma* 345 (1983): 60–61.

Lee, Min. "Joining Forces with the Militant Collective Slon." *Film Comment* (July/August 2003): 38–41.

Lee, Sander. "Platonic Themes in Chris Marker's *La Jetée.*" *Senses of Cinema: An Online Journal Devoted to the Serious and Eclectic Discussion of Cinema* 4, (March 2000): www.sensesofcinema.com.

Lemaitre, Barbara. "*Sans soleil,* le travail de l'imaginaire." In "Recherches sur Chris Marker," edited by Phillippe Dubois. Special issue, *Théorème* 6 (2002): 60–73.

Leutrat, Jean-Louis. "Le coeur révélateur." *Trafic* 19 (1996): 67–72.

Levy, Jacques. "L'audace et l'honnêteté de la subjectivité." *CinémAction* 41 (1987): 125–31.

Liem, Ronco Yaobing. "Chris Marker and *La Jetee.*" PhD diss., Columbia University Teachers College, 1983; University of Michigan, 1991.

Loewinger, Larry. "*La Sixième Face du Pentagone.*" *Film Quarterly* 22, no. 2 (1968–69): 58–59.

Lopate, Phillip. "In Search of the Centaur: The Essay-Film." In *Totally, Tenderly, Tragically: Essays and Criticism from a Lifelong Love Affair with the Movies,* 280–311. New York: Doubleday, 1998.

Lucas, Gonzalo de. "Chris Marker: The Political Composition of the Image. Introduction to the First Image of *Sans Soleil.*" *Formats* 2 (n.d.). http://www.iua.upf.es/formats/formats2/luc_a.htm.

Lupton, Catherine. "Shock of the Old: How the 'Gentleman Amateur' of the Digital Era Uses Not-So-New Media to Map the Workings of Human Memory." *Film Comment* (May/June 2003): 42–45.

———. *Chris Marker: Memories of the Future.* London: Reaktion Books, 2005.

———. "Chris Marker: In Memory of New Technology." *Silverthreaded* (n.d.). http://www.silcom.com/~dlp/cm/cm_memtech.htm.

Mann, Karen B. "Narrative Entanglements: 'The Terminator.'" *Film Quarterly* 43, no. 2 (1989): 17–27.

Mansfield, Charlie. "Identity and Narration in Chris Marker's *La Jetée,* and the Appearance of the Internet as a Symptom of Cold War Anxiety." *Faux Titre: Etudes de Langue et Littérature Françaises* 208 (2001): 179–84.

Marchessault, J. "Sans Soleil." Cineaction 5 (1986).

Marker, Cynthia. "Self-Censorship and Chris Marker's Le Joli Mai." French Cultural Studies 12, no. 1 (2001): 23–41.

Moran, James M. "A Bone of Contention: Documenting the Prehistoric Subject." In Visible Evidence 6, edited by Jane M. Gaines, 255–73. Minneapolis: University of Minnesota Press, 1999.

Michaux, Henri. Plume, précédé de Lointain intérieur. Paris: Gallimard, 1963.

Miles, Adrian. "Chris Marker." http://cs.art.rmit.edu.au/marker/. Accessed 1995.

Mitry, Jean. "Amants heureux amants (Louis Malle et Chris Marker)." Combat 20 (1959).

Möller, Olaf. "Japan through the Looking Glass." Film Comment (July/August 2003): 35–37.

Nacho, Cagiga. CM: Retrato de Chris Marker a 24 imagenes-segundo. Valencia, Spain: Ediciones de la Mirada, 1998.

Naficy, Hamid. "Epistolarity and Epistolary Narratives." In An Accented Cinema: Exilic and Diasporic Filmmaking, 101–51. Princeton, N.J.: Princeton University Press, 2001.

Neupert, Richard. A History of the French New Wave. Madison: University of Wisconsin Press, 2002.

Niney, François. "Des statues meurent aussi au Tombeau d'Alexandre, le regard retourné." Images Documentaires 15, (Fall 1993): 29–38.

———. "L'éloignement des voix répare en quelque sorte la trop grande proximité des plans." In "Recherches sur Chris Marker," edited by Phillippe Dubois. Special Issue, Théorème 6 (2002): 100–10.

———. "L'Heritage de la chouette." Images Documentaires 15, (Fall 1993): 41–44.

Niogret, Hubert, and Olivier Kohn. "Témoignages." Special issue, Positif 433 (1997): 90–95.

Odin, Roger. "Le film de fiction menacé par la photographie et sauvé par la bande-son (à propos de La Jetée de Chris Marker)." In Cinémas de la modernité, Films, Théories, Cerisy Colloquium, organized by Dominique Chateau, André Gardiès, and François Jost, 141. Paris: Editions Klincksieck, 1981.

Östör, Akos. "Sans Soleil." American Anthropologist 89 (1987): 1022–23.

Paech, Joachim. "Anmerkungen zu La Jetée." In "Sie wollen eben sein, was sie sind, nämlich Bilder": Anschlüsse an Chris Marker, edited by Natalie Binczek and Martin Rass, 63–74. Würzberg, Germany: Königshausen & Neumann, 1999.

Patalas, Enno, and Frieda Grafe. ". . . das praktische Beweis für die mise en scène." In Kameradschaft-Querelle, 53–66. Munich: CICIM, 1991.

Peigné-Giuly, Annick. "Que rest-t-il ces images?" Images Documentaires 15 (Fall 1993): 19–22.

Perniola, Ivelise. Chris Marker, o Del film-saggio. Torino, Italy: Lindau, 2003.

Petit, Chris. "Insane Memory." Sight and Sound 4, no. 7 (1994): 13.

Porcile, François. *Defense du court metrage français*. Paris: Editions du Cerf, 1965.

———. "Chris Marker, à la poursuite des signes du temps." *Images Documentaires* 15 (1993): 15–18.

Pourvali, Bamchade. "Chris Marker, cinéaste inclassable." In "Recherches sur Chris Marker," edited by Phillippe Dubois. Special issue, *Théorème* 6 (2002): 111–17.

———. *Chris Marker*. Paris: Cahiers du Cinéma, 2003.

Quandt, James. "Grin without a Cat." *Cinematheque Ontario Programme Guide* (Fall 1993): 4–7.

Queval, Jean. "Chris Marker's Commentaries." *Sight and Sound* (Summer 1962): 152–53.

Rafferty, Terrence. "Marker Changes Trains." *Sight and Sound* 53, no. 4 (1984): 284–88.

———. "Chris Marker." In *The Thing Happens*, 63–74. New York: Grove Press, 1993.

Rancière, Jacques. "Fiktion der Erinnerung." In *"Sie wollen eben sein, was sie sind, nämlich Bilder": Anschlüsse an Chris Marker*, edited by Natalie Binczek and Martin Rass, 27–38. Würzberg, Germany: Königshausen & Neumann, 1999.

Rass, Martin. "Schielen und Stottern—Chris Marker am Horizont?" In *"Sie wollen eben sein, was sie sind, nämlich Bilder": Anschlüsse an Chris Marker*, edited by Natalie Binczek and Martin Rass, 9–26. Würzberg, Germany: Königshausen & Neumann, 1999.

Ray, Robert B. "The Automatic *Auteur*: Or a Certain Tendency in Film Criticism." In *Directed by Allen Smithee*, edited by Jeremy Braddock and Stephen Hock, 51–75. Minneapolis: University of Minnesota Press, 2001.

Reisz, Karel, and Gavin Miller. "'Cinema Verité and the Documentary Film of Ideas." In *The Technique of Film Editing*, 297–321. London: Focal Press, 1968.

Reitz, Edgar. "Das Unsichtbare und der Film. Reflexionen zum Handwerk, angeregt durch Chris Markers *Sans Soleil*." In *Liebe zum Kino. Utopien und gedanken zum Autorenfilm 1962–1983*, 125–32. Cologne, Germany: Köln 78, 1984.

Resnais, Alain. "Chris Marker." *Image et Son* (April/May 1963): 52–53.

———. "Rendez-vous des amis." Interview with Birgit Kämper and Thomas Tode. In *Chris Marker: Filmessayist*, edited by Birgit Kämper and Thomas Tode, 205–14. Munich: Institut Français de Munich, 1997.

"Rest is Silent, The Program Notes." http://www.sva.edu/moma/videospaces/index.html.

Richter, Hans. "Der Filmessay: Eine neue Form des Dokumentarfilm." In *Schreiben Bilder Sprechen: Texte zum essayistischen Film*, edited by Christa Blümlinger and Canstatin Wulf, 195–98. Vienna: Sonderzahl, 1992.

Ropars, Marie Claire. "Sémiotique du film ou sémiotique textuelle? La question de la narration." In *Exigences et perspectives de la sémiotique: Recueil d'hommages pour A. G. Greimas*, edited by H. Parret and H. G. Ruprecht, 645. Amsterdam: John Benjamins, 1985.

Roscher, Gerd. "Der Sprung über die Revolte." In *Chris Marker: Filmessayist*, edited by Birgit Kämper and Thomas Tode, 101–8. Munich: Institut Français de Munich, 1977.

Ross, Kristen. *Fast Cars, Clean Bodies: Decolonization and the Reordering of French Culture*. Cambridge, Mass.: MIT Press, 1996.

———. *May '68 and Its Afterlives*. Chicago: University of Chicago Press, 2002.

Roth, Laurent. "A Yakut Afflicted with Strabismus." In *Qu'est-ce Qu'une Madeleine?: A propos du CD-ROM Immemory de Chris Marker*, edited by Yves Gevaert, 37–63. Paris: Centre Georges Pompidou, 1997.

Roud, Richard. "The Left Bank." *Sight and Sound* (Winter 1962–63): 24–27.

———. "SLON." *Sight and Sound* (Spring 1973): 82–83.

———. "The Left Bank Revisited." *Sight and Sound* (Summer 1977): 143–45.

Rovan, Joseph. "Un mouvement culturel et politique: Peuple et Culture." *Les Cahiers de l'animation* 57/58 (December 1986): n.p.

Sandro, Paul. "Singled out by History: *La Jetée* and the Aesthetics of Memory." *French Cultural Studies* 10, no. 1 (1999): 107–27.

Sauvaget, D. "De L'introversion consideree Comme un des Beaux-Arts: *Si J'avais Quatre Dromadaires* et *La Solitude du Chanteur de Fond*." *Positif* 66 (1975).

Schefer, Jean-Lous. "On the Jetty." In *Passages de l'image*, translated by Paul Smith, 102–7. Barcelona: Fundació Caixa de Pensions, 1991.

Scherer, Christina. *Ivens, Marker, Godard, Jarman: Erinnerung im Essayfilm*. Munich: Wilhelm Fink Verlag, 2001.

Schröter, Jens. "Was ist Film? Zwischenspiele zwischen André Bazin und Chris Marker." In *"Sie wollen eben sein, was sie sind, nämlich Bilder": Anschlüsse an Chris Marker*, edited by Natalie Binczek and Martin Rass, 129–42. Würzberg, Germany: Königshausen & Neumann, 1999.

Seguin, Louis. "L'intimité des cornichons." *Trafic* 19 (1996): 58–66.

Siclier, Jaques. *Nouvelle Vague?* Paris: Editions du Cerf, 1961.

Siegel, Joshua. "Chris Marker Video Premieres." Program notes, The Museum of Modern Art, New York, January 1994.

Sohet, Philippe. "Fixations sur l'image." In *Faux Titre: Etudes de Langue et Littérature Françaises*, edited by Mireille Ribière, 155–69. Amsterdam: Rodopi, 2001.

Spielmann, Yvonne. "Visual Forms of Representation and Simulation: A Study of Chris Marker's *Level 5*." *Convergence: Journal of Research into New Media Technologies* 6, no. 2 (2000): 18–40.

Tailleur, Robert. "Markeriana." *Artsept* 1 (January–March 1963): n.p.

Thiemann, Birgit. "Die Relativität der Dinge und ihrer Begriffe. Chris Markers *Sans Soleil*." *Augenblick* 10 (1991): 25–34.

Thirard, Paul-Louis. "A propos de 'la Spirale.'" *Positif* 180 (1976): 25–26.

———. "*Sans Soleil* Ex-fans des sixties . . ." *Positif* 265 (1983): 62.

———. "Marker, le cinéma et la politique." Special Issue, *Positif* 433 (1997): 83–85.

Tode, Thomas. "Phantom Marker: Inventur vor dem Film." In *Chris Marker: Filmessayist*, edited by Birgit Kämper and Thomas Tode, 31–52. Munich: Institut Français de Munich, 1977.

Torok, J. "Une Phrase qui n'a pas se sens *La Fond de l'air est Rouge*." *Positif* 204 (1978).

Toubiana, Serge. "Savoir posthume *(La Spirale)*." *Cahiers du Cinéma* 265 (1976): 56–60.

Turim, Maureen. "Virtual Discourses of History: Collage, Narrative or Documents in Chris Marker's *Level 5*." *Sites: The Journal of Twentieth Century Contemporary French Studies* 4, no. 2 (2000): 367–83.

Valade, P. "Un Programme de Chris Marker." *Jeune Cinéma* 84 (1975).

van Assche, Christine. "On the Contribution of Videographics." In *Passages de l'image*, translated by James Eddy, 96–101. Barcelona: Fundació Caixa de Pensions, 1991.

Van Wert, William. Review of *La Jetée*. *Cinema* 34 (1974): 56–59.

———. *The Theory and Practice of the Ciné-Roman*. Manchester, N.H.: Ayer, 1978.

———. "Chris Marker: The SLON Films." *Film Quarterly* 32 (1979): 38–46.

Varda, Agnes. "Chris Marker." In "Freunde der deutschen Kinemathek." Special issue, *Kinemathek* 18 (1965): 2.

Veillon, Olivier-René. "L'image dialectique, sur *Le Tombeau d'Alexandre*." *Images Documentaires* 15 (1993): 49–56.

Walsh, Michael. "Around the World, across all Frontiers. Cineaction: *Sans Soleil* as Depays." *Cineaction*, (Fall 1989): n.p.

———. "'My Work Is to Question Images': Chris Marker's *Le Tombeau d'Alexandre*." *Iris* 29 (2000): 103–16.

Wetzel, Michael. "Verwerfungen. Zeitraumreisen in Chris Markers *Sans soleil* und *La Jetée*." In *Once upon a time . . . Film und Gedächtnis*, edited by Ernst Karpf, Doron Kiesel, and Karsten Visarius, 9–37. Marburg, Germany: Schüren Presseverlag, 1998.

———. "La Japonais—Fernöstliche Erinnerungsbilder." In *"Sie wollen eben sein, was sie sind, nämlich Bilder": Anschlüsse an Chris Marker*, edited by Natalie Binczek and Martin Rass, 159–72. Würzberg, Germany: Königshausen & Neumann, 1999.

Wilson, D. "*Le Train en Marche*." *Monthly Film Bulletin* 41 (1974).

Zarader, Jean-Pierre. "Les Voix du dilence d'André Malraux et *Les Statues*

meurent aussi d' Alain Resnais et Chris Marker: Une Marmonie polémique."
Revue des Lettres Modernes: Histoire des Idées et des Littératures 1419–24
(1999): 163–66.

Special Issues, Journals, and Catalogs

"Chris Marker and Armand Gatti." Special issue, *Mirroir du Cinéma* 2
(1962).
"Chris Marker." Special issue, *Image et Son* (April/May 1963).
"Chris Marker." Special issue, *Hefter der deutschen Kinemathek* 18 (1965).
"Chris Marker: Film photographie, voyage, écrit et aime les chats." Brochure
of the retrospective *20 ans de cinéma offensif, 20 ans de fictions documentai-
rées/de documentaires fictionnés*. Geneva, 1982.
Chris Marker. *CICIM* no. 8 (July 1984).
"O Bestario de Chris Marker." Special issue, *Collecçao Horizonte de Cinema*
no. 114 (1986).
Passage de l'Image. Paris: Musée National d'Art Moderne, Centre Georges
Pompidou, 1990.
"Chris Marker." Special issue, *Bref* 6 (1990).
Images documentaires no. 15 (1993).
Time and Tide. London: Tyne International Exhibition of Contemporary Art,
Newcastle, 1993.
Video Spaces: Eight Installations. New York: Museum of Modern Art, 1995.
Silent Movie. Columbus, Ohio: Wexner Center for the Arts, 1995.
Chris Marker. Catalog, XXII Pesaro Filmfestivals, 1996.
"Chris Marker." Special issue, *Positif* 433 (1997).
Clara Bow: Chris Marker. Retrospective, *Cinémathèque française* (January/
February 1998).
Chris Marker. Catalogue, Fundacio Antoni Tapies, Barcelona, December 4,
1998–January 24, 1999.
Théorème 6. Paris: Presses de la Sorbonne-Nouvelle, 2002.
"The Travels of Chris Marker," *Film Comment* (May/June, July/August 2003).

Index

NORA M. ALTER is a professor of German, Film and Media Studies at the University of Florida. She is author of *Vietnam Protest Theatre: The Television War on Stage* (1996), *Projecting History: Non-Fiction German Film* (2002), and co-editor with Lutz Koepnick of *Sound Matters: Essays on the Acoustics of Modern German Culture* (2004).

Books in the series Contemporary Film Directors

The University of Illinois Press
is a founding member of the
Association of American University Presses.

Composed in 10/13 New Caledonia
with Helvetica Neue display
by Jim Proefrock
at the University of Illinois Press
Manufactured by Sheridan Books, Inc.

University of Illinois Press
1325 South Oak Street
Champaign, IL 61820-6903
www.press.uillinois.edu